P

"Vivid with complex characters, *Truth Like Oil* is a heart-affirming novel centered on Nadine Antoine and her two sons—one brimming with potential; the other full of problems. Saddled by the weight of a troubled adolescence, resilient Nadine, a Haitian-American nurses' aide, is intent on her sons rising above the odds trapping so many young Black men in this graceful story that explores race, identity, prejudice, community, and secrets. Emotionally true and beautifully written, *Truth Like Oil* is a timely gift to be shared."
ROBIN FARMER, AUTHOR OF *MALCOLM AND ME*

"*Truth Like Oil* is the moving and ultimately uplifting story of a single woman from Haiti, and her sons—two very different boys—each struggling with the secrets necessary to the preservation of personal integrity. Connie Biewald's honest prose hums with love for her characters as they navigate the complexities of life in Cambridge, Massachusetts. Her graceful rendering of Haiti's influence on each of them grounds the unraveling and reformation of their relationships, mother to son, brother to brother, lover to lover, and family to community. You'll find yourself wondering—long after you've finished the rewarding conclusion—about how Nadine and her boys are doing now, as if you're missing old friends."
TRACY WINN, AUTHOR OF *MRS. SOMEBODY SOMEBODY*

"Full of wisdom and compassion, this emotionally bountiful novel is a thoroughly contemporary portrayal of family in all its flaws and resilience. Connie Biewald's cast of richly developed characters are steeped in place and displacement as they move through layers of yearning and pain toward connection. Strong women learn to love without weakness. Fatherless boys learn to be men. Individuals navigate racial and economic inequities, the vagaries of aging and loss, and the joy and hope of birth. Big-hearted and intelligent, this novel grabs you from the first page and lingers long after the last."
LAURA BROWN, AUTHOR OF *MADE BY MARY* AND *QUICKENING*

ABOUT THE AUTHOR

Connie Biewald has been writing stories in an effort to explore human relationships since she was five years old. She has been a teacher for more than forty years, sharing her love of reading and writing with hundreds of students in the US and Haiti. She is the author of three loosely connected novels that comprise *The Rivertown Trilogy: Bread and Salt, Digging to Indochina,* and *Roses Take Practice.*

Visit her website at *conniebiewald.com*

TRUTH
like
OIL

CONNIE BIEWALD

www.vineleavespress.com

Cover design by Jessica Bell
Interior design by Amie McCracken

A catalogue record for this
book is available from the
National Library of Australia

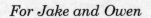

For Jake and Owen

March 2005

Sak vid pa kanpe.
An empty sack can't stand up.

11

April 2005

"Lè w ap neye, ou kenbe branch ou jwenn."
When you are drowning you hang on
to the branch you can find.

79

May 2005

Verite se tankou lwil nan dlo, li toujou anlè.
Truth is like oil in water, it always comes to the surface.

139

June 2005

Wont pi lou pase sak sèl.
Shame is heavier than a sack of salt.

211

MARCH 2005

Sak vid pa kanpe.
An empty sack can't stand up.

Nadine hesitated and pressed a hand against her lower back, the stairs to her second floor apartment looming steep after her long day, the entryway as cold as the late winter air outside. Samba music and the smell of peanuts, garlic, and ginger drifted from behind her downstairs neighbor's door. Then Yara, in a velvety red bathrobe, peeked out, glamorous as always, even at midnight in her own kitchen. The music swelled, and the spices announced themselves as her friend flung the door wide open.

"So late?" Yara said. "When are you going to quit that job and start cleaning houses with me? Changing sheets with no one in the bed is so easy, the money so much better. But you don't listen." She grabbed Nadine's arm, tucked it under her own, and steered her into the warm apartment. "Eat. Have a glass of wine. You'll sleep better. And I have something to show you." Yara patted the pocket of her bathrobe where a corner of white envelope peeked over the edge.

Nadine let herself be shepherded into a kitchen chair.

How good it felt to settle her exhausted bones after a double shift. She shouldn't feel so tired—she was thirty-six not fifty. But her back complained as much as the old people she lifted on and off the commode all day long. Underneath it all Chance's recent refusal to do well in school, to come home on time, to listen to anything she had to say, sapped her energy as surely as a terminal disease.

"*Sak vid pa kanpe*," she said. "This day has emptied me." A bowl of chicken stew, a plate of *pão de queijo*, and a glass filled to the top with pink wine appeared in front of her. She dropped her heavy purse onto the floor.

Yara sat down across from her and refilled her own glass. Nadine, still in her black winter coat, popped a warm roll into her mouth. She loved that cheese bread, crispy on the outside and warm and gooey in the middle, and Yara's stew was one of the best she'd ever eaten, but she would have enjoyed soup from a can if someone heated it up for her.

"Sister, you're a mess." Yara sipped her wine, little finger in the air, then slid the envelope from her pocket, laid it on the table next to her glass, and covered it with the flat of her palm. Her long fingernails shone gold this week with tiny rhinestones glued to them, little stars that sparkled when she gestured. How did she clean houses with nails like that? No doubt her crew of recently arrived family members did the heaviest, nail-threatening work.

"I don't look so bad." Nadine knew her short hair always looked neat. She could stand to lose a few pounds, but her body had a nice shape. Families of patients said she had a "dazzling" smile and the cheekbones of a fashion model. "I'm tired. You remember what it's like to work a double."

"That's what I'm saying!" Yara leaned forward. "You—"

"You don't need to tell me again to quit Riverview," Nadine said. "I know what you think." In the eight years since Yara had left the nursing home and started her own business, she'd made enough money to buy this two-family house from the landlord, hire her cousins to fix it up, and help her two daughters through UMass Boston. In fact, sometimes Nadine had to wonder if her cleaning business was all she had going on.

Nadine swished her cold drink around in her mouth. She wished she could relax—stop straining her ears, listening for Chance's footsteps.

"Have you heard my son come home?"

"No." Yara slipped a photo from the envelope. "Look, it's my grandchild. It's a boy." She pointed at a spot on the sonogram. "My son-in-law, the doctor, sent it to me."

Nadine squinted at a black-and-white smudge. "Very nice," she said. It didn't seem natural or right to be taking pictures of people who weren't yet born. She'd had ultrasound scans when she was pregnant with Henry and Chance, but never a photo to show the world. Why rush such a thing? Yara's daughter, Luiza, knew just where her baby was. Yara's daughter's body was all that baby needed.

Yara plucked the ultrasound picture from Nadine's hand and stared at it, a dreamy smile on her face. "I'll go down to New York when he's born. Until then I'll pray every day for an easy birth."

"Birth is just the beginning," Nadine said. "While you are at it, pray for a long healthy life with enough to eat. Pray he be protected from violence. Pray he find a good job. Pray he stays out of trouble. Do you know that every day I come home to recorded messages from the school? 'Your son,' then they fill in the name—'Chance Antoine'—'was absent from' and they fill it in again, 'second period, third period, any class.' What do they expect from me? Yesterday there was a real message from the assistant principal, telling me to come for a meeting."

Her friend looked up from the picture. "Say to yourself, Chance is a good boy. He is."

Nadine sucked her teeth with a loud *tuipe*, and helped herself to another roll.

Her other son, Henry, always did his best. If he hadn't, he wouldn't be in expensive private college on a full scholarship. Chance had nothing, no plans for next year. She'd made a mistake raising him so loosely, but after all the beatings she'd endured, she vowed she'd never hit her children and had been proud of mostly keeping that promise to herself. And he had been a good enough boy until this year. A favorite with his teachers, Chance's biggest problem had been that "he talked to his neighbors." When she had asked him about it, he said, "When they change my seat to move me away from my friends, I make new friends."

Yes. Nadine wanted to smack him, then and now. And yet she wished she made friends that easily. Yara was her only real friend in Cambridge. But lately, when she complained about Chance, Yara just said, "Chance is a good boy." When she complained about Riverview, Yara said "Quit."

Yara refilled Nadine's wine to the top, where only surface tension kept it from overflowing. Nadine dipped her head and sipped without lifting the glass. She would talk about something else.

"You know that Mrs. Watkins I've been telling you about?" Nadine said. "The old lady who had a stroke—ninety-five years old?"

"The one who only wants white aides?" Yara laughed. "Good luck to her with that. The one who can't talk, but somehow manages to call you a thief. I'm telling you, enough is enough with that job!"

Hazel Watkins's tenacity reminded Nadine of the grandmothers she'd known as a child in the mountains on

Lagonav. Once people passed a certain age, they kept on going, nothing but bones covered with loosening skin, and they still worked every day. "I don't mind the old people. I like the feisty ones, their spirit."

"So what about her?"

"Her son is the boys' old basketball coach, from the center." Mrs. Watkins had welcomed her son with an even colder version of the same hateful squint she directed toward everyone else. Nadine could not imagine looking at her boys that way, even with the way Chance was acting lately. "He told me he's been to Haiti. He tried to speak *Kreyòl* with me."

"Is he handsome?" Yara wanted to be married again before she turned forty and was always trying to find both of them boyfriends.

"Two months she's been in there, and he hasn't shown his face until today. Terrible to abandon his mother like that. She is very angry." He had never come to feed Mrs. Watkins, rub her feet, or bring her the littlest thing to make life more beautiful—her favorite butterscotch candy, a cheerful plant, never mind the communication aid that he kept promising. "Maybe it is because he is a man—men and boys can be so selfish." Nadine envied Yara her money, her beauty, but most of all her daughters. "You have good girls."

"How old is he? His mother's ninety-five! But older men can be better than young ones, more settled, more money, knowing how to treat a woman. What's he look like? Is he short? Is he fat? Is he bald?"

Nadine tried to conjure a clear picture of him. Gary Watkins had a neatly-trimmed brown beard with a touch of gray, wire-framed glasses and a compact body. "He was wearing a baseball cap, so I don't know."

"He's bald then," Yara said. "Older men with baseball caps always are. Anyway, there is a lot to worry about with daughters too."

"Maybe." Nadine listened when Yara spoke. She'd graduated from college in Brazil and studied psychology; she knew a lot about people and their secrets from cleaning their houses. "In Haiti, girls work harder, but if a mother dies the father might send her away. To live with relatives or even strangers who could offer a better life. Too much trouble to keep her if there is no one to fix the hair." Nadine pushed away the image of herself at fourteen in Uncle Maxim's beautiful pink American bathroom, resigned and lonely, using his electric clippers to shape her hair for the first time into the short style she'd worn ever since. She'd collected the hair in a paper bag and burned it in his gas grill. The smell caught in her throat and lingered in the air. When he came home from a business meeting he beat her—for cutting off the hair he liked to touch or using his fancy grill, she never knew.

"Chance is a good boy," Yara said. "Say that to yourself over and over."

Nadine swallowed the last of her wine and pressed her fingertips to her forehead. She massaged her temples with her thumbs.

"Your girls never stayed out all night or came home drunk. The school never called telling you they hadn't come to class. Henry might be a good boy, but Chance is not, and saying something over and over won't make it true." He didn't listen to her anymore. It was as if someone had cursed him. Maybe someone jealous of Henry's success.

"Everyone has problems. Girls aren't any easier. What's easier is someone else's child." Yara stretched, yawned, and shook out her long dark hair. "I love this song!" She twirled out of the kitchen into the living room, where she turned up the music.

Nadine closed her eyes and let the music help her pretend

that she was somewhere far away. When she got upstairs she'd put her feet up, watch her favorite show, *How to Look Good Naked*, where an enthusiastic homosexual man taught women to like their bodies. She'd take a hot bath, throwing in some mint leaves and basil. Then she'd sleep.

"I'm telling you," Yara said. "Quit that job and you'll feel like the young woman you are. You need to dance more." She cleared the dishes to a *samba* beat. The outside door slammed shut; footsteps pounded up the stairs, and Nadine's whole body relaxed. A space opened around her heart; she could breathe easily. With her son home, safe in his bed, she'd be sure to sleep well. Before she could stand up, Yara had the door open calling up to Chance. Even before he appeared in the kitchen, the thick stink of marijuana mixed with the smell of Yara's stew.

"Smells bomb in here!" Chance burst in head bobbing, pants sagging, wires dangling from his ears, eyes bleary slits. "What's cooking? *Manman*. Yara."

"Hey, baby." Yara grabbed his elbows and kissed him on each cheek. Nadine couldn't remember the last time she'd touched him like that.

Chance gave his big dimpled smile and bent to kiss the top of Yara's head. He took her hands and started to move in time with the music. He spun her under his arm. The wine sloshed in Nadine's tight stomach.

They danced a few measures. Chance helped himself to a handful of rolls from the basket Yara held out to him. She handed him a heaping bowl of stew, which he ate standing up in just a few giant bites while bobbing to the next song. Nadine rested her forehead in her hand and imagined how good it would feel to lie down on her pillow. Yara touched her shoulder. "Don't let your heart be angry," she whispered.

Angry? She was exhausted and a little bit drunk. Chance's

phone sounded a bar of his terrible music. Yes, she was angry. Anger was necessary in many situations.

Chance dropped his bowl and spoon into the sink and rubbed his stomach as his phone played the tune over and over. Yara posed like a gangster, folding her sparkly fingers into a strange gesture. Chance laughed, gestured back, and answered his phone. "Yo." He slouched into the next room.

"This isn't funny," Nadine said. "This is nothing to laugh about."

"Chance is a good boy," Yara said. "You are a good mother. Believe it. It's important to believe it."

Nadine slapped the edge of the table. "I'm not stupid."

"You're tired," Yara said. "You need a new job so you have the energy to have a good time."

She was tired. And angry. And scared. But mostly angry.

"The principal said he wouldn't walk at graduation," Nadine said.

"Wouldn't walk" sounded like someone, the security guards maybe, would break his legs. Break his legs and place him at a desk. If only some strong man would care enough about her careless, beautiful boy to do that.

"You'll talk with him—"

"Yo, *Manman*." Chance paused in the doorway with his heavy-lidded eyes and his know-it-all smirk. "I'm outta here. Junior's crib."

"You're not leaving now! It's late." Nadine willed herself to speak calmly, but the wine had loosened her lips. "You didn't even wash your dish after Yara fed you! And where have you been?"

"Junior's crib. Spitting fire." He drummed a measure on his thigh. "But we need to redo the track."

"Always these messages from the school. Only a few months left, and what are you doing? The principal called today. It's very serious now."

Chance sighed long and loud. "Mom, chill. You don't know what you're talking about."

Yara fanned herself with the ultrasound picture and patted Nadine's arm, her forehead wrinkling in concern.

Nadine turned on her friend. "This is a good boy?" She shook Yara's hand off her sleeve. "I know I would never waste the opportunity for schooling! You!" She blocked the door to the hallway and shouted at Chance. "*You* don't know what *you're* talking about!"

He filled a glass with water. "I said, chill." Nadine knew not to go on about the years she spent lugging water on her head, first up the mountain paths in her village, and later, after Uncle Maxim took her to Port-au-Prince, through dusty streets from the communal tap. Once those words began to spill out, they wouldn't stop. Chance flicked his wrist, the water flowing, and drank. She watched, clenching and unclenching her fists at her sides, breathing hard.

"You must go to school tomorrow. We have to meet with that man."

"I already been meeting with him. Seriously, relax." An insolent grin stretched his face. "They never keep track of seniors in the last semester. Junior has a session scheduled at a studio. I gots to be there."

"You think you are some big shot? More special than any other person? You need to go to school!"

Music blasted from Chance's pocket, the same tune twice. He flipped open the phone and started talking the kind of English she had never learned in her ESL classes.

"Aye, homie. You got the whip? Word? You trippin'! I ain't trying a hike over there." He rolled his eyes. "Yeah? You burning? Aight den. I be there."

He knew Haitian Creole, French, English, and even some Spanish, yet he chose this ghetto talk. When she had expressed her concern to his white teacher back in seventh grade, the teacher said not to worry; she called it "code switching," said Chance spoke proper English when he needed to, that kids wanted to fit in with their friends. She made it sound as though he were clever to have another language. Teachers had always loved Chance and been wary with her, until it was too late, when even they had to say, "He isn't working anywhere close to his potential"— their words, not hers. She had failed. She had failed him and herself. She should have beaten him.

"For real?" Chance, his back toward her now, spoke into his phone. "'S good. One."

Exhausted as she was, Nadine would never be able to sleep. She gripped the door frame and avoided Yara's pity-filled gaze.

Chance filled his glass again, drank the water in one long swallow, and set the glass in the sink next to his dirty bowl. Nadine stood unmoving between him and the door.

A flicker of shame crossed his face. He turned back toward the sink, ran a sponge around the rim of the glass, rinsed it and put it in the dish drainer. "Aight. Later." He brushed past her, answering his singing phone. The outside door slammed.

Nadine waited, relieved when Yara's only comment was the clatter of pans at the counter.

"I need to call Henry," she said. She would make him tell her what to do with his brother and wouldn't let him go on and on about Miami rice and Creole pigs and all the policies he was learning about that made the US rich and Haiti poor. Henry was a good boy. A smart boy.

Henry took advantage of the morning emptiness of the dorm's computer room to study his little brother's disturbing Myspace page. His mother's hysterical phone call in the middle of the night had made sleep impossible. He'd never heard her so upset.

At the opposite end of the counter that stretched along the windowed side of the room sat the mountainous guy everyone called Bear. Henry tried never to look too closely at Bear's red beard, flecked with unidentifiable crumbs. The guy's smudged glasses, unwashed hair, and strong yeasty smell made Henry sick. People had a responsibility to those around them to look and smell their best—it was a matter of respect. So many kids at this school acted like it was beneath them to give a shit about their appearance. Bear's flannel shirt was ripped at the arm hole. When he typed, it gaped, revealing a slice of mottled skin and red armpit hair. If Henry had ever worn torn clothes, his mother would have scolded him until his ears hurt.

"Been up all night working on this paper for linguistics," Bear muttered. "You do it yet?"

Henry nodded. He was not a procrastinator. In fact, he was extremely proud of his paper on the development of Haitian Creole and had already emailed it to the professor. He shifted in his chair, hoping the back of his head would discourage conversation. He gnawed on a sparerib left for him in the middle of the night by his roommate, realizing too late that John-o had neglected to include a napkin. Still chewing, he looked at his fingers and considered his options, finally wiping his sticky hands on his pants, up near the waistband under his shirt, before touching the keyboard.

"You're not allowed to eat in here." Sage, that self-righteous, vegan white girl with locs, plopped herself at the computer right next to Henry's. He purposefully helped himself to another rib, holding it between his thumb and index finger. He'd lick them clean later. She could have chosen any of the other twelve computers. Maybe she wanted to keep her distance from Bear. He couldn't blame her for that.

"Hi, Bear," she said.

Henry angled his monitor away from her. The photos Chance had posted of himself smoking blunts, sucking on fifths of Hennessy, hands splayed in front of his face in gang signs, and especially the references to packing heat all seemed to shout, "arrest me." Their old coach had told Henry last summer that the Cambridge Police monitored kids' Myspace pages. Sage extended her already ridiculously long neck slowly, as if he wouldn't notice. When he turned his head to confront her with narrowed eyes, she had the decency to blush and straighten up. He repositioned the package of ribs to the spot between them on the computer table, took his time smoothing the foil and even longer to raise one to his lips. She breathed a disgusted little sound and focused on her keyboard.

"My boyfriend 'borrowed' my laptop and won't give it back, even though I told him I had a paper due this afternoon. He won't answer his cell."

"Maybe you need a new boyfriend," Bear offered.

Henry clicked on a music video Chance had posted— Young Jeezy. The words tore through the air. In his rush to silence them, Henry smeared barbecue sauce on the mouse. He wiped it with his sleeve. The blotchy streak on his cuff looked like dried blood. He hoped it wouldn't stain.

Sage laughed, a bubbly delighted sound.

Over winter break Henry tried to talk some sense into Chance. "Keep your eyes on the prize," he told him. "You've got a couple of classes left. Don't screw it up."

"I'm not like you," Chance had said. "I don't want to go

to some fancy-ass college. It's cold and white enough in Cambridge, Massachusetts."

"I'm not talking about college. I'm talking about a high school diploma."

"Ma thinks teachers really give a shit if seniors go to class." Chance scoffed. "I need a couple of English credits, and Ms. Lorenzo likes me. She let me hand in lyrics instead of essays. A D's all I need, and she gon' gimme that."

Sage's keys clicked. She rolled her lips in and out, biting the top, then bottom, making no secret of the smirk she was half-pretending to hide. Henry wanted to scream, to leave, but he stayed in his chair at his sticky computer because at that moment he couldn't stop looking at the mess Chance was proudly broadcasting as his life. Henry's face twitched just below the surface, and he hoped it didn't show.

"Are you okay?" Sage had stopped typing and pretending not to look at him. She'd turned her whole chair to face his.

"Finish your paper." He closed the Myspace site.

"No, really, you look—"

"I'm fine." He stared out the window, past the computer screens, across the campus to a group of barefoot kids dancing on the lawn, which until a few days ago had been splotched with snow. The five of them joined hands around a huge tree and began to circle it. No doubt they were chanting something, some Indian mantra, but he couldn't hear it. He flash-backed to orientation when, after a yoga class, as he attempted to roll up the borrowed mat, he'd told the girl next to him, Sage, that he hated the way people said "Have a nice day" all the time. She looked at him quizzically, then laughed. "*Namaste*," she said. "Not have a nice day. *Namaste*. The spirit in me bows to the spirit in you." Everyone thought it was hilarious, mumbling, "Hammaniceday" and bowing to each other. Henry had jammed his half-rolled mess of a mat onto the rack, dislodging a few of the properly stored rubber rolls. Sage had reached out as if to touch his arm, but he'd jerked away. "They're not laughing AT you," she'd said. "It's funny, that's all."

Why had this school paid for him to come here? His guidance counselor had pushed it so hard. More diversity than any other small liberal arts college, the admissions materials boasted. All year he'd pretended not to be lonely, perfecting a look of contented detachment. He liked his roommate, John-o, though they didn't hang out. He liked Tiberius and Mr. Roy Washburn, the older guys from North Minneapolis that he worked with in the dining hall. In fact, sitting around with Tiberius after a work study shift was the only time he really felt relaxed, and the guy was what—forty? Older than his mother.

"You could smile once in a while," Sage said. "People would respond."

He concentrated on keeping his reply civil. "Good luck with the paper." He pushed his chair back, crushed the foil together around the bones, and stood.

"No, wait, Henry. I didn't mean to piss you off."

"I'm not pissed off."

"You sound pissed off to me," Bear said.

Henry clamped his mouth shut.

"You look pissed off." Sage smiled and reached toward him. He stepped back. Full of that pretty girl sense of privilege, she thought she could touch people whenever she wanted and they'd like it.

She tilted her head and made her blue-green eyes huge. "Maybe you could try not to look so angry all the time. You intimidate people, walking around like that. Do you want to scare people off? I mean, what are you trying to prove, really? That you're some kind of thug?"

"What?"

Thug, a substitute for the N-word as far as he was concerned. He'd been accused of trying to prove things before—like how smart he was, which by fifth grade he knew enough to keep undercover. Wrecked his own diorama of Toussaint L'Ouverture. He'd been punched in the face for acting white. Some of the Jamaican kids said he, like all Haitians, stunk. Other folks, even teachers, still believed Haitians caused the AIDS epidemic. A kid from Taiwan had asked him if he'd ever drunk human blood in vodou ceremonies.

"Henry, listen..." Sage said. "I'm just—"

"Don't worry about it." Henry tossed the ball of bones across the room into the trash basket.

"You could recycle that foil," Bear observed.

"Three point shot," said Sage.

"Later." His African-American Lit class started in ten minutes all the way across the campus. He swung by his room to grab his books and jacket, dashed down the stairs instead of waiting for the elevator, and cut across the sloshy, partly-frozen lawn.

Brownish grass squashed underfoot. Mud splattered his sneakers. He approached the tree dancers and imagined Sage watching from the window. Damn her for always making him more self-conscious than he already felt. The stench of incense burning near the base of the tree seared his nose and throat. Three out of the five dancers actually wore tie-dyed shirts. All five chanted with eyes closed. One of the girls opened her eyes, let go of her friend's hand, and held hers out to him, a crazy disoriented smile on her face.

Sage and Bear were probably talking about him right now— look at that angry Black man walking across the campus like a thug. Sometimes anger was the only thing that made sense. What made Sage angry besides factory farming? He tried to picture her life before college and couldn't. The girl spun past again, hand still outstretched. Three point shot, Sage had said. Why? Thinking he'd respond? That because he's Black he had to be into basketball? Fuck her. Fuck this place. Fuck it.

The girl dancer, and now the one next to her, circled and beckoned. What was he doing here so far from home? Barefoot people wouldn't be dancing around trees at UMass Boston, and not just because there were no trees.

Fuck it. He dropped his books and extended his hand. What was he doing? He felt a welcoming squeeze from each side. The group's momentum pushed him round and round the tree. He'd be late for class. Were Sage and Bear watching? What would they say? Chance would laugh his ass off—that loud throaty contagious howl. Henry closed his eyes, breathed in the pungent smoke, hummed along with the chanting, gripped the fingers of the girls' warm hands and surrendered to the dizzying orbit. He wasn't about to take his shoes off, though.

Yara pulled up next to a dirty heap of snow in front of *Manbo* Sivelia's blue suburban house. "Good luck," she said to Nadine. "If you have a chance, ask her about my grandson's birth. If there's anything I should be doing besides praying?"

You could make your own appointment, Nadine thought. *You can afford it.* She had problems enough of her own to talk about. But Yara had given her a ride all the way down to Randolph so she agreed. "I'm going to pick up a few things for the baby," Yara said. "I'll come back for you in an hour?"

The house had been a dull tan the last time Nadine had been there. Now it was blue, her favorite color, not exactly her favorite shade but nevertheless, a good omen. She fingered the roll of bills in her pocket—twenty-five dollars Sivelia had said on the phone. The price, like the price of everything else, had gone up.

"If you aren't finished then, no problem," Yara said. "I can wait. Go on."

Nadine set a foot on the damp pavement, breathed in the smell of wet snow, and willed herself toward whatever it was she might learn. Icicles hung from Sivelia's roof, and the loud sloppy tick of their dripping filled the silence Yara left behind after driving away.

Before Nadine pressed the bell, the little woman opened the door, grabbed her with strong, wiry arms and kissed her cheeks. "*Cheri! Ou lage m. Sa fè lontan depi m pa wè w.*" She shook her head, and the beaded ends of her gray braids clicked softly.

The music of Sivelia's voice wrapped right around Nadine's heart. Yes, Nadine had let her go. Yes, it had been a long time. Henry was barely walking when she'd come here last, and Sivelia had warned her about devils in disguise, devils dressed in three-piece suits with handkerchiefs in their pockets and matching bowties. She'd done all but say the deacon's name. Yet, if Nadine had heeded the warning, she wouldn't have Chance. Henry wouldn't have a brother.

Manbo Sivelia held both of Nadine's hands and stared into her eyes. Her kind face had aged. The flesh near her mouth sagged. The skin around her eyes had loosened and wrinkled. Her grip was strong, and her fingernails pressed into Nadine's palms.

When Nadine was baptized at the Full Gospel Church, she'd had to renounce vodou. When she felt Chance kick the walls of her womb and she could no longer hide her growing belly, she knew she had to leave that church. She adjusted to her self-imposed exile in Cambridge by working hard. She cared for Henry, saw her social worker, and kept a small distance between herself and others. Someone, especially anyone Haitian, was sure to know Deacon Joseph or Deacon Joseph's cousin or aunt or nephew or godchild, so Yara was her only friend. That small distance stretched big. She lit candles at home, alone, the way she'd done so much else in her life. With Sivelia's delighted face before her, Nadine wished she had come sooner.

Framed school pictures of smiling children covered the hallway's walls. The pale carpet was new. A round glass table near the basement door still held a plate of Sivelia's business cards, a vase of plastic flowers, and the Ninja Turtles lunch box she used for collecting fees. Nadine tucked the twenty-five dollars into the lunch box. When Henry came home from daycare excited about Ninja Turtles, and she remembered that lunch box, she'd taken comfort in her previous association—small as it was, it seemed auspicious. She'd found the cartoon on TV and they watched it together; even Chance, a toddler who almost never stopped moving, sat still for it.

Sivelia, with a tilt of her chin, directed her down the freshly painted stairs to the basement peristyle. The dim, empty room spread out around the metal support column, the *poto mitan,* and the two wooden chairs and small table beside it. Bottles and candles clustered at the base of the column. *Manbo* Sivelia waved Nadine into a chair, lifted a blue bottle and splashed liquid onto the floor three times, before handing it to Nadine to do the same. She seated herself across from Nadine, knees almost touching, and wrapped a string around a small white candle, covering the whole outside surface, pressing it in place with a manicured thumbnail. When she finished, she lit the candle.

"Something is troubling you," said Sivelia. "Is it money? Love?"

Nadine laughed. She wished she could sit forever in this immaculate, candle-lit space, Sivelia's open, listening face before her. "Always money, always," she said. "And no— love does not concern me, too busy for love. But the biggest problem is with my boys."

"Boys. Ah. Henry is grown now, no? You have another boy, yes? They are almost men. This is not an easy time for a mother."

A *pànye* placed on their knees made a surface for the card casting. Sivelia shuffled a worn deck of playing cards while Nadine pictured the *pànye* full of shelled and roasted peanuts ready to skin for peanut butter or clumps of coffee beans glazed in melted sugar, ready to pound, so many uses for the flat baskets. As Sivelia laid out the cards in rows, Nadine missed her village so much everything inside hurt.

The candle flame sputtered and flared as *Manbo* Sivelia considered the cards. She pointed to them with her long red fingernail and spoke, working her way through the configuration. Her face blurred and shifted.

"*Manman!*" The sound of her own voice startled Nadine. She saw her brothers lined up in front of her parents' tomb, beckoning her. The tomb she had helped pay for.

"Tell me what you see," Sivelia said.

Nadine's chest heaved, as tears trickled, then flowed down her face.

"My brothers," she said. "Onaldo, Kervens, Jonas—all of them standing next to the tomb."

"Yes." Sivelia studied the cards. "Your son, he needs male energy. You do what you can, but it is not enough for a young man."

She tapped a jack of clubs and a jack of spades. "Your

brothers, your sons' uncles, when you think of them, what do you see? What are they telling you?" Nadine let out a loud breath.

"They are calling me."

"Then you don't need me to be telling you," *Manbo* Sivelia said. "The message could not be more clear. You must return home and bring your sons."

She swept up the cards. Nadine cut the deck. Sivelia laid them out once more and examined them. "This is very interesting," she said. "Again, quite clear. The time is right for thinking about a change in your work. Have you considered this?"

"My friend is always telling me to quit my job," Nadine said.

"Your body is tired. You must rely more on your brain. Pray to *La Sirèn*. Make offerings to her. She is known to help singers and actors with their voices, do you want to sing?"

"No," Nadine said.

"You will make money using your voice. If not singing, then speaking, speaking truth. *La Sirèn* will help you. She will bring you wealth—like riches from the sea. She will show you the way, how to navigate the next months, even years. And she will help you find your way back to Lagonav."

Nadine couldn't go back to Haiti—too much need, too much gossip. She couldn't face a village full of people who thought they knew her story but had it all wrong. They would not want their version to be corrected. How could she go and not talk about Uncle Maxim? How could she go without the piles of gifts and money the family would expect? And Henry might agree to go to Haiti but Chance wouldn't. Chance wouldn't even go across the street with her.

Sivelia dealt the cards one more time. "Do you have any questions?"

"My son Chance. Why is he so rude? Why doesn't he go to school? After his brother left for college in September, he became trouble. Is someone envious of Henry's opportunities and punishing me by putting a curse on his brother?" If anyone was responsible it was Deacon Joseph's wife. Maybe she had found out about Chance, her husband's unclaimed son. Nadine couldn't say her name out loud.

The *manbo* leaned over the rows of cards. Nadine wished she could see whatever it was Sivelia saw. Finally, Sivelia said, "No, it is no kind of curse."

Nadine closed her eyes and breathed a relieved thank you, but the *manbo* went on. "It is very simple. Your boy has been having a difficult time. He needs more family. You are not enough anymore. You must take him home. Both boys must go home."

Nadine nodded, her throat too full to say anything.

"Trust in *La Sirèn* to carry you all back across the ocean. The visit doesn't have to be a long one but it has to *be*—if you want your sons to thrive, especially the younger one. You don't want to go?"

Nadine kept her expression neutral. She didn't answer, though it was clear to her that Sivelia and the spirits knew what she was thinking.

"Your life here is too lonely," Sivelia said.

Nadine didn't need the spirits and *Manbo* Sivelia to tell her that. She'd isolated herself inside her secrets since Chance was the size of Yara's coming grandchild, and, working to make a life for herself and her sons, had somehow gotten used to it.

"Pray," Sivelia commanded. "Come back to see me. Have faith."

Later, when Yara asked about her grandson's birth, Nadine couldn't admit she'd forgotten to bring it up.

"All will be well," she told her. "Pray."

"Nothing else?" Yara raised her perfectly shaped eyebrows.

Nadine wished she had something specific and helpful to say. "Have faith?"

Yara nodded.

"Have faith," Nadine repeated for her friend's sake and her own. She hadn't meant to make a question of it.

Nadine waited near an arrivals board at Logan, willing the moments to pass. "Landed," she read next to Henry's flight. Airports hurt her stomach. When Uncle Maxim brought her at fourteen from Haiti, speaking no English, they landed first in Miami. She'd stood at the top of the escalator, a moving cliff, unable to take the next step. Maxim gripped her upper arm—his hand fit all the way round as he dragged her through immigration; she was nothing then but bone and bruised skin.

That girl, sitting in the back seat of a big, quiet, air-conditioned car, saw streets so black and smooth, they looked delicious. Buildings made of glass glittered and shone. That girl, scared as she was, couldn't wait to go to school. But she had waited. She had waited months until the church ladies shamed her uncle into sending her. He thought she would get into trouble at school, fooling around with boys, but those white and Cuban boys had no interest in her, and she couldn't even talk with them. Only serious, sweet-tempered Lucien, who worked at the Haitian bakery, made her laugh and brushed his fingers against hers when he handed her the boxes.

Henry had a slight gap between his front teeth just like

Lucien, and was just as careful with his smiles, as if he were born with a limited number and had to save them for the most deserving situations. But when he was thinking or worried, his brow furrowed just the way her older brother's had—his uncle Onaldo—five small wrinkles between his eyebrows. She used to trace them with her finger while she teased him into a better mood.

The opaque glass doors opened, and Henry stepped through, shrugging his small duffel bag higher on his shoulder. He wore his sport coat and a white shirt with a necktie. He looked very studious in his big black-framed glasses, and neat with his closely shaved head. She opened her arms wide, wrapped him in a hug, kissed him on each cheek, then held his face between her palms and kissed his forehead and nose. His cautious smile dissolved.

"*Manman*, you're steaming up my glasses."

"When we get home we'll have *fritay* and *pikliz*, like you wanted," she said.

He looked past her and from side to side. Looking for Chance.

"I told your brother to be home for dinner. I'm sorry we have to take the train." She stopped at the sign for the shuttle bus. "Can I carry that?"

"*Manman!*" Henry nudged her hand away. "I can manage my own bag."

Fried food tastes best fresh from the oil. Chance's portion sat cold on grease-soaked paper, under the *kouvrepla*. Henry flipped through the small pile of mail his mother had saved for him, all junk. She scuttled around the kitchen, banging dishes, running water, turning up the radio, as if trying to fill the space where she and Henry would be making conversation if either of them could think of something ordinary or calming to say. His mother shut the cupboard door on the dried dishes. The talk show host rattled on in *Kreyòl*.

"I should sleep," his mother said. "I have to be up early for work."

Henry dumped the mail into the recycling bin. He might as well go to bed too.

Way downstairs a door slammed and footsteps clomped their way. Chance burst through the apartment door. *Manman* gave Henry a look he couldn't read, a wince. He took it as a worried warning, but watching her uncover the fried fish, potatoes, and plantains and poke at them, as if she actually cared that Chance's food was cold, he wanted to shout at her. His brother didn't need someone waiting on him; he needed someone to kick his ass.

Chance filled the kitchen doorway and yanked out an earphone; it dangled, tinny, thumping music leaking out, as he swaggered toward Henry. "What's good, bro?" Henry stood, feeling his mother's anxious stare over his shoulder. He forced a smile. Chance grabbed for his hand, middle, ring and pinky fingers folded in some complicated shape that Henry reflexively tried to imitate. Chance pulled him close with his other hand and thumped his shoulder.

His little brother had at least eight inches on him. That wasn't right. Their mother had to notice his slitted red eyes. Chance scraped a chair across the linoleum and fell into it. He tossed aside the *kouvrepla* and shoved a whole sweet potato into his mouth.

"*Sa bon, Manman.*" Crumbs fell from his lips.

Henry sat steaming. Which was worse? Chance chewing with his mouth open, spitting food, or his mother watching with a faint, but pleased, smile as though all that mattered was that her boy was eating the meal she'd prepared? Had she already forgotten her desperate call, begging Henry to come home? He'd spent his whole savings on this spring break trip. He wanted to see for himself how things had deteriorated since December. He wanted to help out.

Chance finished the *fritay*. "So, you chilling with me tonight, or what?"

Their mother hovered in the small space between the sink and the table as if she didn't know where to settle; nervous exhaustion emanated from her every pore, weed's sweet stink surrounded Chance.

"Mom, go to bed," Henry said. "Get some sleep."

"Are you going out with your brother?" she asked. She wanted him to. She would be able to sleep imagining him as some kind of chaperone. Yeah, right.

"Hell yeah, he's coming." Chance slapped Henry's back. "Let's go."

How many times had they crossed the streets of their neighborhood side by side, Henry under strict orders to hold Chance's hand, to keep him safe? Even after youth center dances, when middle school kids were required to be picked up by someone, it was Henry, only a year out of middle school himself, who went over to walk his brother home, listening to him jabber about the girls he'd danced with and speculate which one liked him the most.

"Watch your head," Chance warned Henry, ducking at the low spot halfway down the stairs to Junior's basement. He shouldered open the door. "What's poppin'?"

Junior and Razz sat close together sunk deep into a sagging couch, Junior breaking up weed on the spiral notebook of lyrics resting on his thighs, Razz peeling the wrapper from a Dutch. They were an odd pair, Junior big, dark, and slow moving with soft, round cheeks; Razz, scrawny and pale, almost white looking or Puerto Rican, with meticulously cared-for facial hair. These days he wore it in a perfect chin-strap.

Chance lifted a bottle from the table in front of them and squinted at the label. "What's this shit, yo? 99 Bananas?"

"This clown sweats it." Junior wagged a thumb at Razz. His deep laugh shook all of his enormous body, but he kept his knees steady so as not to spill the weed. "Hey, college boy. Was going on way up in the North land? Got any snow-shoes and shit? Any brothers out there?"

"A few," Henry said. "But most be working in the cafe-teria. Or they janitors and guards and shit. A few Black foreign students—straight from Africa—sons of bankers and daughters of dictators." His words flowed, unconsidered and unedited; he relaxed into a chair. The dim light from Junior's aquarium and a couple strings of old Christmas bulbs softened the dark.

"Welcome back to the hood." Junior picked a seed from the weed and threw it at Henry. "Razz, twist up, my dude."

Razz's spit was all over that cigar, licking it before peeling off the outside leaf, again before splitting the inside paper and tossing the tobacco. That wasn't all. His drool soaked the blunt as he rolled, expertly crimping it with his lips, licking it again to seal the whole thing. Henry had gotten used to smoking a pipe, on the rare occasion he indulged at school.

"Weed any good out there?" Razz handed Henry the blunt. "Check this out."

"S'okay." Henry held it to his lips and tried to ignore how damp it felt. Probably wouldn't even be able to get the thing to catch, he thought. Razz flicked the lighter and Henry inhaled a deep lungful of delicious smoke. Edges dissolved. The world felt far away and irrelevant. All of it.

Chance took a swig from the bottle and shuddered.

"Monkey piss!" Henry let his brother's laugh, rumbly and musical, roll over him. He leaned back, closed his eyes, and ran his fingers over the nubby fabric covering the arms of the chair.

"Fucking monkey piss," Chance said again. "What's left after the bananas run through the monkey. All fermented and shit. That's probably how they make it. A fucking factory of pissing monkeys. There's a job, yo. Holding the bottle under a monkey's dick. Then another one lets loose. You be running back and forth." He acted it out, a few steps one way, then the other, waving the bottle. They all hooted, loud and long. Henry couldn't remember the last time he'd had a whole-body, stomach-aching, side-wrenching, gasping-for-air, mindless good time like this.

"Yeah, don't be spilling it. Less you want to be fired from your monkey piss collecting job," Junior said.

"You be laughing," Razz said, "But that shit's 99 proof. Tastes better and better."

Chance knuckled Henry's head and passed him the bottle. "Brought him to check out our beats," Chance told his friends. "He thinks I don't do nothing but get high."

"He don't know the half," Junior laughed.

"**B**e easy," Henry warned as he and Chance stumbled their way up the stairs. "Easy, bro."

Chance thudded against the wall, laughing loudly, then folded into a heap on the second floor landing.

"Door's right here," said Henry. "Get your ass up and on into bed. Come on."

"Sooooo ... I say, it's better to have a gun and not need it, than need one and not have it."

"Shh." Henry tugged at his arm, hauling Chance partway

to his feet. "Do you want Mom to hear you? Or Yara?" When had his little brother turned from the boy who spent evenings at the park organizing games of manhunt and werewolf, with a kid or two on his shoulders, into this wannabe gangster fantasizing about guns?

"Two hundred bills for a deuce-deuce, cheaper if it has bodies on it." Chance's words echoed in the stairwell. "Razz knows a dude—"

"Shut the fuck up," said Henry, sweating in his effort to find his keys while keeping Chance standing. He managed to jiggle the key into the lock, pull the door knob the necessary fraction of an inch so the lock could turn, and twist the key, all with Chance balanced heavily against his hip. The door fell open, and he shoved Chance inside.

The smell of wax and Florida water washed over them—Mom lighting her candles again. Henry knew better than to believe any of that nonsense. Vodou, Christianity—it was all the same, opiate of the masses. His notebooks were full of images of Karl Marx, Ho Chi Minh, and John Brown. He propelled Chance past the kitchen.

"Hang on a minute," Chance protested and lurched away. "I gotta get me some food. My stomach's saying it won't be letting me sleep 'less I fill it up."

Henry followed. In the deserted kitchen, on the table, their mother's *veve*-like picture of sprinkled sugar—its symmetry disturbed by something in the night, the sleeve of her nightgown maybe—reproached him. How long had she sat up praying and waiting?

"The abolition of religion as the illusory happiness of the people is required for their real happiness," Henry muttered, partly to prove to himself that, high as he was, he could still remember the whole Marx quote. "The demand to give up the illusion about its condition is the demand to give up a condition which needs illusions."

"Huh?" Chance pulled open the refrigerator and bent low to study the contents, his face oddly illuminated in the dimness of the room. "Is that what they're teaching you out there on the tundra?"

"That's what I be teaching them!" Henry said. "Or I would be, if anyone gave a shit."

"You all about revolution," Chance said into the refrigerator. "But you got a problem with guns. Everyone knows nobody be just giving up power, handing it over." He stood up, holding a container of leftover stew. "You the one telling me to read Malcolm X. Didn't he say 'No one be giving you freedom. You gotta take it?' You need firepower, man. You know, if you got shot with a deuce deuce, bullets bounce off your bones." He forked cold stew into his mouth and flashed a huge close-mouthed grin, cheeks bulging. He stabbed a chunk of sweet potato and held it out to Henry, eyebrows raised.

Henry pushed his hands up underneath his glasses, massaging his eyeballs and eye sockets. Chance's goofy generosity made him feel mean. Chance had gotten busted for cheating in almost every one of his classes, sharing his answers on tests, until teachers automatically forced him to sit in isolation. Why would anyone want to copy Chance's papers? The world was full of idiots. "I'm going to bed," he said.

"Soon's I finish this, I am, too. What time is it anyway? Guess I won't be making it to class."

"Mom's working 7-3. She'll be up in an hour." Henry moistened a finger and touched it to a whorl of sugar in the middle of his mother's creation. "Won't she make you go to school?"

"She tries." A short laugh escaped his nose.

Henry, too tired for an argument, headed toward the bedroom they'd always shared. He imagined his mother awake and listening.

He threw himself onto the bed, and squeezed his eyes shut against the graffiti Chance and his friends had painted on the bedroom walls. He pretended to sleep, but after a few minutes of rustling sounds, he turned his head and saw his brother's legs sticking out from under the other twin bed. Chance wriggled out, emerging with a flat, t-shirt wrapped package in his hand.

"Henry, I know you ain't asleep."

Henry opened one eye. His brother jittered in front of him, chewing on his lips in attempt to stay cool.

"I got something for you—a late Christmas present or early, depending on how you want to look at it. Either way, you gonna be smiling."

Henry rolled away from him, pillow pressed around his face.

Chance pried the pillow from his hands and threw it across the room. He sat on the edge of the bed and lifted the shirt and its contents from the floor. Henry rolled over and tried to pull the sheet over his head, but it was bunched under Chance.

"Henry, look what I got for you. Don't ever say I didn't give you nothing."

Chance whisked the t-shirt from a brand new laptop, and with a flourish presented it to Henry on the flat of his hand as if it were a tray of fancy food he'd spent hours preparing.

"You're shitting me," Henry said.

"Well, don't just be sitting there. Log on."

"Where'd you get it?"

"All's I know it fell off some truck."

"You steal it?"

"I didn't," Chance said. "Don't start with the self-righteous bullshit, alright? I'm helping my friends out. It's all business. Here." He opened the laptop and set it on Henry's legs.

Henry hesitated. No more computer room. He could do his work in private. And other things too—keep an eye on Chance, listen to music, watch movies, chat with people without Sage or anyone else sticking their long noses where they didn't belong.

He ran his fingers over the keyboard.

"They can probably trace stolen computers." Henry had tried not to say it, but the words came out anyway. Once Chance had a rap sheet he'd never get a student loan or a job.

"Yeah, but they don't. You think any big company cares about someone losing their computer? They know they gonna sell another one. Anyway, I told you, it fell off a truck. Finders keepers." Chance slapped him on the back, his breath warm near Henry's face and stinking of stale weed and rotten bananas, his body leaning in close.

Henry pressed the power button. The screen lit up. Heads together, they watched it boot.

Nadine switched off her alarm without opening her eyes. She thought she heard Chance and Henry talking, but groggy from her restless night, with a long day of work stretching ahead, she couldn't summon the energy to confront them.

No one yelled at her to get up. She should enjoy a few extra minutes alone on her comfortable mattress. Even now, years and years after leaving Haiti, she could hear uncle's woman cawing her name over and over—Naaaaaa-diiiiiiine—until she stood her skinny body up from her pile of rags, grabbed the water bucket, and stumbled down the path. "*Fè vit tifi!*" the woman squawked at her back, and Nadine would hurry off just to distance herself from that hateful voice. She enjoyed a few moments of peace on the road, the empty bucket swinging light from her hand, dirt road cool under her feet, freshness of night yet to be burned away by the rising sun.

She'd shoulder her way through the crowd of kids clustered around the spigot. Back home in the mountains of Lagonav she'd been happy to wait her turn at the water, splashing her friends, trading elastics, sharing *kenèp, grenadya,* or *mango* picked along the steep path to the spring. In Port-au-Prince she'd had no friends, and if she took too long getting back with the household water, Maxim's woman beat her. Better to brave the loud protests and rough shoves of the women and kids as she maneuvered her five gallon bucket under the tap. Nadine heard the talk of those who belonged in that neighborhood calling her *restavèk, dezòd, tèt kwòt.* She missed her mother's hands in her hair, braiding, twisting.

She willed the water to glug faster before the tall girl with the beautiful yellow scarf jabbed her in the back again with the point of her elbow, before another voice behind her called her a stink butt or said she had rotten teeth. Her teeth were strong and shiny. Her mother had made sure of that. Every other kid in the village sucked and chewed candy when they could. If she had candy, her mother made her brush her teeth afterward with soap. They had no right to call her rotten teeth. They'd never even seen her teeth because since she'd come to Port-au-Prince she hadn't once smiled. And she never would.

Finally, the bucket full, she heaved it away from the spout, twisted her one other skirt into a coil, the *twòkèt,* a cloth nest on her head. *Sa se twòkèt la; chay la dèyè.* This is the *twòkèt;* the load is on its way. She squatted and with her thin, muscled arms hefted the bucket onto it. In Port-au-Prince that load loomed much larger and weighed more than the forty-pound bucket of water. She whispered the proverb to herself as she hung on tight, every muscle working hard, praying no one pushed her. Back in the village friends would lift the buckets for each other. Here, a scrawny girl with bulgy eyes stomped close, threatening a shove.

Nadine jerked back, sloshing water over the edge of the pail. It streamed down her arm onto her blouse and people laughed. She narrowed her eyes; at twelve, she had perfected this look, and her body, under its burden, moved with a tight and angry grace. A path opened for her through the jeering women and kids, and she made her way to the small house she would never call home.

Uncle Maxim, his wife, and three sons lived in a beautiful house with wrought iron gates, tiled floors and ceiling fans, and heavy wooden furniture from the United States. When her father sent her to Port-au-Prince, this was the house he'd imagined his daughter sleeping in. Instead Nadine lived in a one-room, dirt-floored block house with her uncle's bitter mistress and her children who were always coughing. She wasn't allowed to call them cousins. He introduced her to the children in the beautiful house as cousin, so perhaps it was the woman's children he was pretending weren't his.

"This one never smiles," Uncle said, pulling on Nadine's cheeks. "What would it take to make you smile?" He gave her blue lollipops and *bonbon guarina*, Coca-Cola. He sat in the tiny yard, next to the woman's hibiscus flower, in the one good chair and pulled her between his legs, tickled her ribs, cupped her growing breasts. He pinched her nipples while the woman peeked through the petal-shaped openings in the concrete block of the house and sucked her teeth. Nadine winced and squirmed, but Uncle just laughed.

"You're my favorite, little sour face," he said. "I'd bring you to live with me but my wife and children would be jealous."

His words filled her ear with their damp heat. He licked her neck, and she held as still as she could, staring into the hibiscus blossom.

Sometimes a hummingbird came to drink and, watching its shimmer against the ruffled pink flower, she could lose herself in appreciating the bird's tiny perfection. She wished for the bird when Uncle took her hand and slid it inside his pants. "I'm going to make you smile one day," he said, as she vowed he never would.

"I'm going to bring you with me to the United States," he whispered, and moved her hand faster over his penis. He twisted her nipple.

She wouldn't scream or acknowledge in any way what he was doing. She imagined the blur of the hummingbird's wings. "When I can arrange it all, you will be the one to come with me. You will smile then."

She wanted to go to America. Most people did. But, in the same way, she had wanted to go to Port-au-Prince, and imagined when he'd arrived to fetch her that her world was about to open up. Instead, *chay la dèyè*. How could leaving her father, her brothers, which had felt so miserable, seem easy in comparison to all that followed? It made her wonder if America might be like Port-au-Prince, but worse.

Even now, so many years later, she didn't understand why her uncle chose her. Did she carry a curse? He had a wife, the one mistress she knew of in Port-au-Prince, and another in Miami. He wasn't an unattractive man, and he had money. There were many beautiful young women who would have been willing to please him in return for a trip to the United States. Why a hungry niece?

There was no point now in regret. Henry and Chance had opportunities they wouldn't have had back home. But on all the nights when her back screamed and she couldn't sleep, or early on a rare morning when she allowed herself this extra time in bed, she thought about her father dying without her there. She thought about her parents' tomb she'd paid for but only seen in pictures, her family waking up each day in the mountains, sweeping their yards, weeding their corn and cassava, carrying their *epina*, peppers, and cabbage to the market.

Get up, she thought. Before a big loneliness comes and joins you.

At home she'd be sharing a bed with at least three other people, more if they were small—siblings, cousins, nieces, nephews. While she loved her pillows, sheets, thick comforter, and expensive mattress, she would sleep better with a toddler curled beside her or a sister-in-law gently snoring within arm's reach.

Maybe Sivelia was right and she should take the boys back to Lagonav for a visit. But no. What had she done with her big opportunity? How would she explain leaving Maxim? Or Henry and Chance with two different fathers she never saw? Or spoke about? Since the coup and the ousting of Aristide, the political situation was unstable. Instead of settling down, it seemed to be growing worse. A visit wasn't possible.

She'd dreamed that Maxim had died and that she was responsible for tying his jaw shut, but flocks of hummingbirds swarmed from his mouth, pricking her with their needle-sharp beaks, blinding her with their beating wings. She rubbed her cheeks, relieved to find them free of punctures and scabs.

Maybe she should be praying to *Èzili* and *La Sirèn* for a husband. Yara would say so. Sivelia would say so too. Yes, a husband might be a useful influence on Chance—right here in the US, eliminating the need for a complicated return home. She'd prayed for a man that wakeful night, when little

Henry wheezed with asthma. Deacon Joseph appeared and not only took them to the emergency room, but calmed her afterward with comforting touches that led to lovemaking and Chance's very existence. It remained a mystery why she had allowed that to happen, what magic he had used on her, he was almost old and not handsome. Exhaustion had crumbled her defenses and her common sense.

The deacon was a stern and powerful man and just a train ride away. She had never asked him for anything. Might she ask him to give Chance a talking to? No, that would open a whole new box of trouble. She hadn't spent all these years alone, only to tangle up her life with his now.

She had to get up. She had to think about the future, make plans, forget about Lucien, Deacon Joseph, and relatives who had forgotten about her. Living on Lagonav, her brothers were okay, far from violence in the cities. Hunger allowed people at least a chance of survival, killing more slowly than a bullet or machete.

Her boys stared up at her from their framed pictures on her bedside table—Henry with his glasses, neatly shaved head, collared blue shirt, and solemn expression; Chance with cornrows—there was always a lineup of girls ready to braid his hair for him—heavy-lidded red eyes, and lips pressed together in a know-it-all smirk. How had she not noticed he was high on drugs? She was a fool. She laid the picture face down, careful not to break the glass.

She stretched her sore back and opened her purple curtains to consider the sky. Since the spring time change, it was very dark again in the morning before her early shift. Another thing Americans couldn't leave alone. Why change clocks just to confuse people?

She cleaned the kitchen from the night before, glad to see the boys had eaten, drank her coffee, considered knocking on their bedroom door to say goodbye and tell Chance to go to school, but all was quiet. She didn't want a fight. She and the principal kept missing each other—phone tag, people called it, like some kind of game. She checked her tomato seedlings, marveling that they managed to push up through the dirt with those threadlike stems and delicate leaves. They must be stronger than they looked.

*H*azel Watkins *opened her eyes and pressed them shut again. One worked, but the other drooped, not quite open, not quite closed, no matter what she tried to do with the muscles of her face. After a lifetime of mornings, waking ready to tackle a long list of tasks, the world waiting to be reshaped by her capable, busy hands, that moment of preparing to jump into her daily routine persisted. Heavy tomatoes and peppers that had begun as seeds on the tip of her finger turned into gleaming jars of relish lined up in ready rows. Flat pieces of fabric cut, tucked, pleated, and sewn into aprons, blouses and slacks for herself or curtains for her mobile home. Every floor and countertop dust free and shining.*

At night, she'd relax in her red Barcalounger, the one she'd gotten for practically nothing at the flea market, her double scotch on the rocks on a coaster beside her, listening to Glenn Miller, Bing Crosby, Tommy Dorsey—music had never gotten any better than that—and doing Sudoku until the ice melted in her glass. She'd drink the cool mouthful of water, wash her glass, and after checking the stove, the faucets, the windows, and the lock on the door, get herself ready for bed. In a perfect world, there would be no need for sleep, such a waste of time.

At Riverview Manor, sleep was a survival technique. In

her dreams, when she was lucky, she found herself making bread or baiting a hook with a big, fat night crawler, or burying a dead gopher under her lilac bushes. When she was lucky, her dreams felt real and her waking life receded into only a passing nightmare. This useless body was not her. If someone did not straighten the crooked blind, which she was forced to stare at whenever she opened her eyes, she would go crazy. They were constantly finding subtle and devious ways to torture her. People stole and screamed and turned the heat up too high. At home she could keep as cool as she wished. In her spotless and streamlined mobile home, she had perfected the art of loneliness.

"Mrs. Watkins?" Fat Black Nadine approached the bed. Hazel breathed in the fragrance of chrysanthemums, distinct and bitter—she loved that smell, but the woman carried no flowers. "Time to get you moving a bit. Cleaned up. Ready for breakfast." Hazel tried harder to squeeze her eyelids together.

"And breakfast has arrived!" Ronnie, a twitchy little man— Puerto Rican, Hazel thought, but Dominican, he said—with ugly spider webs tattooed over both arms pushed the food cart halfway into the room. "Hey, beautiful."

Hazel glared and prepared to scold him for his audacity, realized he wasn't talking to her, and ducked her head to hide her embarrassment.

"I'm too old for you," Nadine said.

"You hungry, Mrs. Watkins?" Ronnie pawed through the stacks of plastic-covered plates to find the one with her name on it. Some tasteless glop.

"Put the food over there," said Nadine. "She's not ready. Mrs. Watkins, I'm going to wash you up now." Hazel lifted her face toward the cloth. One cheek registered the cool dampness, the other felt nothing. She concentrated, willing her skin to recognize the nubbly texture of terrycloth, the

pressure of the aide's hand as it moved over her affected side. Maybe she felt something or maybe she just thought she did.

"I like older women," Ronnie said. "Besides you're not much older than me—you hit thirty yet?"

"Thirty-six." The aide made a sharp tuipe *sound—sucking her teeth. "You like older women, you're working in the right place."*

Ha! That was funny. If her mouth worked properly, Hazel would smile.

"You got that right!" Ronnie winked at Nadine, grabbed hold of the cart, and followed it out of the room.

The aide made that sound again. Very expressive. So many situations called for just that response. "Today you have speech therapy. Took them long enough to get it started. I know you have a lot to say."

Darn right, Hazel thought. The woman's hands settled on her thighs, warm even through the fabric of her nightgown. She steeled herself to suffer the indignity of diaper removal and the washing of her most private parts. She would never let herself relax into accepting such care as routine. The speech therapist would help her formulate the words necessary to convince Gary to get her out of this place.

Henry lay curled up, tight and furious, facing the wall, listening to Chance's even breathing. He was on vacation, should be sleeping late. Instead it was his brother, who was supposed to be in school, snoring peacefully. What a deluded asshole, so cocky and sure he'd get away with stealing computers, playing with guns. Too charming for his own good. While Henry ground away at footnoted papers with page-long bibliographies, Chance scribbled a few rap lyrics, performed them for his English class, and got the same grades. While Henry took out the trash, Chance threw his arms around their mother, dancing her around on the rug Henry had just vacuumed, and soaked up her weary smile like a self-satisfied sponge.

Relax, he told himself. Relax. When he concentrated on his toes he unclenched them, but as soon as he moved on to relaxing another muscle, his toes clenched again. Chance was always on him to chill, but he couldn't leave their mother to do it all on her own.

Chance uncoiled into a noisy stretch clearly intended to wake Henry if he'd been asleep. When Henry didn't react, Chance began to hum, then croon, "Wake up, wakey, wakey." He leaped up and began belting out Bone Thugs-N-Harmony, "1st of tha Month."

Hand clamped on Henry's shoulder, Chance rocked him back and forth, "Okay!" Henry tried to shrug him off.

"Chill. Didn't think you'd want to be sleeping away your vacation." Chance retreated to the middle of the room, bobbed his head, bounced his shoulders, tapped his feet, and hummed.

Henry lifted himself onto an elbow. "What's on the agenda for today?"

Chance kept singing about getting up and smoking weed.

Henry wouldn't roll his eyes. He'd come home to hang out with his brother, not to alienate him further. Maybe they'd play some ball, pick up DVDs at the library or the movie store, go to the Galleria Mall and check out the new fitteds at Lids.

Chance grabbed a pair of pants and a shirt and clomped to the bathroom, leaving both the bedroom and bathroom doors open. It was as if he didn't want to deprive Henry or the rest of the world the opportunity to hear him piss. Henry retreated back under his blanket to wait for him. Maybe while they were at the mall or library he could persuade Chance to read something and finish it, instead of dipping into *The Autobiography of Malcolm X* between swigs on a bottle or pulls on a blunt.

The water stopped running. Henry slipped on his pants from the day before for the walk to the bathroom. Chance was already clattering around in the kitchen. Henry picked up the toothpaste. When he'd lived at home he'd kept it squeezed from the bottom, neatly rolled. Chance crushed it from the middle.

Mall first? Or hoops? He'd do whatever Chance preferred.

"You up for hanging with Junior and Razz? Got beats for you." Chance appeared in the bathroom door.

The idea of sitting in a basement subjected to their ragged music was not how he'd pictured spending a day, but what the hell. "Okay."

They strode into the feeble March sun that did nothing but soften the surfaces of the filthy snow heaps, just enough to wreck shoes and wet feet. At least it was warmer than Minnesota. A couple of blocks from Junior's, Chance tensed and sidestepped. The sidewalk in front of them was dry; he wasn't avoiding a puddle. Henry twisted around to see Chance slumping behind him as if trying to hide, then scanned the street. No puddles and no cops. Just a small person heading their way with a dancing swagger.

Chance's breath quickened. "Set me a pick. Get cross the street, yo."

"Hey, that's Rosie." Henry hardly recognized their old neighbor with her short hair and baggy clothes and gangster walk.

"Ro-Z, you mean," Chance muttered. "Like Jay-Z. Think

she all that. Rapper chick now. Singing songs that hate on men. Come on, cross over. She don't like me these days."

"What? Last summer she sweat you—your fan girl."

"Sweat me too much. She's extra."

Rosie/Ro-Z, close enough to recognize them now, called out to Henry. "You back! Long time, brother."

She lifted her little, sharp face and Henry pressed his cheek against hers. "What happened to all your hair, Ro?"

Chance shuffled past her and motioned Henry to keep moving. Neither he nor Rosie had even looked at each other.

"You know, the chemo." She waited for a perfectly timed moment, while Henry registered his horror and concern, then let loose with one of her legendary shrieks of laughter. "You should see your face! Just fuckin' witya."

Henry forced a laugh. Behind her Chance jerked his head in the direction of Junior's, then began walking.

"Got better things to do now than be messing wit my hair. You remember how much time all those college apps be taking, right? And I got my music—"

"What's up with you and my little brother?" Chance had already turned the corner. Henry knew the way to Junior's. He'd catch up.

Rosie rolled her lips in and out, caught them in her teeth, studied the toe of her sneaker. Her expression hurt to look at so Henry studied the sneaker too. It was a plain red one, like a little kid would wear—looked generic—so uncool it was cool.

Just as he opened his mouth to say, "See ya' around," she spoke. "Ask him, Henry. It wasn't good. I'm alright now. But your brother's an asshole."

She gave his arm a pat. "I'm late. If you want to chill some time, shout me a holler. Number's the same. I'd love to hear about life after high school."

"My take on it might not be what you're hoping to hear."

"You might have some survival tips." She grinned. He'd always liked her smile, not quite smirky, but with an edge of something, mischief might be the right word. "I'm a little scared to leave this town, but I gotta get out and see something different."

"It is different," Henry said. "First survival tip—go to Philly or New York or Atlanta or DC, where you got some Black people."

"My first choice, Smith College."

Henry laughed. Who was he to be giving advice to anybody?

"See you, Ro. You got my number too."

Henry jogged to Junior's, Rosie's words, "Your brother's an asshole," echoing in his head, just the way she'd said them. He called Chance an asshole and worse countless times, but hearing her say it—Rosie who'd played basketball with the boys for hours and gave everyone the benefit of the doubt, reluctant to call foul, even against the most egregious shoves and grabs—bothered him.

He descended into the smoky dark of Junior's basement. Chance, Razz, and Junior sprawled on the couch, passing a blunt, laughing. The music blasting from the speakers was not theirs. Chance shot him a look. Junior offered the blunt.

He could accept it. Or not. He could ask Chance about Rosie right there in front of his friends. Or not. He could leave. Or not. The world was full of choices.

"Have a seat, my man," Junior shouted above the music. He waved the blunt at Henry and the beanbag chair. "Get comfortable."

Chance pushed himself up out of the couch cushions and

sat at the computer. The music stopped. Henry took the blunt, inhaled deeply, and lay back in the chair, ears ringing in the sudden silence. He'd do it—confront this cocky kid, as soon as he released the smoke from his lungs. Just as he opened his mouth to speak, Chance's voice leaped from the speakers, confident, strong, the beats behind it more sophisticated than Henry would have expected. Junior and Razz moved their shoulders to the music. Henry passed the blunt to Razz. His brother concentrated on the computer screen. Chance rapped about capitalist elite and the media and George W. Bush, nuclear weapons in North Korea and the war in Iraq and Blackwater and the assassination of Rafic Hariri. When the song ended and Chance, his fingers playing with his earlobe, finally looked toward Henry, the glint of pride in his eyes reflected the lump of pride in Henry's throat. Henry nodded, with a thumbs up, and Chance clicked on the next track.

*H*azel's left hand obeyed her desires more readily than the cramped, clawed right, so it was with those fingers that she pushed letters into wobbly words. If she relied on her left hand enough, when she got home she'd be able to cast a fishing line ambidextrously. When one arm tired, she'd have the other. She could see better from the corner of her left eye too. It didn't droop as much as the right. She tilted her head closer to the tray and looked for an H. But why bother spelling "home" again? Most people in this place didn't stop long enough to notice what she'd written. Even when Gary or that Nadine read her words, they did nothing but exchange rude glances they thought she didn't notice.

She pushed the bulk of the tiles to the corner of the tray and overshot, knocking a few to the floor, hopefully none she needed. The cleared space waited as she struggled to pick up an A and resorted to sliding it into place. She nudged over-lapping tiles flat, and after examining the array multiple times, found two L's and added them. As she pressed an O with her index finger, ready to drag it into the lineup, her sleeve brushed the ALL, destroying her last ten minutes of work. Her head sank back into the pillows, both hands heavy and useless on the table, framing the mess on the tray. A croak escaped her, rasping and horrible, but Hazel Watkins was not a quitter.

For the next forty-five minutes she poked at the tiles. Fat Nadine looked in on her once and seeing that she was busy with the letters, approached the bed.

"ALL OF YOU CA..." Nadine read. "If I'm not back, you ring for me when you finish, hear? Your speech therapist will be here any minute. Need the commode?"

Hazel ignored her.

Another forty-five minutes and three additional words later, Hazel studied her sentence. She was short an L but had expressed what was on her mind well enough. She pressed the bell for Nadine. Her lips might not form a proper smile, but a self-satisfied grin filled her chest as sustaining as fresh air in the lungs.

Hazel had waited only a moment before an unfamiliar girl whipped into the room, words spilling from her mouth, and shoved Hazel's tray aside, making nonsense of her message. A scream stuck in Hazel's throat, and the girl, rattled on, oblivious. "Kristen Barker...here to help you...speech exer-cises...each day..." Her white-blonde hair, scraped back into a ponytail, revealed an endless forehead.

ALL OF YOU CAN GO TO HEL. Little Miss Kristen Barker, too. She was still talking. Slower now. She perched on a stool near the bed as if she might stay for a while.

Kristen Barker had a habit of wrinkling her nose, as though

she smelled something unsavory, heaven knows there were enough bad odors in the Manor, but then Hazel realized she was just trying to keep her too large glasses in place.

Those can be adjusted, Hazel wanted to say. She had a little kit, complete with tiny screws and screwdriver, in her wallet. Of course, no matter how prepared she was with the proper tools—and Hazel had always been and still was a believer in the proper tools—her clumsy, useless, twisted fingers couldn't fix this girl's glasses or anything else.

"We'll start with a variety of exercises to strengthen the muscles you need for speech. They may be difficult for you, but trying is what's important."

Kristen Barker's lips shaped themselves around each word with excessive care, yet her tone was flat. "We'll begin with those that help to improve the control and strength of your tongue." She held her face too close. Hazel could smell her minty breath and wondered what her own breath smelled like. Maybe Kristen Barker's nose wrinkling wasn't just to keep her glasses on. She tried to remember if she'd eaten anything odoriferous for breakfast. A little oatmeal, a couple of prunes in a thick sweet syrup. A long time ago. It would be lunch time soon. The days here were measured out in meals.

"Mrs. Watkins!" Kristen Barker sounded more lively now, even frustrated. "Please. We don't have much time. We'll begin with a tongue reach. Stick your tongue out as far as you can and bring it back in." She demonstrated. Tongues were ugly things, wet and seamed with bluish veins on the undersides, even on this pretty little towheaded girl. They looked like a species of slug she'd hate to find in her garden. She watched her own hideous attempt to extend her tongue reflected in Kristen Barker's glasses. When had she become so old, so very unattractive?

"Eight times, Mrs. Watkins. Here we go."

Hazel closed her eyes and followed instructions.

"Next the tongue raise. You place the tip on the ridge behind your upper teeth and keep it there while opening and closing your mouth. Are you with me?"

Hazel's dentures sat in a case on her bed stand.

"Oh!" The girl blushed. "You should be doing these exercises with your teeth in. I'm sorry. I should have noticed.

"Next time I'll bring a mirror, so you can see how you're doing," Kristen Barker said. "Now, tongue up."

Hazel groaned.

"I see you're working hard." Nadine carried a stack of Hazel's clothes, freshly washed and folded. "Now, let's see, what did you want? You buzzed me?"

"We're almost done," Kristen Barker whined. "Just give us a moment, please. So we can finish here!"

"I see Mrs. Watkins is tired now," Nadine said. She slipped the clothes into a drawer, closing it with a decisive thump.

With an irritated, "I'll be back tomorrow, same time," Kristen Barker rolled back on her stool and left.

Even through closed eyelids, Hazel saw Nadine's shadow looming over her, blocking the relentless, phony fluorescent light. She could fall asleep in that warm dark shade.

"Mrs. Watkins," Nadine said. "Why'd you buzz? You need the commode?"

Hazel tipped her head toward the tray.

"Oh, yes, you wanted to tell me something. This is a mess."

Hazel opened her eyes. A smile played at the edges of Nadine's lips as she pulled the tray close between them.

"So, you were saying?" Nadine shifted tiles to spell ALL OF YOU CA... "Go on. I will remind your son. I will insist that he bring you that computer he keeps talking about."

Hazel spotted the N and willed her hand toward it. Once achieved, she would have to edge it along with a finger and *then the G and the O and the TO HEL. Nadine waited. One wouldn't guess she had more work to do than time to do it. She stood, attention focused on the letters, no jiggling or foot tapping or even a glance at the door. She waited and when Hazel finally finished, Nadine would be rewarded for her patience by reading GO TO HEL. Hazel let her arm fall limp against her side. She closed her eyes. If something's worth doing, it's worth doing well. If she had the proper letters, she might take pains to finish the sentence. Or not.*

"I will give your son a call," Nadine said. "I won't wait for him to come in."

Henry stepped aside to let his mother lead the way into the receptionist's alcove outside Vice Principal Johnson's office. Ms. Travers nodded an unsmiling hello at Nadine, but when she saw Henry, her narrow brown face split into a grin. "Henry Antoine! Look at you all dressed up. You here to apply for a job?"

"You know why we're here." Henry shook her hand. "Don't you?"

Ms. Travers bit her lip and nodded, squinting. "Your brother. Couldn't be more different from you. Determined to fail, that one. Though he does have a sense of humor."

His mother raised her chin and glared. Henry touched her arm.

"He's no stranger to this office. We've gotten to be great friends while he sits in that very chair waiting for Mr. Johnson. I told him I even started calling it Chance's chair. Have a seat in Chance Antoine's chair, I tell people when they come in. If he comes while you're here, and he probably will, I tell them, you'll have to get up." Henry looked at the molded plastic seat and imagined his brother slouched down, legs splayed and stretched halfway across the small room.

"You don't sound like you're his friend," Nadine said.

Ms. Travers snorted a light laugh and answered the ringing phone.

"This isn't funny," said Henry, immediately regretting his words as evidence of his lack of a sense of humor. "Can you let Mr. Johnson know we're here? I have to catch a plane." He surprised himself he sounded so assertive. His mother's appreciative look warmed and agitated him. He plunked down his stuffed nylon duffel bag.

His mother stood rigid and formal, clutching her giant purse to her belly. "I'll stand," she said.

Mr. Johnson's door cracked open and the vice principal himself appeared without being summoned. Henry had always liked him, a young, light-skinned African-American guy who'd gone to Yale. He seemed to be everywhere at once—wrestling matches, dance performances, the cafeteria, striding unhurriedly down the hall, acknowledging students by name.

"Ms. Antoine." Mr. Johnson leaned toward his mother, hand outstretched. She had to adjust her grip on that ridiculous purse in order to shake his hand. What did she keep in there anyway? The back of Henry's throat itched. What was he doing here pretending to be a grown up, a parent, an authority figure? He'd been a student here less than a year ago.

"Henry." His own name in the vice-principal's voice, warm and familiar. "How's college?"

Henry wanted to ask him how he'd managed Yale, get some advice. "S'awright." He gripped Mr. Johnson's hand.

"Okay, then. Head into my office. Ms. Travers, please check Chance's schedule and get him down here."

Had Chance even gone to school?

Henry and Nadine seated themselves at two sides of a square table. Ms. Travers and Mr. Johnson conferenced in whispers just outside. Nadine fiddled with the clasp of her bag. He wished she'd leave it alone.

His brother swaggered into the room, followed by Mr. Johnson, who pulled the door shut with a decisive metallic click. Chance shot Henry an odd glance, half-question, half-warning, and dropped into the chair across from him. Mr. Johnson sat to Henry's right, across from their mother. What a week it had been—his mother's despair, Chance's unwillingness to communicate, his own inability to tell anybody about anything that mattered. Maybe he'd appreciate Minneapolis when he got back.

Mr. Johnson positioned a calendar in front of Chance and flipped the pages, counting. "We've got forty-eight school days until graduation. Show up. Three weeks until April vacation. Make the most of your week off. Get yourself to school every day before and after. That isn't too much to ask. Drop out now, and you'll end up spending more time than that working for a GED. You feel me?"

Chance rolled his eyes. Tendons in his neck quivered.

Yell at the kid, Henry wanted to say. Be more of a hard ass. Forget about trying to relate to these punks. Maybe if he acted more professional, kids like Chance would take what he said more seriously.

Henry couldn't figure out where to look. Chance leaned back in his chair and studied the ceiling.

"Chance is a good boy," his mother said. "He can do the work."

"Yes," Mr. Johnson agreed. "He's a fine young man. A smart young man. I'd like to see him living up to his potential."

"I always tell my boys school is important," Nadine said.

She straightened her shoulders and raised her chin. "Henry listened."

Chance rocked forward, chair legs struck the floor.

"Chance is a smart young man, making some stupid choices," Mr. Johnson said. He stood and leaned over Chance, hands flat on the table, tie dangling. "At this point, you need to *choose* to graduate. You need to pass English."

"I'm passing English," Chance muttered.

"That's not my understanding," Mr. Johnson said. "Ms. Lorenzo says you haven't completed any homework assignments this semester. Do you hear me? *None.* That is completely unacceptable."

Ms. Lorenzo was a notoriously easy teacher. Henry had gotten so much extra credit in her class that he'd had a 125% average.

Chance's hands clenched. He smacked the table hard, right next to the principal's long fingers, and leaped up, sending the chair clattering across the floor.

"I am not my brother!" he yelled.

Mr. Johnson shot to his feet and reached toward Chance. "Relax now. Chill."

Henry sat motionless, overwhelmed by the desire to say the right thing, flooded with a crippling combination of bewilderment and rage.

Chance punched the file cabinet, and the loud metallic thud filled the room. He stared at Henry.

"I am not like you," he said in a kind of choking sob, and fled; the door crashed shut behind him.

"Maybe you could talk to him." Mr. Johnson broke the silence, looking Henry in the eye.

"Me?"

His mother and the principal both nodded.

"Me?" Henry said again, voice shrill. He'd been trying to talk to him all week long.

I'm his brother, not his mother, Henry almost said. I'm his brother, not his school administrator.

"I'm not his father!" he shouted. "I'm not his fucking father." He stood.

"I need to get to the airport." His flight wasn't for hours, but he was glad he had all his shit with him so he didn't have to stop at the house. In one long motion, he stood, kissed his mother, and left. In the outer office he grabbed his bag, hoisted it to his shoulder without acknowledging Ms. Travers, and raced down the stairs.

The corner of his new laptop rubbed hard and wrong against his neck. Out on the sunny sidewalk he set his duffle down. He caught his breath and repacked, wrapping the computer in protective layers of clothes.

Nadine made her way from the high school to an empty bench in front of the public library, the day blurring around her. Students streamed from the high school doors toward the lunch trucks parked at the curb on Broadway. They elbowed their friends, laughed loud, took up so much space on the sidewalk. She hoped the principal would punish Chance for his rudeness, but feared he wouldn't. If Chance passed by she would slap him, embarrass him in front of his friends. Who was she fooling? She wouldn't do that. That was the problem. A good mother, a strong mother, would.

She loved her boys with every bit of herself. But love was not enough. If she had disciplined them better, stayed in a church, found them a father, one wouldn't be failing and the other wouldn't have run off back to the middle of the country, with such a quick goodbye.

Women raised good children without the involvement of men. Even when children knew their fathers, the men always seemed to have something more pressing to do than change a diaper or help with homework.

Henry's father, Lucien, had been no older than these passing students when they met. She was already living in Boston when she heard he'd moved to Fort Pierce to try to start his own bakery, been arrested for a small traffic violation, and deported. No one knew she'd ever been with Deacon Joseph. Even Yara assumed that Henry and Chance shared a father. She'd almost convinced herself. Lying by omission was easy when the truth was so painful. "Your father in Haiti," she'd say to Henry with both boys in the room, the few times the subject came up. How little her sons knew about her life. How little she knew about theirs. Did they talk about it between themselves? What would they say? Nadine had no idea, locked out of the mystery of brothers. Did they ever wonder about dates and timing? She'd led them to believe that Chance was conceived during this vaguely-described father's visit to Cambridge, when, planning to stay, he realized he couldn't stand the New England winters, and besides, he was needed back home by elderly parents.

The sun's warmth and the weight of her sadness anchored her to the bench. She checked her watch and saw that she had two hours before work. She closed her eyes and forced herself to breathe and think happy thoughts: watching from the porch while Chance and Henry played so seriously in the patch of yard behind the house with their little plastic army men and tiny Haitian flags on toothpicks, taking them skating at that freezing cold rink, her embarrassment as she clung to the wall eclipsed by the pride she felt as her vigorous little boys whipped around on the slick ice.

Footsteps stopped in front of her and a shadow blocked the light. She opened her eyes. Gary Watkins.

"Hey, there's life outside the Manor!" he said. "What are you doing here?"

Before she could decide how to answer him, he went on. "I just had a meeting at the school about a youth center kid who—never mind. Nice day, right?" Behind his glasses his watery blue eyes widened. He adjusted his baseball cap. His beard had grown bushy and his mustache almost covered his mouth. "You know, I was just thinking about you."

Why would he be thinking of her? Did he know about the meeting she'd just had at the school? How could he? He seemed to take her puzzled silence as an invitation to settle himself close to her on the bench. She lifted her hips enough to wriggle a couple of inches away and forced a smile.

"I was thinking about you because I need help. To clean out my mother's trailer. It's got to be done. I was thinking I could pay five hundred bucks. Know anybody? Or maybe you'd do it yourself?" He paused. "Shouldn't take more than a day."

Five hundred dollars for a day of cleaning?

Gary Watkins waited, head tilted, eyebrows raised.

"Your mother wants to go home," she said, relieved to talk about his problems instead of her own.

"She won't be going home. We both know that."

Nadine barely knew this man. When you show people your feelings, you give them an advantage. She forced herself to look right through his glasses into his eyes. "We don't know. What we know is that she needs to have a way to communicate and she wants a computer. I left you a message about that. Did you hear it?"

She left no room for him to respond and didn't care. "If you have five hundred dollars for cleaning, couldn't you buy her a computer? She worked at an insurance company. I'm sure she could relearn to type."

Gary laughed. "Okay. Okay. I'll get her a computer. Want to come with me now and pick it out?"

"And why couldn't she go home if you hired some help for her? It's what she wants. When the spirit is happy, the body is more likely to improve."

"How's Chance doing anyway?" Gary asked.

The slam of his fist into the principal's file cabinet echoed in Nadine's head, alternating with Henry's angry swearing about not being his father.

"What?" Gary Watkins asked. "Tell me what's going on. Maybe I can help."

He had been important in her boys' lives at the youth center. He had experience with teenagers.

"Why don't we grab some lunch and go to Microcenter. My car's right over there. You can fill me in."

"I have work."

"I'll take you to work. I'll come with you—with the computer we're about to buy."

She had no better plan for the next two hours. Hazel Watkins would get a computer and she might get some helpful advice. If the right moment showed itself, she would ask again about home help in the trailer.

Gary Watkins waited in the car while she picked up her work clothes. At Microcenter, he bought a laptop while she stood watching the TVs, not wanting to seem too interested in the amount of money he was spending.

"I know you haven't eaten lunch," Gary said. "Let's get a bite at Camie's. Best patties around. You ever go there?"

A fish patty, flaky and warm, would soak up the acidic morning coffee she could still feel sloshing in her nervous stomach. "I usually cook."

Gary raised his eyebrows. "I loved the food in Haiti. You ever make Haitian spaghetti—with those little black fish? Or hotdogs? Is that the kind of food you cook?"

He liked Haitian food. Who wouldn't? Was he inviting himself to her house for a meal?

"I am hungry," she said.

"Okay, let's go." He talked fast. "If you don't feel like eating patties, they've got chicken and beef and goat, fried, stewed, however you like it. And *legim*. The best *legim*—big hunks of meat. And it's just a few blocks from here."

Nadine had to swallow the saliva that filled her mouth as he recited the menu. She really was very hungry. She actually laughed.

At Camie's, Gary greeted the bald man behind the counter in *Kreyòl*. The red Formica tables stood empty. A TV blared from high up in a corner. Nadine couldn't smell anything cooking. They ordered and sat down. The man disappeared into the kitchen.

"Wait'll you taste this food," Gary said. "You'll have to tell me how it compares to your cooking. So what's going on with our boy?" He leaned forward, elbow on the table, chin in hand.

Our boy? Nadine bristled at his presumption and warmed at his interest.

"I don't understand it. Something changed. He stopped doing any school work. He began spending time with different friends. I think it's that music—such a bad influence."

Gary laughed. "It's not the music. Why do people always default to that ridiculous explanation for kids' behavior?"

"You're laughing at me? Have some respect," she fumed, then lowered her voice. "Do you think it's easy to be a mother? Do you have children?"

Gary took off his glasses and polished them with a napkin before answering. "No." He drank some water. "Never really wanted to. My father died before I was born so ... I don't know. I never had one. I missed the idea of a father, but not an actual person, know what I mean?"

She didn't really, but she nodded so he would keep talking.

"And maybe because I never had a role model, I never aspired to doing it myself. I have enough kids to deal with in my job. Tell me more about Chance."

"I just met with the principal—that's why I was sitting there." She told him about the meeting.

The counterman/cook set plates of food in front of them—rice and beans, plantains, the stewed vegetables, and meat. It tasted good, but it was *legim* made in the United States—no real *epina*. Lots of carrots and was that, cabbage? The tender hunks of meat fell apart at the touch of her fork. She'd never even seen meat like that when she lived in Haiti.

"Is it good?" Gary asked.

"*Koupe dwèt!*"

The man behind the counter smiled over at her.

"Chance knows how to put in effort when he wants to," Gary said. "He was the heart of the team back when he played ball. Other guys listen to him. A hard worker. Whenever the gym was open he'd be in there practicing."

"When did he stop playing?" Nadine asked.

"About a year and a half ago maybe?"

Nadine tried to remember back. That was around the time he started to talk about making music with the boys in the basement. No matter what Gary Watkins thought, she blamed the music.

"And then this past fall he stopped seeing Rosie Richard," Gary said. "They were always so close. I think something might have gone down between them. She's working with me at the center these days. I'll see what I can find out."

Rosie Richard, the girl from around the block. Nadine hadn't thought of or seen her in years. If Chance was having problems with a girl, she'd know about it. No matter what

Gary Watkins said, she blamed the music and those *dezòd* boys that he spent time with making it. Or herself. Or the lack of a father. Gary Watkins said he didn't miss his father.

"This is a nice connection," he said. "Don't you think? You help with my mother. I help with your son."

"I wonder if my boys miss having fathers," she said.

The TV trumpeted an ad for Viagra. Gary bit a plantain and didn't seem to notice. "Ask your doctor if your heart is healthy enough for sex," the TV announcer shouted. "Take advantage of the most effective erectile dysfunction treatment available today."

She wasn't squeamish about bodies, in her work she couldn't be, but sitting across from Gary Watkins in a Haitian restaurant, worrying about Chance, thinking about their fathers, listening to the TV man talking about a remedy for soft penises was uncomfortable or should have been, if she weren't so anxious about her sons.

"Fathers?" he asked.

Nadine folded her paper napkin and rested it on her empty plate. Gary scraped up his last bite of fried goat and chewed. He swallowed the goat and took a long swig of his water.

She fussed with her napkin. "Yes. Neither of them knows their father."

This was the first time she'd said that sentence aloud, and here she was saying it to a man she barely knew, telling him, complete with Deacon Joseph's name. It felt good.

"You've been through a lot," Gary said. "Strong lady." He had taken his glasses off and was studying her with a rapt face.

She hadn't even told him anything about her childhood. "We'd better head over to Riverview, or I'll be late," she said.

He matched her stride as they walked to his car; his arm bumped against hers. She didn't mind. She could use another friend.

*H*azel breathed in Nadine's chrysanthemum scent and forced open her eyes.

"Mrs. Watkins," Nadine said. "Your son brought you something."

Fat Nadine, unlike some of the others, took a moment to read the letter tiles before sweeping them away.

GET ME OUT OF HERE.

"I don't blame you. This is no kind of place to be spending so much time. You need to work hard with the therapists. Cooperate. Look here. Look what your son has."

Gary plunked a thick plastic rectangle onto her tray and opened it. A pleased-with-himself smile filled his face. A laptop computer.

Nadine was still talking. "I'm sorry nobody gave you this sooner, but what is that American proverb, 'Better late than not ever?'" She turned toward the laundry cart and began restocking Hazel's closet with supplies.

Hazel stiffened. Rage shot through her. Too late. Much too late.

"Maybe this will make communicating easier," Gary said.

Caring what his mother had to say would make communication easier, she wanted to tell him. Showing up would make it easier. He pushed a button to turn the computer on and the screen lit up. His face glowed like a little boy's.

"This way, when you touch a letter to spell a word, it will remain on the screen. I can get software that will allow you to type the most commonly used words with one stroke, but I have to look into that, and I didn't want to keep you waiting any longer." He was busy clicking and typing and admiring the computer.

Look at me, she thought. Look at me. Do I look happy about this?

"Try it. Type something." He raised his eyebrows in naked expectation.

His vulnerability tangled her thoughts. What would happen if she typed *"darn you"* as she was inclined to do? She should teach him a lesson about procrastination. Wait too long and...it's too late. It's no good. But what was that saying he used to argue with her—put off until tomorrow what you could do today because it might turn out you don't have to do it at all? He counted on things being too late. Look how long he procrastinated on getting married, having children.

But this was her son.

If she refused this gift, it wouldn't teach Gary anything. It would be cutting off her nose to spite her face. She'd learn how to use this darn thing. Why not? She used to touch type, and the keyboard was just like a typewriter. Her fingers found their places. Even her compromised hand felt at home. It took so little pressure to move a key.

She typed her two words, faster than she would have ever expected of herself all these years after retirement and after a neurological event to boot. It was like riding a bicycle. Her body remembered. She'd eaten her dinner. Next time she'd make it to the toilet.

His face softened. *"You're welcome,"* he said. *"I'm sorry I didn't get to this sooner. I don't know why I'm such a procrastinator."*

Hazel rubbed his bare arm. She would feign forgiveness since he'd finally delivered. She'd never liked the way men looked in short-sleeved shirts, but her son had beautiful arms, and she'd always liked the capable look of a man's wrist in an old-fashioned watch. A warm loosening filled her chest, sudden—like finding the knot of yarn that with one pull untangles the whole skein. She turned back to her typing. She would begin with that very simile.

"Whoops," Gary said. *"You must have hit delete by mistake."*

Her last words were gone.

Her chest tightened again—a snarl of rage and despair.

"Pay attention," Gary was saying. "This is important. Control Z. Like this. It undoes your last action. If you make a mistake or change your mind, just hold down the control key and type Z, like this." Her words magically reappeared. "I always thought it would be nice to have a Control Z for real life," Gary said. "There were plenty of times I could have used it. Know what I mean?"

He pressed Z again and again the letters returned. No white out or retyping necessary. No incorrect carbon copies. No trace of a mistake. She pushed his hand out of the way, eager to try it herself. So much to learn, but she had time.

She would write her memoirs. Her fingers tapped the familiar pattern of the keys; even the affected hand cooperated. She hunched closer and peered at the screen. It was darn slow, finding the words, typing the letters.

I was born a month early in Wethersfield, Connecticut in 1910, the fourth girl child, a disappointment from the start, they told me—a sickly jaundiced girl with a dangling extra finger that my father chopped off. When my brother was born a year later, he was welcomed with great enthusiasm—the big healthy son everyone wanted. Well, that scrawny baby has outlived not only the three older sisters, but also the younger brother and a husband. I arrived a month earlier than anyone expected, and I appear to be staying longer than anyone expects as well.

When people meet an old person like me, they want to know the secret to a long life. They want to know what to eat, what to drink, what not to eat, what not to drink. Should they exercise? Should they take medicine? Well, I say to them, if you want to live a long life the secret is very simple. Don't die. I want to die, and I can't. I keep on living.

I wake up and there is a new number on that calendar if someone has remembered to tear off yesterday. And I will say that after manicures and pedicures, the thing they take most seriously around here is keeping calendars and clocks correct. They don't want us—the residents—to be more confused than we already are. I am not confused about dates. I am confused about why I am in this place when I have a perfectly good home of my own. I would like to go home and plant my garden before it is too late for anything to grow this year. I would like to go home now—not tomorrow, not next week. NOW!! !!!

The exclamation points continued for an entire page. Holding that key down Hazel felt better than she had since her accident.

She clicked to a blank page and began to type a conversation. This is my story. Of my life. I have decided I will write the story of my life. In here I have time. Like men in prison who write their books.

She waited for Gary's response, straightened and turned her stiffened neck and aching shoulders, to see his face, but he had already left. If he'd said goodbye, she'd been so absorbed she hadn't heard him.

Henry shivered on a bench by the river under a low gray sky, hands pushed deep into his pockets, neck pulled into his coat, duffle bag beside him. He had five hours until he had to be at the airport. Cracked slabs of ice on the Charles sloshed up against each other. Better take a break from worrying about Chance and think about himself. He'd stop by the center and see if Coach had any summer job possibilities.

He waited for a break in the Memorial Drive traffic and dashed across one lane at a time, hesitating on the broken white lines between cars. He sprinted the last bit and running felt so good, even with his duffle on his shoulders, that he kept jogging along the sidewalk. As he passed Junior's house, he slowed his pace and listened for music leaking from the basement windows. He used to know his brother. Even as recently as last year, he knew his brother.

Sacrificing his already soggy sneakers, he cut across the field near the youth center, right through a scuttling flock of Canada geese. They rustled and flapped out of his way with honking complaints and furious snapping at his legs. He hung onto his duffle, arms close to his body. Fucking birds. They could fly anywhere, but here they clustered on a muddy field in Cambridge and made a nuisance of themselves.

Tucked behind a playground like a secret, the youth center waited—a one-story brick building, the side wall a colorful street scene Henry had helped to paint when he was in sixth grade.

He hadn't been at the youth center since August, before he left for school. The December break had passed in a blur of days at the public library finishing his incompletes. In high school he'd spent more effort hiding his good grades than he did on the work itself. He would never be one of those suck ups with hands always waving in the air. "Call on me!" He wasn't prepared for sitting in college classes full of those kids. He knew his silence was affecting his grades, but every time he convinced himself to throw up a hand, his heart pounded harder than it was pounding right now after running for miles.

He peeked in the youth center's windows. At this time of day the kitchen and the game room were deserted, but he figured Coach would be in his office. Instead, at Coach's desk, tapping at a computer, sat Rosie/Ro-Z. He rapped on the glass, and she whipped her head around and glared in his direction. He considered a duck and leave, but when she recognized him and her scowl melted, he waved. She met him at the door.

They stepped forward, back, forward again, not sure whether to hug or kiss each cheek Haitian style or dap, and ended up laughing in a half hug.

"Shouldn't you be in school?" he asked.

"Internship," she said, and launched into a long story about Coach traveling to Haiti with a group of teachers and getting all excited about connecting Cambridge kids, especially Haitian-Americans, with kids in Haiti. Literacy for all. If the afterschool kids knew they were writing for a purpose, they might be more into it.

Henry sucked his teeth. Another story of white people going to Haiti when his mother had never found a way to go back home, even for a short visit.

"Kids in Haiti need books in *Kreyòl*," Rosie said. "You know that most of their education, for rich kids or kids lucky enough to even go to school, is in French? And most folks there don't even speak it."

"I know that," Henry said. "Just wrote a paper about it for linguistics. But kids here can't write in *Kreyòl*. Even if they're Haitian."

"That's where I come in. And maybe you? I'm helping write the grant, and there's money in it for translation." She grabbed his sleeve. "Hey! Come work with me this summer. I don't know anything about linguistics or translating. I'm just trying to get this ill project going."

He did need a summer job, and this one sounded better than scooping ice cream for tourists and students or mowing lawns for people rich enough to have one, but in the moment, before he could think about planning his own future, he wanted Rosie to tell him what she knew about his asshole brother.

Typical. Chance's problems, Chance's personality, Chance's needs, always trumped his own. Always had. Always would.

"You never called me," she said. "Your break must be almost over. I really want to hear how they're treating you out in the heartland."

"Weather's cold." He shifted from foot to foot. The whole conversation would go better if they weren't standing in a doorway. "You got time to shoot some hoops?"

"Hell, yeah!"

He should tell her about feeling trapped on a campus smaller than his high school because he had no disposable income to explore the city. He should tell her about his serious lack of friends. But when you came back to your roots you were supposed to say everything's good, I'm making it, I'm living up to all you expected of me.

He followed her down the unlit hallway toward the smell of sweaty socks and new plastic emanating from the gym doors. Shiny red mats lined the walls. The floor gleamed.

"Like the new floor?" Rosie asked. "Looks like wood, right. But it's vinyl." She pulled out an enormous ring of keys from the pocket of her cargo pants, unlocked a closet and grabbed a ball, bounced it, rejected it—too flat—and chose another.

"That one's good," he said, and she threw him a bounce pass.

Her keys rattled and her little-kid sneakers squeaked as she raced across the floor.

Henry palmed the ball, ready to dribble down the court, then remembered his dirty sneakers. Rosie followed his downward gaze.

"Don't sweat it. Go on," she said.

He tossed his coat onto the bleachers. They looked new too, a step up from the splintery version where he'd sat watching his brother grab rebounds and sink three-point shots. The heart of the team, Coach had always called Chance.

Back when Chance played ball, their mother working longer hours than she did now, the only family member watching had been Henry. At the end of a game, Chance bobbed among the crowd spilling onto the court, dribbling through his legs, trash talking, headed straight for Henry, who acknowledged him with a nod of quiet pride.

Rosie dribbled the ball hard and fast like a jackhammer.

"Okay, hold up. Game fifteen?" Henry asked.

"How about eleven? Shoot for it."

Henry squared up and shot. The ball clanked off the back of the rim. Rosie grabbed it, checked it to Henry, then dribbled past him. Henry sprinted ahead, pivoted, and blocked her shot. She snatched the ball again and scored.

Evenly matched for the first game, she won by just one basket. She was small, but fierce, and she wanted to win more than he did, but Henry couldn't let her win two in a row and played hard enough to beat her by four.

"Two out of three," he panted.

"I can't," she said. "I got to get back to work."

Henry attempted to clean his fogged up glasses with the edge of his sweat-soaked t-shirt. Rosie put out her hand. He laid his glasses on her open palm.

"You're going to work with me on this job this summer, right?" she said. "And you could supplement it with work for the Mayor's Program. Coach basketball, do crafts. Get your application in. I'll focus on the grant."

Henry felt luck gather in his chest—a rush of happiness, unexpected and too unfamiliar these days.

In front of the hallway trophy case, they both stopped. Chance figured prominently in most of the basketball photos, his smile huge—cocky or just easy and open, depending on how you looked at it.

Rosie turned away.

"Come on, Ro, what's up with him? He's acting the fool. Gonna get himself arrested. He barely shows at school. I came back to see what's going on."

Little Chance grinned at him from the pictures. He'd grown much taller since they were taken, and those rounded cheeks had thinned, but the smile was exactly the same.

"I don't want to talk about your brother." Rosie stepped away.

"You know what happened, don't you?" He grabbed her arm. "Tell me."

"He needs to grow up. That's all. He needs to grow up and take responsibility. He thinks his shit don't stink. He thinks he can get away with murder. He thinks he can do whatever he wants to whoever he wants and they'll still be there for him. Fuck Chance Antoine!" She ripped away from his grip and tried to hide her face. "Your brother needs to learn that life is not a joke. Fuck it, Henry, I've got to work. Don't talk to me about your brother. You want to know what happened, you ask him. I'm gonna tell Coach Watkins to get rid of these photos if he wants me to work here."

APRIL 2005

"Lè w ap neye, ou kenbe branch ou jwenn."
*When you are drowning you hang on to
the branch you can find.*

Henry dropped into his usual seat next to the door of the windowless box of a classroom. They'd left it for him, the chairs already full of people who, at eight AM on Friday morning, did not want to be sitting in Introduction to Linguistics. Their collective lethargy solidified into a heavy silence. One girl examined the ends of her hair. A boy chewed a cold slice of pizza. Another studied his cell phone. Several rested their heads on the desk arms of their chairs.

Sage burst in, glowing and out of breath, grabbed an empty chair and maneuvered it into the small space beside him. She brought the smell of a sunny morning and melting snow and something else, licorice. Before sitting down she rooted around in her bag, arranging a travel mug, a plastic bag of seeds, a pink pen, a highlighter, and a battered spiral notebook on the desk. Henry watched her without turning his head. She held an elastic between her teeth and bunched her long damp locs into a ponytail. He glimpsed her tongue as she grabbed the elastic from her mouth and snapped it around the hair. Finally, she sat down and sighed, stretching her long legs. Her purple ribbed tights emphasized the shape of her kneecaps. Some people took so much time to arrange themselves—as if they were moving in. He'd wondered if Sage had taken the class just to be near him, but she did seem into it, hand always raised, alert as a ferret.

Professor Kim entered, laptop under his arm, chatting with a tall, Black man in a dark suit. A bright silk scarf, yellow, red, and turquoise, graced the man's neck. Henry had never seen a man, even a tree-dancing hippie, wear a scarf like that. The visitor nodded at the class, eyes behind gold-rimmed glasses, taking in each student. Henry didn't realize he was expecting something from the man until the visitor's gaze moved past him, on to Sage. He shrugged away a shiver of disappointment, and took out his computer.

"Good morning," Professor Kim said. "We'll be deviating from the syllabus this morning. I trust no one will be too disappointed. My esteemed colleague from Boston is in town on his way to a conference, and I persuaded him to honor us with his presence."

Henry straightened and strained forward, rising a bit in his chair. Sage nudged him in the leg with her toe and widened her eyes. He settled himself, strangely comforted by the fact that someone in the room knew he was from Massachusetts, too.

"Professor Edmond will speak to us about Creole languages in general and Haitian Creole in particular." Professor Kim smiled right at Henry.

Sage kicked Henry again. If this had been on the syllabus, it might not seem so surreal—a visiting professor with a crazy scarf, from Boston of all places, speaking about the language his mother had first loved him in, in this dreary room in a college in a city in a state where no one knew him.

Professor Edmond fired up his PowerPoint presentation and began his talk. "Today I will begin by giving you some historical background. We'll explore some language myths and do some debunking of those myths. I'll end with some lessons from the past that we can use to create a better future."

Henry leaned forward so far that he rose off his seat. He'd covered some of this in his paper. Professor Edmond's accented English poured over Henry like warm rain.

"To begin, I'd like to ask you what comes to your mind when you hear the word 'Creole?'"

No one raised a hand, unusual in this place. The boy across from Henry peeked up from his laptop screen. Sage turned her head toward him. The guy on his left who'd worn sandals all winter and sported a long scraggly goatee swiveled his head in Henry's direction too. Was everyone waiting for him to say something? He wouldn't. He was not going to tell a whole class of strangers about his mother's proverbs and jokes, or that Haitian way of scolding Chance and him, or vodou, or Haitian church.

Someone coughed. People shifted in their chairs. Henry stared at his computer. Half of Chance's face showed behind the blank page he'd opened to type his notes. Every couple days he thought about calling his brother, but there was no way to casually mention Rosie's rant, and he couldn't think of another way to do it. He clicked to close the window.

If Chance were here, he'd speak right up with whatever popped into his head.

"Let me ask the question in another way," Professor Edmond said. Henry released the breath he hadn't realized he'd been holding. The class focused on the professor again. "What do you think would come to the minds of most North Americans when they hear the word, Creole?"

Sage raised her hand, of course. "Kind of like a cartoon language."

"Cartoon language?" Professor Edmond tilted his head and stroked his chin.

"Yes, like you'd hear island characters speak in a cartoon."

"Hmm."

Sage looked worried and fiddled with her pen.

"Other thoughts?"

The goateed student volunteered. "Not really its own language. Made up of pieces of lots of different languages."

Hands began to wave.

"That it's simple. For people who aren't literate."

"Easy to learn since it's only for basic communication."

Henry's ears and cheeks felt hot. Professor Edmond just nodded, then turned to look at his first slide, an image of the Haitian flag. Henry thought of the little flags his mother bought Chance and him every May for Haitian Flag Day. He still had them somewhere. He'd never thrown them out.

"Haitian Creole is the Creole with the largest community of speakers. It emerged in the 1650s." Henry began to type as the professor defined Creoles and talked dizzyingly about how various linguists fit them into theories of human language development. He'd gotten an A from Professor Kim on his paper about Haitian Creole, but saw now how much more he could've added, if he'd known.

The professor began a comparison of English and Haitian Creole, asking and answering technical questions about lexicon, morphology and syntax. Henry typed as fast as he could, trying to capture every word.

"The way you measured humanity was in language. Europeans were 'enlightened,' yet making Africans into beasts of burden. They had to turn them into beasts, by 'proving' they were beasts." Henry's hand shot up. His own understanding of the professor's point filled him. He couldn't wait.

"Yes?" The professor paused and with narrowed eyes considered him.

Henry ignored the flicker of regret that he'd raised his hand and spoke. "So one way they justified enslaving people was to 'prove' their language was inferior!"

"Exactly." Professor Edmond smiled before launching into the second part of his talk: the historical roots of anti-Creole myths. He mentioned a book, *Silencing the Past,* by Trouillot, and Henry made a note to request it at the library right away. He'd felt this kind of energy listening to good music or watching an overtime Celtics game or flirting with a hot girl, but never in a class.

"Most nineteenth century views on Creoles were shaped by the same racism that characterized slavery. Even today, as suggested by your answers to my initial question, many think of Creole as broken French and the people who speak it as belonging to a race that is linguistically inferior." He flashed a list of myths about Creoles as inferior to other languages. "Would someone volunteer to read?"

Sage waved her hand; her breast close to nudging Henry's shoulder. The professor called on a less eager student three seats away from them. Sage pouted, then consoled herself with a sip from her travel mug.

According to the *Dictionnaire des Sciences Anthropologiques*, 1889, "Creole languages result from the adaptation of a language, especially some Indo-European language, to the (so to speak) phonetic and grammatical genius of a race that is linguistically inferior." Henry winced. His fingers wouldn't type those words.

Professor Edmond nodded, unsmiling. "Another volunteer?"

Sage's arm shot up again along with most of the other students'.

The professor called on the boy with the pile of pizza crusts on his desk. "Creole grammar 'imposes so little strain on memory and calls for so little effort from those with limited intelligence.' Saint-Quentin, 1872."

Henry swallowed hard, his throat suddenly tight.

"One more?" Professor Edmond called on Sage.

"As compared to the languages of civilized people [i.e., Europeans], the dialects of people considered primitive ..." The words ran together.

Henry knew the professor was making a point of the ridiculousness of this thinking, but his classmates' comments earlier and the way they read these quotes like pronouncements of absolute truth, made him sick. The room, already stuffy, tightened around him. He considered stepping out, took a huge breath, louder than he'd intended. His classmates were all glancing his way while trying to appear not to, but Professor Edmond seemed to pay him no special notice.

The next slide lit the screen—selected articles of the 1987 Haitian Constitution, two of them highlighted.

Article 5: All Haitians are united by a common language: Creole. Creole and French are the official languages of the Republic.

Article 32-2: The first responsibility of the State and its territorial divisions is education of the masses, which is the only way the country can be developed. The State shall encourage and facilitate private enterprise in this field.

Henry's breath evened out. He copied them onto his laptop as another student read them aloud.

"So," Professor Edmond said, "I will leave you with four very pointed facts." He read the slide himself.

"Point number one: The still widespread practice in Haiti is to teach and test students mostly in French, even though most Haitians speak only Haitian Creole." He paused, scrutinizing the class. Henry tried to catch his eye.

"Point number two: Fewer than 10% of students who enter primary school in Haiti will make it through high school. Less than 10%!"

He looked around the semicircle starting from the other side. Henry itched for some acknowledgement of connection. Professor Kim had to have mentioned that he was Haitian, even if he hadn't known he was from Massachusetts. And what about the paper Henry had written, which had touched on at least a couple of these ideas? Maybe that was it. Maybe Professor Kim had described Henry's paper, and Professor Edmond thought it sounded juvenile and undeveloped.

"Point number three: Countries with the least use of the mother tongue in education are among the worst off, both in academic achievement and in national development."

The professor adjusted his scarf. The turquoise and red splotches were flowers.

"And point number four: In order to be effective in Haiti, instruction must be carried out in Haiti's national language of Haitian Creole. This is an indispensable condition for 'education for ALL' in Haiti."

Henry's scalp prickled. This sounded like the thinking behind Coach Watkins's book project and his own summer job. This shit really mattered. He searched his brain for something to say, a question that would stand out, impress, start a meaningful dialogue of any kind. He could ask if the professor knew about the project.

"Thank you," Professor Kim said. "Unfortunately, our time is up and Professor Edmond has a plane to catch."

Students slapped shut their laptops and rustled on their jackets, bumping toward the door, before Professor Kim finished speaking. Maybe they took the fact that the class had run over by five minutes as permission to be rude.

"How'd you like that, Henry?" Sage, gathering her possessions, stood in his way. "Interesting, huh? You speak

Creole, right? Can you teach me some words? Besides *sak pase*, I mean. Everybody knows that. And," she began to sing a Wyclef song, complete with dance moves.

Professor Edmond walked out with Professor Kim. Henry would never have the nerve to pursue him, especially if he was in a hurry.

"Go ahead and listen to Wyclef if you want to learn Creole," Henry said. "Why would you want to learn it anyway? How many Haitians do you know?"

"You," she said.

"I speak English." Henry stepped around her. "Later."

By the time he left the building the professors were halfway across the quad, Professor Edmond's scarf fluttering in the light breeze like a wave goodbye.

Since Henry's departure one long week before and the meeting with the principal, the silent emptiness of the apartment felt more ominous than welcome. Yara was away in Queens, helping with her grandson—though the birth had been easy, he wasn't sleeping much—so there was no one downstairs welcoming her home with food and reminders that Chance was a good boy.

Upon opening the front door Nadine paused, hoping to hear the throb of a bass line in the stairwell. She longed for sound—even Chance's music, maybe especially Chance's music.

She hadn't seen him since the day he stormed out of the meeting. The school hadn't left any messages so maybe he was going to class. When she called Henry, he told her not to worry, to give Chance space and time to cool off; he was staying in Junior's basement. When she called Chance, she heard the recorded message. She tried it over and over, feeling her agitation grow each time she couldn't get through.

After checking her tomato plants she dialed Yara's number, listened to her message in Portuguese, and hung up partway through the English. Yara would see her number and call back when she could.

Such an empty house. In her mother's *lakou* on Lagonav, there was never a lack of company. The same was true at Uncle Maxim's in Port-au-Prince. Uncle's Miami house had been lonely much of the time, but even he had his American business partners come by, and when he was away in Haiti she would invite Lucien and an occasional girlfriend. People weren't meant to live so alone. Her brothers would feel sorry for her even though she had a television, a refrigerator full of food, and clean running water.

She'd turn on the radio for company and use this time to get some laundry done. Her back insisted she lie down, but she told it to wait until the clothes were in the washer. All those stairs, her back whined. Nadine was an expert at convincing her back, and every other body part, that they really didn't ache or burn. She lifted the basket of dirty uniforms from the floor of her closet. Only partly full, this load was hardly worth the trip to the basement. She might as well add some of Chance's, even though he'd told her not to, that he was man enough to take care of his own mess and didn't need anyone waiting on him. Besides, his jerseys and undershirts needed to be turned inside out and washed on the delicate cycle in cold water, and he didn't trust her to do them right. She, who had scrubbed the red-brown Lagonav dust out of white church clothes with her hands when she was a child, wasn't a good enough laundress for his Celtics shirt!

The boys' cave-like bedroom needed an airing. She threw open the curtains and raised the window a few inches. The evening sun shone on the two beds, Henry's made neatly, unslept in for a week, Chance's also unslept in for a week, a tangle of sheets and blankets. She stumbled over a basket-ball; it rolled into a corner. Chance's dresser drawers hung open, clothes spilling out. She picked up a smoky, sweaty t-shirt from the floor and tossed it into the laundry basket with some balled up socks, underwear and a pair of jeans. Something fell from the jeans' pocket. A little notebook. She plunged her hand into the other pocket and removed a plastic bag full of tiny bunches of dried up leaves—they had to be marijuana buds—and another plastic bag with smaller bags of buds inside it. Her lower back spasmed.

She did not settle in the USA and work so hard only to have her boy turn to drugs. If that was, in fact, what he was doing. She tucked the leaves and the notebook into her own pocket, lifted the basket and pushed through her pain, down the stairs to the basement. She tossed the clothes into the washer. With her elbow, she slammed the lid, then realized she'd forgotten to add detergent. She clung to the smooth edge of the machine and took three deep breaths while whis-pering relaxing messages to her back.

After adding detergent and starting the wash, she allowed herself a few more long, careful breaths as she listened to the water begin to fill the machine. She talked herself up the stairs, basement to the first floor, first to the second, into her kitchen where she dropped onto a chair. She set the bags and notebook in front of her. Names and numbers—dollar amounts—filled the pages. Money paid, money owed. Ten dollar increments. He was a drug dealer.

She needed advice. Who could tell her what to do? The bags and the notebook sat on the table blaming her, shaming her. She considered calling the vice principal. He might have had experience with this sort of thing. She thought of calling Henry, but she hadn't talked with him all week, and echoes of "I'm not his fucking father!" still rang in her ears. What would the deacon say if he knew his bastard son was selling drugs?

The questions that haunted her pressed harder than ever. Would Chance be a good boy if he'd been raised in the church? Would Chance be a good boy if she'd beaten him when he deserved it? Would Chance be a good boy if he'd grown up hungry and carrying water and feeding the goats on Lagonav? Maybe not, but he wouldn't be a drug dealer, that was for sure.

Far below, the front door squealed open and banged shut. She listened for the footsteps. It had to be Chance, her bad boy. She shielded the pile of evidence with her arm, sat up straighter in the chair and waited, ears attuned. The footsteps with their distinctive pounding/shuffling tread belonged unmistakably to her criminal son.

Chance burst into the apartment and made his way toward the kitchen talking on his phone. "Word, I got that. Hit you up later. Be easy." He poked his head in the kitchen door, nodded, still talking, and walked on past, leaving a cloud of alcohol and weed behind him.

The first time he'd laid his eyes on her in a whole week and all he gave was a tilt of his head! She snatched the bags of weed and the notebook and followed him to his room.

The door hung open a crack. His back to her, he tapped out another number on his phone. Nadine shoved the door with her shoulder, startling him into pivoting toward her, his bloodshot eyes wide.

"What the f—!" At least he did her the favor of catching himself before he cursed.

Nadine shook the bags at him. "Are you going to tell me about this? You are a big drug dealer now?"

Chance grabbed for the bags. She jerked them away.

"Mom, chill! Where you be getting that? Give it here."

"Your pockets." Her voice sounded strangled and shrieky, unfamiliar.

Chance seemed to notice his jeans had disappeared from the floor and began kicking clothes around in a half-hearted attempt to locate them. "Why you even in my stuff? Where my pants at?"

"Your stuff?" She couldn't stop yelling. "Criminal stuff." She followed behind him as he circled the room.

"Mom, where are the pants?"

"They're in the washing machine. I was doing you a favor, Mr. Big Shot."

"I told you, I wash my own clothes!" Chance whirled to face her. "What else did you find in the pockets?"

"This?" she screamed, flapping the little notebook at him. "Is this what you want?"

"Yes!" He caught her arm, gripping it tight, and tried to pry her fingers from the book.

She flailed her arms, struggling to pull free. His menacing look scared her, but his criminal dealings scared her more. She would not give back that notebook.

"Mom, chill! You're going to get hurt!" He squeezed her arm so hard there would be bruises.

"The way you make your bed is the way you will lie on it," she hissed. *"Jan w ranje kabann ou, se jan w kouche."*

"I don't need your old sayings, okay? Leave me alone! I'll hurt you!"

"Oh, oh, you're going to hurt me now," she taunted. "Go ahead, big drug dealer man. Hurt me. Is that what you want to do?" Nothing could hurt worse than his lack of concern for his own future. He might as well put marks where they could be seen on the outside of her body, instead of hidden in her heart.

They stared at each other. She wouldn't back down.

Chance's grip loosened. "I don't want to hurt you." His

voice shook. The edge of his lip trembled. "You're my mother. I don't want to hurt you."

She rubbed the sore spots on her arm.

"You're my mother," he said, tears in his voice. "I would never hurt you. I love you. I was planning to get your name tattooed on my neck."

"Don't do that!" she said.

"Give me the bags and the notebook, please."

"No. I'm not a fool. I know you are breaking the law."

His voice turned angry and serious again. "You don't know anything about this. Let me get straight with what I have, pay off my debts. You've got to give me those buds."

What would Henry tell her to do? Yara? Vice Principal Johnson? If Chance didn't pay his debts, would big dealers come after him? He was right, she didn't know anything. She threw the bags and the notebook at him and left the room to return to the basement.

Chance is a good boy, she whispered, body shaking as she put the clothes in the dryer. She would take them out when they were done and fold them in warm stacks. She would set his pants, shirt, socks, and underwear neatly on his bed. He would look and smell fresh and clean when he wore them to school in the morning.

In her dreams Hazel walked. She cleaned, baked, sewed, gardened, fished, and shot gophers neatly through their furry heads. Awake, she tried—really tried—to be cooperative in speech therapy, physical therapy, life in general, but she never had been a cooperative person. How could she start now at ninety-five? Some things were just too much to ask. Springtime had arrived out of her reach behind sealed windows; she needed to get her hands into the thawed dirt.

Organ music spilled from her TV, and a minister with molded black hair and a red face yammered on. Sunday. The worst day. No therapies, just bored uselessness. A constant parade of loud visitors through the hall, complete with shrieking children, and those aides always leaving her door open.

She remembered her computer. She could reach it, right there on the table.

Hazel pressed her lips inward against her gums. Sometimes she thought sensation had returned to her face. When she poked at the inside of her cheek with her tongue, she felt it. "Home," she said to herself with effort. It was time to go home. She could say the word. She could feel her face.

She could feed herself, sort of. Only crusts of toast, juice from a canned pear, and smears of egg yolk remained in front of her. She'd managed with just a small spill of prune juice on her sleeve, nothing serious. The day before, once Nadine had helped her out of bed and got her into position with the walker, Hazel had made it to the toilet. By the time she got there, she'd peed her ridiculous diaper, but the bowel movement floating in the bowl was something to be proud of. Yes, those gophers better not get too comfortable in their holes. It was only a matter of time. And effort. But no one could say Hazel Watkins was afraid of a little hard work. Well, they could say it—people could say anything—but it wouldn't be true.

"Good breakfast this morning."

Hazel smelled sunshine, clean sheets unpinned from the clothesline, and opened her eyes. Gary. Spring air clung to him. She wanted to press her nose against his jacket, but as usual, he stood a safe distance away from the bed, just out of reach.

"Home," she said.

"*You can't say hello?*" *Gary said.* "*Good morning, Mother. Looks like you were hungry.*"

She was glad to see him. He brought the outside in to her and he was smiling, only kidding about the not saying hello thing, maybe. Hard to know. Everything seemed so hard to know these days, especially with Gary. He was up to something.

He switched the breakfast tray with her computer. "*Here you go. Now we can talk.*"

Gary stood, shifting from one foot to the other, hands in his jacket pockets. What did he want?

"*Mother, I'm not sure how to say this,*" *he mumbled.*

"*Look at me,*" *she typed.* "*Not at the floor.*" *How could she hear his muttering?*

Nadine burst through the door all smiles and purpose. Gary shifted his gaze to her and a sappy grin erased his agitation.

"*A visitor!*" *Nadine said.* "*Good morning. I won't interrupt. Just let me grab this tray.*"

Go ahead, interrupt, please, Hazel tried to say with her eyes.

"*No problem,*" *Gary said.* "*Let me help.*" *Their arms bumped as they reached for the tray at the same time. Nadine grabbed it first and gave Gary the same look that Hazel often felt like throwing his way, if she had the ability to shape her face— chin tucked back, eyebrows drawn together, a slight frown, all saying* "*What ARE you doing exactly?*"

"*Your mother has been taking herself to the toilet,*" *Nadine said.* "*And she spends many hours working on her computer, writing her story.*"

Hazel brightened. Yes. Convince him that she is improving. "*Home,*" *she said again. The word slipped from her lips already formed, whole, perfect.* "*Home. Home.*"

Gary scowled. Hazel typed "*Home. Time to go home.*" *She* could communicate and take care of herself, but he wasn't even looking. For the computer to work, the listener had to pay some attention. Nadine ignored her too, face turned to Gary.

"Hey!" Hazel smacked her tray. Their heads jerked around. Both stared at her. Her pleasure tweaked one side of her mouth upward. She could feel it. She allowed herself a moment to bask in her success.

"Hooooome!" she shouted. She'd planned it to sound assertive, the voice of a woman who was used to giving directions that people followed. Instead it sounded too loud, desperate, pleading. She turned away from both of them. Her heart beat fast beneath the splotch of egg yolk that dirtied her blouse. She would not cry. She closed her eyes, felt the butt of her rifle against her shoulder, early April, time enough before planting to eliminate those pesky gophers and dig a few new beds.

Her son's voice from far away. They must have stepped out into the hall to talk about her. She strained to hear. "...Trailer..." He never learned to call it a mobile home, no matter how many times she corrected him. "...Help clean out..." Nobody's home was cleaner than Hazel's. He'd better not be talking about her mobile home. Her breathing was so fast it hurt. Maybe she was having a heart attack.

"Helllllll meeeee," she called.

Nadine appeared. "Shh, Mrs. Watkins. Shh. Everything is okay."

Hazel squirmed under the weight of the aide's hand on her shoulder. She tried twisting out from under it, but Nadine pinned her with two hands and put her brown face right up close, nose almost touching Hazel's. Her breath smelled like cinnamon. Her body like chrysanthemums. Gary's face floated behind Nadine's. Why was he talking with a nursing home aide about his own mother's business? An uneducated foreigner?

"Now, look here. Breathe with me."

Hazel writhed and swiveled her head. Nadine exhaled near her ear and whispered. "Shh, no need to be upset, Mrs. Watkins. Don't worry."

Hazel turned her head again, away from Nadine's voice and found herself nose to nose once more. Cinnamon and chrysanthemums. Autumn. Pumpkin pie.

Nadine breathed in slowly and deeply, then exhaled, her hands warm on Hazel's shoulders. Hazel opened her eyes, stared right into Nadine's and found herself following the aide's breath. Nadine's nostrils flared wide. Hazel felt her own opening. Nadine's ample bosom rose. Hazel tried to do the same with her own skinny chest, withered and drooping old breasts. When did she get so old?

"Mrs. Watkins, shh, no need for crying. Everything is alright." Nadine's voice soft and soothing. "Would you like a foot rub? It will help you feel better."

She never cried. Foot rub? Nadine did give a very nice foot rub.

Hazel nodded. A foot rub might help.

Nadine's tone changed. "Come here. This is very simple. I will show you how to rub your mother's feet. Hand me that lotion."

Gary's voice. "I don't have much time."

"Then it will be a short foot rub."

"No," Hazel said.

"She doesn't want one," said Gary.

"She wants one." Nadine held her hand out for the squeeze bottle.

Gary slouched to the foot of the bed. Was he really going to stand there and massage her feet? She didn't want anyone *touching her who didn't want to. She thrashed her feet in protest.*

"Okay now Mrs. Watkins," Nadine soothed. "Relax."

Hazel gave one more feeble kick. This woman put some kind of spell on her, that voice, her warm, slow hands. Nadine put spells on Gary too if he was actually standing there preparing to rub her bony old feet. Maybe some kind of Haitian vodou magic. Nadine cupped Hazel's heel in one hand and pressed her fingers into the ball of her left foot, instructing Gary to copy her on the right. Nadine's touch, confident, strong, singing up through Hazel's sole to her still racing heart. Gary, tentative, tickling. She fought the urge to kick at him. He was trying.

Nadine gave a few more instructions that Hazel half heard. "This is nice, right?"

Hazel nodded, eyes closed.

"You can do this for your mother when you visit. It feels good and helps her circulation."

"I bet your feet get tired, on them all day," Gary said.

What was he talking about? She was lucky if she walked to the bathroom. All day? Hazel peeked at him. He was watching Nadine. Was Gary flirting with the aide now?

"It helps mood, insomnia, more problems than you can imagine. Mrs. Watkins, you have a good son," Nadine said as she left the room.

Gary bent over her feet. When did he get to be so bald? Suddenly, she remembered his baby head, that spot where the skin pulsed in and out, where one hard poke could injure the brain. She'd thought something was wrong with her son, until the nurse explained. His skull had formed as promised. She'd never done anything to damage his developing brain.

"Oh, Airy," she said.

He looked up, startled, hands frozen on her foot.

"Aaank ou."

He smiled. "You're welcome."

She thought he'd stop then, but he continued, rubbing each toe, the balls of her feet, her ankles, pressing with more confidence. "Maybe I should go back to school to learn massage," he joked.

Nadine had explained to Hazel as she pressed a particular toe, that it connected with the kidney or the stomach or some other organ and helped to relieve stress or depression. Hazel considered Nadine's ideas a bunch of foreign hocus pocus, but she wasn't going to say anything that might make her stop, or Gary either.

Henry didn't mind his work-study job. He scraped the edges of the tray of mac and cheese with the giant metal spoon and plopped a helping onto a plate without looking at the girl who asked for it.

"Hand me the empty," said Mr. Roy from behind him. Tiberius slid a full pan into the empty spot.

Henry liked these guys more than anyone else he'd met at school. Mr. Roy Washburn, soft spoken and thoughtful, counseled him on investing in the stock market, and Tiberius, who reminded him of Chance with his constant singing and trash talk, gave advice about love. Their words of wisdom amounted to pretty much the same thing.

"You know, it's not a bad idea to look for a rich woman," Mr. Roy had said more than once. "Then invest in real estate and slow-growing stocks. You can do it without the rich girl—I did—but it takes awhile to save that money to get you started. If my wife had come from money, I'd have already flipped a house or two and wouldn't be here still slinging hash at fifty."

"Now's your chance," Tiberius would badger Henry. "Plenty of well-off hotties at this place. Daddy's the head of a bank in Tanzania or an internet company in Ireland or an insurance company right here in the Twin Cities. Look around."

"I'll have that broccoli and tofu." Henry looked up to see Sage, a sparkly knitted scarf flung around her neck, its fringe dangerously near the surface of the bowl of soup on her tray. She smiled. Her teeth could be in a toothpaste commercial. Even her lips glistened. "Hi, Henry."

"Hi." Behind him, Tiberius hummed the tune to Sonny Boy Williamson's "Eyesight to the Blind." Tiberius had sung that same song often enough after work as they sat around on overturned milk crates that Henry could hear the lyrics in his head and knew Tiberius was ragging on him.

"Hey, brother, you're holding up the line there. Give the lady her broccoli." Tiberius laughed.

"Uh, you're not going to use that cheese-coated spoon, are you?" Sage asked. "Cause I don't eat any dairy."

It never failed. Just when Henry felt a flicker of interest in her, she'd say something like that.

"Wouldn't think of it," he said with an edge in his voice. Why would he, when the broccoli and tofu had its own tongs, right there in the tray? If she weren't so entitled and so self-absorbed, she'd see he hadn't had a chance to switch utensils.

"I'm just kidding," Sage said. "Guess I'm just trying to find a way to talk to you, connect, you know. And I keep messing it up. Sorry. I mean I'm not kidding about not eating dairy, but I—oh never mind."

The line lengthened and grumbled behind her. Henry realized he hadn't served her yet and fumbled with the tongs and a plate. "Not too much," she said. Tiberius passed behind him singing about pretty rich girls being fine.

"Keep the line movin'," Mr. Roy called from the back.

Henry handed Sage her food over the sneeze guard. Their fingertips touched as she accepted the plate from him, and he felt a cool charge travel through his body as if she'd done something weird to his blood, iced it, stopped his heart and breath.

"Hey, I'm starving here," said the next guy in line. "Give me a few big scoops of that mac and cheese, before I pass out."

It seemed like slow motion, the way Sage pulled her clear gaze away from Henry's and lowered her plate to her tray. He didn't know if she was having the same difficulty breathing, but because her smile faltered a bit, he guessed she might be.

"What time do you finish work?" she asked.

"Around nine."

"I'll be out on the patio. It's actually a beautiful night, for April in Minneapolis."

"I've got a lot of work," Henry said.

"Can you two save this for later in the bedroom?" the hungry guy said.

Henry filled his plate and handed it to him.

"I'll be on the patio," Sage said, "whether you decide to join me or not. But I hope you will." She pivoted out of line and crossed the cafeteria.

He liked her short, scuffed boots, her lacy gray tights, and her skirts which were form-fitting and flowing at the same time. No one else wore skirts like that. He liked the way she walked. She didn't stomp or sashay or make any kind of big deal out of it. She wore her clothes and her body too, as if she'd chosen them because they made her happy.

He served the next person and looked up to see she'd settled with friends, facing away from him. Bear sat beside her, his meaty arm resting on the back of her chair.

"I hope you will," Tiberius falsettoed as he handed Henry a full tray of broccoli.

"Fuck you." Henry smiled.

Tiberius ran his mouth the rest of the shift, just like Chance. As Henry washed pots and trays, he wondered what nonsense his brother was up to back home. Only a couple of months, Henry would be back in Cambridge and could try again to reason with him—not as a father, but as an older brother, who had somehow survived freshman year in a bougie private college in the heartland, a real accomplishment. Even Chance had to see that, whether he'd admit it out loud or not.

He dried the last pot and hung it in its proper place. Mr. Roy locked the kitchen. Tiberius shrugged on his coat. "I know you heading for the patio." When Henry didn't respond, he said, "You heading for the patio, right?"

Henry, reluctant to admit it even to himself, gave a small nod. Tiberius raised his hand for a high-five. Henry answered with a feeble slap.

Tiberius frowned. "What's wrong, man?"

"You have some fun now," Mr. Roy said. "You're in college. You're young. Opportunities everywhere you look."

"I want to hear all about it tomorrow," Tiberius said.

"I don't," said Mr. Roy. "Gentlemen don't talk about what they doing with the ladies."

Sage sat in the dark at one of the round metal tables, talking on her phone. Henry hung back watching, too far away to understand actual words, but close enough to hear the cadence of her voice, her bright laugh. What was he doing? In a matter of weeks, okay months, he'd be out of here. He didn't want to start anything now with mountains of work to get through. And if he were going to start anything, why her? Besides the pull of her lovely kneecaps and brilliant smile and alluring smell, besides the lust, he ached to know what exactly she found compelling about him. He crossed the deserted patio, past the chained up stacks of chairs, to where she sat waiting. When she saw him, she stopped talking abruptly and put her phone on the table. She turned it off.

"Hi."

"Hi." Henry sat down in the chair next to her. It froze his ass. He could see his breath and hers.

"Nice night," she said. "Look at the moon over there. I think it's just past full." Backs toward the building, they looked out over the shadowy, deserted lawn.

"Yeah."

"Henry, I was thinking, we should do something sometime."

"Like what? Aren't we doing something now? Hanging out in the moonlight on the patio."

"You make it sound romantic," she said.

What should he say next? Chance would see this as an opportunity to pull her close and jam his tongue into her mouth. Or at least say something to move things in that direction. The jewel on the side of her nose glittered. Her lips looked wet and kissable. She was waiting for Henry to respond.

"I think this is the first time we've ever sat down together," he said. "Without a lot of people around. I don't know much about you, really, except that you're a vegetarian."

"Vegan," she corrected.

"Okay."

"Do you have a problem with that?"

"No."

She tilted her head and raised her eyebrows.

"Well, maybe a little. To me it's like being a picky eater."

"Oh. Well, I can tell you more about why it's good for both you and the environment. It's probably the single most important thing a person can do to combat global warming." She sounded heated. He wished he hadn't said anything. "I mean ... so much is out of our control, but this one thing ..." She trailed off.

"I didn't mean to hurt your feelings," he said. Or inspire a lecture, he thought.

"You didn't," she said quickly. "Well, maybe a little." She pouted, then laughed at herself. "You're so serious. I don't know anyone around here as serious as you."

"Really?"

"Is that a cultural thing?"

"What?"

"Are Haitian people serious?"

Henry laughed. "How can you ask that?"

Sage picked at a fingernail.

"You don't think every culture has its serious side and its silly side?" Henry asked.

"You think I'm racist. Shit, I'm bleeding." She sucked her torn cuticle.

"Aren't we all? It's a racist world. But I wish you could stop seeing me as the Haitian guy and see me as Henry." He realized how much he felt this as he heard himself say it. "Yes, I'm Haitian. But I don't think of you as THE white girl...white girl with locs, maybe, white girl with locs and a diamond in her nose."

He watched his own hand reach out and touch the jewel above her right nostril and then her hair. He lifted a bunch of her hair, closed his fingers around it and let it slide through his hand. "You don't see too many of those." The hair didn't feel right. It reminded him of the wool sweater he'd shrunk in the drier by mistake—matted and coarse. He never liked locs on anyone except maybe Bob Marley, couldn't shake the idea that they were the result of careless hygiene. On a white girl, who made it a project, spent money to look like a dirty hippie, they looked bizarre. The nose stud was kind of sexy, though.

"I get a lot of shit for it," she said.

"Why do you do it?"

"I don't know."

"Maybe you like pissing people off." He ran the tip of his finger along her jawbone, resting it on her chin.

"Maybe I like to 'push boundaries and break stereotypes.'"

"Now you sound like some PC manifesto." He suddenly realized what felt wrong. "Have you gone out with Black guys before?"

"I never had the chance."

"There you go. You're admitting it. You're interested in me cause I'm Black. You have to be because what else do you know. Nothing!" Henry's anger surprised both of them.

"No," she protested. "No, that's not why!"

His thighs and ass were now frost bitten, in stark contrast to the heat in his groin. His fingers were numb. It was not a beautiful night. It was fucking Minnesota in early April. It was most certainly not romantic.

"Well maybe a little," she said finally.

"What?"

"Maybe it is partly because you're Black. I've never known anyone like you. So serious. From the east coast. I like the things you say in class. Everyone else seems like they're talking to impress the teacher, but you only talk when it matters—when you're so excited or angry you can't help yourself. And people really listen. You're not afraid to contradict the professor."

Henry scratched his head and turned his face to hide his pleasure, but she must have glimpsed it anyway. She leaned toward him and rested her hand on his sleeve. "Listen, will you go out with me? One date. Have you ever been to the mall?"

He hadn't gone during orientation when they offered the trip to the Mall of America, largest retail shopping mall in the United States, with over 520 stores and a theme park. He was in his room recovering from the embarrassment of his first conversation with Sage back at the yoga class. He was sure she remembered it, and hoped she would never ever bring it up.

She didn't wait for him to answer. "They have everything there, but what I want to do with you is play mini golf. Have you ever played?"

"I played regular golf once in high school when I thought I might want to be on the golf team. I sucked."

"Mini golf is different. Want to go? Want to go on Friday? I can drive."

"You have a car?" He'd never had a friend who owned one.

"At my aunt's. She lives pretty close. That's one of the reasons my parents wanted me to come here, since I told them I wanted to be far from home. I go to her house every Sunday for scrabble and supper—always vegan waffles and bacon."

"Bacon?"

"Vegan bacon from adzuki beans and buckwheat. She's not even vegetarian. She figured it out for me."

Why did this girl make life so difficult for herself and people around her? Maybe a person went to the trouble to make fake bacon for the same reason they'd turn white people hair into dreads, but he had no fucking idea what that reason might be.

She must have said where she was from back at orientation, but he couldn't remember.

"Home is...?"

"California. Marin County."

"I've heard of that."

"Just north of San Francisco. The other side of the bridge."

He'd never been to San Francisco. He'd never been anywhere besides Cambridge and twice to New York City and now Minneapolis.

"The Golden Gate Bridge," she said.

"Oh, yeah." Everyone knew what that bridge looked like, spanning the opening to San Francisco Bay, towers wrapped in fog. "That's cool."

"It's beautiful there. I miss the smell of the eucalyptus trees. Sometimes I buy cough drops cause I'm homesick. I don't even care if they have corn syrup in them. But I don't miss my parents or my sister."

If he asked about her family, he'd end up talking about his and he didn't want to even think about his brother. He had to finish reading *Don Quixote* and write a response—only one page, but still...

Sage scraped back her chair and stood suddenly. "Do you want to come Friday, or not? I'm not going beg you."

If he didn't go with her, he'd be doing homework or hanging out smoking bud in the dark behind the cafeteria while Tiberius ragged on him about having nothing to do on a Friday night.

"Okay."

She nodded, gathered up her phone, books, travel mug, and bag. She paused as if waiting for him to head back to the dorm with her, but he didn't move. "Bye," she said.

He watched her start to walk away, shoulders hunched around her armload of books, and realized he'd been waiting for her to insist they go back together.

"Hey," he said.

She stopped, too far from the dim light spilling from the dining hall for him to see her expression.

"Hold on." He caught up to her. "Can I carry something for you?"

Her raised eyebrows said, "Really?" as clearly as her voice would have. He held out his hands. She dumped her stack of books into his arms and smiled.

Maybe she was only interested in him because he was so different from her. Maybe he'd suck at mini golf. But walking beside her across the deserted and dark campus, he was a helpful person with Friday night plans.

"How far is it around this lake?" Nadine asked. "I've been on my feet all day." She didn't often come over to this part of Cambridge, but since returning from her daughter's, Yara had started a regular exercise routine, tramping around Fresh Pond.

"Yes, but this walking is different." Yara bent to tighten the lace of her special sneakers, bright and wide with a thick cushiony sole. "You need some good shoes."

"These are good shoes," Nadine held up a foot in its plastic clog. "On my feet all day, I have good shoes! How far is it?" She felt naked without her purse, left in the trunk of Yara's Toyota. If she needed a breath mint or band-aid, she'd be out of luck.

"About two miles. We won't even notice, we'll be talking so much. Come on." Yara tucked her arm under Nadine's, drew her close, and pulled her along. Nadine matched her steps to Yara's.

Green tinted the willow trees, and magnolia buds threatened to burst. Yellow fringed the branches of a large bush.

Dogs splashed into the small pond, Fresh Pond itself caged in by a chain link fence.

A shirtless man sprinted past. "He's easy on the eyes," Yara said. "Do you think he's too young for me?"

"How about him?" Nadine pointed at another man walking a big slobbery dog. "He's more our age. You can have him. I don't like dogs."

"So how's Chance doing?" Yara asked.

Nadine's throat tightened. She told her friend almost everything, but she did not want to admit her son was a drug dealer, not to Yara with those successful daughters and now a perfect new grandson.

"Things aren't good?" Yara asked. "I'm sorry. I should have called you from New York, but that baby cries most of the night and Luiza is so tired. Her husband is working all the time at the clinic." She reached over and patted the back of Nadine's hand. Nadine pulled away, wrapped her arms around herself, and picked up the pace, staring straight ahead. Yara never did miss a chance to mention that her son-in-law was a doctor. A white woman with fluffy hair and a fluffy short-legged dog to match passed Nadine, but greeted Yara with a huge hello that flowed immediately into a stream of conversation. Nadine stopped to wait.

Yara and the woman laughed. The breeze carried a chill. People in this country sure did love their animals. She watched Yara from a distance. On a different day, Nadine would have introduced herself, but she couldn't muster any friendliness to strangers, especially these skinny, laughing white women, who hired people to clean their houses, care for their kids and aging parents, and didn't worry about the cost. They must pay very well for Yara to afford the life she had.

Yara headed toward Nadine, shaking her head and laughing. "That little dog ate all of a birthday cake," she said. "And she had to take it to the grooming place to wash the icing from its fur. I clean for those people."

"Did you have to clean up the cake mess then?" Nadine sounded mean.

"No, no," Yara said. "It was this morning. Today I had other houses." Yara took her arm again. "So tell me what is bothering you."

"Whose birthday cake was it?"

"Her son's. She had to buy another. Can you imagine? You saw that tiny dog. How could it have reached the counter? I'm surprised it isn't sick.

"Hello," Yara said to a stooped older man. "Beautiful day, Mr. Norton."

The man shuffled to a stop. Yara, her arm through Nadine's, paused too, jerking Nadine midstep.

"Yes," he said. "Beautiful day. I couldn't spend the whole of it at my desk. If I don't get up and move once in awhile, I won't be able to get up at all." He chuckled.

"How is the book coming along?" Yara asked. Nadine groaned inside.

"Slow. This chapter requires a great deal of research."

Nadine gave Yara's elbow a tug.

"Good luck with it," Yara said. "I'll see you tomorrow."

"Yes. Enjoy the beautiful afternoon."

"Do you know everybody?" Nadine asked. "Do you do more for that old man than clean?"

Yara stopped. "What are you saying? What are you thinking? I have sex with him? Massage him? Just come out and say it, if you do."

Nadine flushed. "I'm sorry. I'm not serious." But even as she said she wasn't, she realized she was. "I don't know how you make so much money housekeeping only."

"I clean for many, many wealthy people. At least twenty houses right in this neighborhood. They pay well and give me extra at every occasion. And you know I'm a business woman with many people working for me. You really should leave Riverview," Yara said. "You can make your own schedule. Be around when Chance is out of school. Keep your eyes on him. How is he, anyway? You were about to tell me."

"People in this country think they can buy everything—cleaning, cooking, massages, care for their children and mothers, even love. I've been thinking—"

A woman in a blue tracksuit jogged in place next to Yara. "How are you?" the woman panted. "The couch under the windows works so well. You're an absolute genius with space, Yara. The entire room opened up."

Yara smiled.

"Next week, can you take a look at the TV room? I'd like to change things around in there." The woman fluttered her fingers at Nadine, winked, and jogged away. "Have a nice walk," she called back.

"I'm sorry." Yara draped her arm around Nadine's shoulders. "What were you saying?"

Nadine studied the folks walking toward them. "Do you know these people? If you do, I'll wait to talk until you are finished talking with them."

"Nadine." Yara raised her eyebrows. "You need to relax. Enjoy yourself. Listen to the birds. Look at the flowers."

Yara didn't know the approaching couple, but she did say hello and comment on the weather. When Nadine had first moved to the States, she hadn't understood peoples' tendency to rush past each other without greetings, so different from Lagonav, but she'd gotten used to it. She'd become part American, lost in her thoughts, alone in her troubles.

"Maybe we should have walked somewhere else, "Yara said. "It's so crowded here on a nice day. I'd forgotten."

They strode along, side by side, silent for awhile. Nadine picked up her pace to match Yara's and began to enjoy the rhythm of their steps and her quickening pulse. Birdsong poured from trees and bushes. "I wonder what the birds are saying," Nadine said. Maybe she should tell Yara every- thing. It might make her spirit lighter.

"They're singing, not saying anything."

"They have to be saying something." Nadine was sure of it. Their warbling sounded desperate when she listened hard enough, identifying a particular bird's voice from among the whole tangle of sound.

"Probably basic things," Yara said. "Like, 'There's food over here ... I want to have sex with you ... Stay away from my nest.' What do you think?"

Nadine listened to the loud mix of trills, twitters, and cheeps. They were so small, the birds, their tiny feet holding tight to the branches thick with buds about to burst, their songs big with everything in their miniature hearts. "I think they must be saying more than the basics," Nadine said. "If only we could understand them."

A boy whizzed past on a scooter, an older boy running beside him demanding a turn. "Stop right now, or I'll kick your ass."

"You'd have to catch me to do that!" The younger boy whipped ahead, swerved around a woman with a stroller, the older boy close behind, cursing. Obviously they were brothers.

Yara didn't believe in secrets. She would think Nadine ridiculous not to have told the boys from the beginning about their fathers. Yara didn't understand the silencing power of shame.

Nadine's little toe hurt—and the back of her heel. If she complained, Yara would tell her to wear different shoes. She wanted Yara to say that her feet ached too, but Nadine knew they didn't, so she swallowed her distress and continued walking.

Henry waited for Sage in the vestibule of the dorm as the top of the sky turned that rich just-after-sunset blue. He'd tried standing outside, but the freezing wind bit through his thin sport coat. He didn't know what people wore for miniature golf but Yara, his mother's friend, always complimented his jacket, and even though she was old, she was fun and always dressed with style. Topping his ironed jeans and white t-shirt fresh from the package, the jacket seemed just right. He'd sprayed himself with his roommate's aftershave and now realized he smelled like some strange combination of coconut, caramel, and chocolate; fine for a candy bar, but not so fine for a man on a first date.

A rusty Honda Civic, blotchy with unpainted bondo, pulled up, horn blasting before it slowed to a stop. Sage, hunched over the steering wheel, didn't look his way.

He opened the passenger door and leaned in; she was picking at her fingernails and jerked back, startled. "Whoa! You're here!"

He felt like an overeager fool and chided himself for not waiting upstairs.

"Want to drive?"

Why would he drive? It was her car. And he'd never bothered to get a license. No point in spending the time or money when buses or the T took him wherever he needed to go, but suddenly he felt foolish about that too.

"You know where we're going," he said.

"Okay, true." She patted the seat. "I'll drive then. Get in."

Deep in his pants pocket, his phone vibrated. He ignored it.

"Just a short ride," she said. She fussed with the CD player, and the Black Eyed Peas sang out. Chance would laugh his ass off if he knew Henry was on his way to mini golf with a girl who liked those posers, but Henry didn't mind them.

Sage bobbed her head to "Where is the Love?" and watched the road. A lot of fine leg in glittery stockings showed between the hem of her little skirt and the top of her beat up pink Uggs as she worked the gas, clutch and brake.

Henry's phone vibrated again, and he switched it off. Probably his mother. She'd be happy to hear he'd been on a date.

They sped down the highway, past the airport. Last time he'd been out this way he was fresh off that fucked up meeting with the principal, so agitated he couldn't do anything on the plane except stare out the window and remind himself that Coach Watkins said he'd check in with Chance.

"What?" Sage asked. "You'd rather talk to yourself than to me?" Her forced smile didn't quite cover the actual hurt in her voice.

"Don't take it personally," Henry said. "I don't know why I do it. I think of something and the next thing you know I'm having an actual conversation—what—were my lips moving?"

"Hands too," Sage said. "Who were you talking with?"

"My brother." Henry answered.

"What were you saying?"

"Sorry," Henry covered her beautiful knee with his hand. The sparkly stuff felt prickly. "It was a private conversation." When he realized how funny that sounded, instead of feeling embarrassed, he surprised himself with a self-accepting, relaxed laugh.

"Okay," she said. "But I'm really interested."

"Something happened between him and a friend. Maybe it's not a big deal, but I keep thinking it might be and I don't know how to ask him about it. I keep practicing in my head." He imagined telling her, 'My brother's a criminal.' The one Black guy she's talked to at school and his family fits a racist stereotype.

The mall was ridiculous, like so much about the messed up world—a monument to consumerism and people's desperation to make themselves feel better by spending money—but the sheer vastness of it, the Cambridge mall he knew on mega-steroids, impressed Henry. Sage led him up to the third level. Moose Mountain Adventure Golf appeared before them—rocks, trees, logging train, life-size animals— all made out of some kind of plastic.

"I saw a moose once," Sage said. "Up north."

Henry considered the cartoonish moose head before him. "Do they look that corny in real life?"

Sage stopped a few yards short of the ticket booth and followed his gaze. "Moose look silly and majestic at the same time. You wouldn't think it was possible. You know how people have animal totems? Well, the moose is mine."

"Totems? No. Don't know nothing about that."

She studied him for a long moment. "Well, let's play. This is all my idea, so I'll pay for us." He didn't argue and accepted the golf club and ball she handed him.

They advanced to the first hole. She showed him where to set the ball and how to score. The club had a nice weight to it, and he found himself under par on the fifth and sixth holes.

"You're a natural," she said.

Didn't make sense that successfully sinking a ball in a cup made him feel so all around good. He was winning so far. Some of these holes were trickier than they first appeared with odd hills and valleys and obstacles, but he enjoyed the challenge. When Sage told him she could take pictures with her phone and asked him to pose in the fake logging truck, then showed him the photo, he barely recognized his relaxed grin. He looked like someone having fun.

They thought about getting something to eat after, but places were beginning to close up.

"There's great leftovers at my aunt's," Sage said. "She brought home all this food from a party they had at her analytic institute. She's a fancy therapist, though you wouldn't know it to look at her. There's even a case of wine, champagne, I think. Want to come over?"

She took his hand and swung it as they wandered.

"Okay."

As they passed the closed Apple store, he felt his lips move, about to engage in another animated conversation with his brother, and shut his mouth. Too late, she noticed. She just smiled. The rare pleasure of being known flooded through him, and he squeezed her hand.

A few songs later, they pulled into her aunt's driveway. He hoped he wouldn't have to meet the woman. From the little Sage had told him, he didn't think she'd mind that her niece was out with a Haitian guy, but he didn't want any complications when the evening had been surprisingly successful thus far.

"My aunt's at her girlfriend's," Sage said. "Isn't this a great kitchen? Sit down."

A TV show kind of kitchen: long stretches of cleared counter, cabinets and floor of pale wood, hanging pots of gleaming copper, giant refrigerator and stove, shelves of cookbooks, and a comfortable red couch strewn with pillows. So much space, but cozy, too. Weird. This girl definitely had money in her background. Tiberius and Roy would be glad to hear it.

He shoved a few pillows aside and sat at one end of the

couch. She opened the refrigerator and began pulling out trays of party food. "This champagne is nice and cold." She brought him the bottle. "Go ahead. Open it."

No reason to feel ashamed that he'd never opened champagne before. He took his time, examined the wire trapping the cork, saw he'd need to untwist it. He'd seen champagne plenty of times after the big sports wins—players showering in it. "Is it going to mess up the floor?" he asked.

"Don't worry." Sage brought over two glasses. "Go ahead."

He thumbed the cork, and it shot up with a satisfying pop. She positioned her glass under the spray of champagne which was nowhere near as dramatic as he expected.

"To new experiences," he said.

They clinked glasses and took big swallows.

"Henry," she began, then burped.

He burped back to ease her embarrassment. They drank and burped again and poured and drank and burped and laughed. They had to put their glasses down. Sage gulped air, tears running down her red face. Henry, miniature golf pro, champagne opener, could also be the kind of guy who wrapped his arms around a girl, pulled her onto his lap, and kissed her laughing lips. Her body melted into his, her firm ass against him, anchoring and arousing. He avoided touching her hair, remembering the odd texture of it, but he touched her everywhere else, nothing odd about any of that. She kissed him back, hard, and rolled her butt in beautiful ways and whispered in his ear how delicious he smelled, how sexy he was.

"Wait," she said. "I'll be right back." She untangled herself, tugged her shirt into position and disappeared, probably to the bathroom to do whatever girls do in there at times like this. He wondered if she expected to fuck, a little worried about what it would mean if they did. But if she sat back in his lap, he'd shove those worries aside.

His phone jabbed into his thigh. He'd be more comfortable with empty pockets. Out of habit he checked his messages before putting it on the table. Seventeen from his mother! One from Chance. Couldn't be good. He listened for Sage and tried to gauge whether he had time to hear any of them. He accessed the message.

His brother's imagined voice. *Checking messages from home when you're about to get it on with a lovely lady?* Then the recorded voice, the real voice, more scared than cocky. "Bro, I'm in jail. They're charging me with a felony. This is my phone call and you're not picking up."

The asshole. He'd done it now. Henry leaped up, banged his shin on the low table in front of the couch. Shit!

Sage returned, barefoot and barelegged in a soft blue clingy dress. He was sure she had nothing on underneath. "What's wrong? Are you okay?"

"No, no, I'm not. Sage, I'm really sorry. I've got to take care of some business. Family stuff."

She froze. "What?"

"I've got to go."

He hadn't even taken off his jacket so he didn't have to look for it. He pocketed his phone and barreled past her to the door.

"Wait, where are you going? I'll give you a ride."

"I can walk. I just—I need to think."

Confusion and concern mingled on her face. He wanted to explain, but couldn't.

"I'll call you," he said.

Out on the deserted night sidewalk, he told himself to slow down. Fuck it. He broke into a jog. Running would clear his head. He'd only gone a few blocks when a cop car decelerated beside him. He swallowed the fuck you in his throat and clenched his fists to keep from flipping the cops off. He should slow down, take pains to show he wasn't a suspicious character. Fuck these fuckers. He ran harder, and the car sped up a bit. Rage trumped fear; every time his soles hit the pavement, he stomped on the man. They followed him all the way to the college entrance. Inside the gate, near the guard booth, he gulped air and watched the cops drive off. The security guard, an older Black man, approached him with concern.

"Those aren't exactly clothes for running," he said. "You alright?"

Henry's head ached. He couldn't catch his breath. If he looked at the guard, he might cry.

"I'm alright," he gasped. "Just tired."

"You go on and have a good night now, okay?" Out of the corner of his eye Henry saw the guard make a move to pat his shoulder, then stop short and turn back to the booth.

His phone vibrated. He straightened and pulled it from his pocket. Sage. Fuck all these people. Everybody wanting something from him. Assuming things. He switched the phone off.

The pink and white flowering trees lining the courthouse sidewalk, filling the air with sweetness, gave Nadine no pleasure, only itchy eyes and aching sinuses. Chance ignored her, talking on his phone, in that street language she could barely understand. But she understood too well that careless laugh. How dare he laugh on his way to a courtroom!

"He was a perfect gentleman, ma'am," the tired bondsman had told her when he finally arrived in the lobby of the police station, as if that would comfort her. And it had. For a moment. "He has beautiful manners. Not like some of these guys." *Se depi yon ti pye bwa piti pou w drese l.* Don't ever let a child grow up before you teach him manners. A bud of maternal pride blossomed in her chest before she leaned over to sign the paperwork and saw Chance's criminal pictures—front and side views. Her eyes blurred and her fingers, always strong when helping the old people, could barely hold the pen.

She'd handed the man the money. Two hundred dollars bail, forty for his fee. His smile was tired and sorry. She sat in the plastic chair and stared at the door by the cubicle where a policeman sat protected by Plexiglass. She had waited and waited, willing her boy to appear, wondering if she'd recognize him.

Chance had slipped out through another door. "Meet him outside, Ma'am." The policeman's voice had crackled through some kind of microphone. She felt cheated. They'd let him out the back.

She thought that a boy who'd been arrested would look ashamed, head down, *I'm sorry, Manman*, on his lips. No. This boy says "Yo, dawg," to her, no matter how many times she says, "I am not a dog," and "Please don't say yo." This boy leaps up the courthouse steps ahead of his mother and answers his ringing phone. This boy is rude. Angry as she is, she'd die for him if it would do any good. *M ap bay lavi m pou pitit mwen.* I give my life for my child. He swaggers along the sidewalk free of cares. Perhaps she should have left him in jail for the weekend.

Now, she scraped her tongue against the roof of her mouth in an attempt to relieve the itchiness. In Haiti she'd never heard of such a thing as allergies to flowers. Chance loped ahead, as if he didn't want to be seen with her. She had begged him to dress nicely, but he snarled that it didn't matter, that if she didn't like how he was dressed she didn't need to come, that he had gotten himself into trouble and he was responsible for getting himself out. Just before he slipped his phone into his pocket, she heard him arrange to meet someone in the courtroom.

She stood behind him in the long line waiting to pass through security. In the dingy, echoing lobby, Chance emptied his pockets, dropping the phone and clattering a handful of change into a plastic dish. His belt, buckled low around his thighs, set off a repeated beeping. He slid it from the belt loops, whipped it onto the conveyor belt, clutched his sagging jeans with the other hand and slouched through the metal detector.

The guard squinted at the picture of the insides of her huge purse, as Chance headed for the elevator without her. The security officer then searched through her things, unzipping her cosmetic bag and sewing kit, as if she were the criminal. Mother of a criminal, though she still didn't know why he'd been arrested. If it weren't for Henry's panicked phone calls predicting this day for months, she might have convinced herself there had been a mistake; it was probably for selling marijuana—she'd seen the drugs herself. He stomped ahead making sure she knew that becoming a man was serious business she could not possibly understand.

They crowded into a dirty elevator. Most of the people wore suits and carried briefcases or stacks of manila folders. No one else in the elevator appeared to be a criminal or a criminal's mother. The people in suits let Nadine and Chance exit first, like guests of honor. Nadine mumbled a thank you. Chance said nothing. He found his name on a computer printout tacked to a bulletin board. Courtroom A. She followed him down a hallway over scuffed linoleum, the same brown flecked pattern that gleamed in the nursing home corridors. This floor hadn't been tended to.

A bored-looking man in a uniform stood just inside the door of Courtroom A. Chance passed him, scanned the room as if looking for someone, then slid onto a bench.

"Shouldn't we make sure this is the right place?" Nadine whispered.

Chance shrugged.

"Want to ask the man?"

"You're the one worrying," Chance said without looking at her. He slipped his phone from his pocket and studied it as if wanting to make a call. "You ask."

The man by the door was the only official in the room. The benches around them were filling up, but the whole area in the front, the chairs and tables on the other side of the railing, was still empty.

The uniformed man said that indeed this was the room where arraignments took place. Yesterday morning Nadine had never heard that word before. Just since Friday night so much new vocabulary: bondsman, booking, bail, and those were just the words that began with b.

They waited. A light brown-skinned young man with an acne-scarred face and a bandaged hand sat right behind Chance. He was breathing hard as if he'd just run up the stairs instead of waiting for the elevator. He whispered urgently in Chance's ear. The words ran together. Nadine had never seen him before, though she'd met many of Chance's friends. She encouraged him to invite them over, made them *fritay* and *pikliz*. Junior, Razz, even Donnie, the one Henry said was not to be trusted, she treated with kindness. Donnie, with his dimples and his neatly braided hair, was the one she'd imagined Chance had been arrested with.

"I don't snitch," Chance said when the man paused.

The man who was not Donnie nodded and sat back. Nadine turned to glare at him, and he nodded again, expressionless.

Chance's sneakers might be spotless, but he was not going to make a good impression in his oversized hooded sweatshirt and baggy blue jeans. She wished she could have dressed him the way she had when he was small—Chance and Henry in their pressed white button down shirts and little jackets, dress shoes shining, for the first day of school.

The people in suits went through a little gate in the railing and chatted in pairs or small groups. Some fussed with stacks of paper. It was all so casual. She wanted to scream at them to hurry up. If their sons had been arrested, they wouldn't be smiling and taking their time. Everyone on the benches was Black or brown. The people in suits up in front were all men, and about half had brown skin.

"All rise."

A woman judge, large and white, with blonde hair cut close to her head, took her place up at the big desk.

Nadine wondered about lawyers who helped criminals, how much they cost and how to get one. A good lawyer could work miracles—look at her immigration lawyer. She should have called him. But everything had happened too quickly. She still didn't know exactly what Chance had done. Instead of sleeping late on Sunday mornings, she should go back to church where she could ask a pastor for advice. Chance fiddled with his phone. She hoped he had the sense to turn it off. If only he would look at her. Maybe Chance would go to prison. When she thought of Henry listening to her messages, hearing the terrible news she had for him, she felt weak and sad.

One after another people were called to the front. Many had driven cars without licenses or insurance and had to pay fines, arranging payment plans for fines as small as fifty dollars.

The judge called the next name, and the acne-scarred boy approached the railing. Chance straightened beside her. Nadine wished she hadn't missed the boy's name. He was accused of beating someone, taking a wallet and phone, then running and assaulting the police officer who had chased him.

A short white man, one arm hanging like a broken wing, useless against his side, who seemed like he might be the boy's lawyer, began talking about Not Donnie. He was twenty-three—not so much a boy. He lived with a grandmother who was mentally ill. He brought her groceries. He cared for two younger sisters. He had not skipped bail when arrested previously. He was not a risk.

They called Chance's name next. He had no lawyer standing next to him. The State of Massachusetts was charging her son. What chance did one Haitian boy have against the whole state of Massachusetts? He'd been with the other young man during the attack, but it wasn't clear what they were saying he'd done. He ran off and turned his jacket inside out. He had drugs in his pocket. Where was his lawyer?

She wanted to stand up and shout that he had been well-loved. He was always a good boy. She wanted to seize his hand and drag him home, scold him, feed him, tuck him into bed. He was a foot taller than she was, at least twenty pounds heavier, and her hand fit inside his. The back of his neck, that neck she'd pressed her nose against hundreds of times after baths and haircuts just to breathe in the delicious baby smell of him, said this is how it is to be a man.

Then he was beside her again. "Why aren't they giving you a lawyer?" she whispered.

"Didn't you hear? Weren't you even listening?" His voice was an angry hiss. "They've assigned me one, but she's in another courtroom. She'll meet with me later. You can go. Go home. Please. Please just go home."

The bailiff frowned and reprimanded them with a jerk of his head.

Nadine bit her lip to stop it from quivering. She would not cry another tear over this disappointing boy. She clung to her cushion of a purse and kept her eyes on the judge until she dared a sidelong glimpse at Chance. He rubbed the soft bristles of a small makeup brush between his thumb and index finger. It wasn't hers. He could've gotten it from any of a long line up of girls. Rosie Richard, maybe. Wonder about the owner of the brush dissolved into memories of Chance with his thumb in his mouth, playing with the ends of her hair the same way, unable to fall asleep without her. He really had been little once, a small, satisfying weight that cuddled into her.

The judge announced a break for lunch, and everyone scrambled to stand up as she left the room. Chance took his time on his way to the door, nodding to this one and that one, bumping fists with so many of the young men in the courtroom you would think he was at a party.

A skinny white woman with a careless hairdo and a stack of folders with papers sticking out every which way rushed toward them. She held out a hand to Chance. "I'm your lawyer, Diana Klein." Chance unclenched his fist and stuck his hand out several moments too late.

"I'll handle this," he muttered out the side of his mouth toward Nadine. "It's my problem. My lawyer. Wait here."

The last people flowed out of the courtroom. Chance's words hung in the air.

Nadine stepped back as if shoved, a hot pounding in her head. She needed water, a place to sit. The white woman lawyer touched her arm.

"Are you his mother?"

"Yes." It hurt to squeeze the word out of her tight throat.

The lawyer stared up at Chance over her glasses. "She's coming in."

"I have the right to meet privately with my lawyer."

"If you'd like to meet with me privately, we'll do that right afterward. Follow me." The generous motion of her arm swept Nadine toward another door in the back of the courtroom. Chance hesitated, his face stony and still.

"Chance! Sorry, man, got here as soon as I could."

At the sight of the person behind her, Chance's hard expression relaxed.

Nadine whipped around, startled by the oddly familiar voice speaking her son's name.

"Don't worry about it, Coach, you're just in time." Chance reached for the man's hand, and after a series of grabs and gestures, wrapped his arms around Gary Watkins, pounding him affectionately between the shoulder blades. Gary smiled at her over Chance's broad shoulder. Nadine's knotted up stomach relaxed. If anyone else she knew were seeing all this, her son in court, she would be ashamed, but Gary Watkins already knew him.

They all followed the lawyer who outlined her plan to separate Chance's case from Not Donnie's. Chance would have to be very careful not to get in trouble while awaiting trial. If he did, "If you are caught with a joint this big," she held her thumb and forefinger less than an inch apart, "you will go to jail. I hope you understand that. As for school, they have a policy that you are not allowed to attend while awaiting trial for a felony charge. I'll try to get this moving as fast as I can, but in the meantime, there will be an expulsion hearing at the high school, and you'll have to attend an alternative program."

Nadine hugged her purse and stared at the lawyer's hands, mind spinning. The scene, already unreal, seemed like a twisted nightmare of random pieces of her life. Her son knew Gary Watkins—well enough to call him to help in a crisis. She wished they knew a more effective man. She really had to go back to church; for years she'd been meaning to find a different one, but wherever Haitians gathered someone would know Deacon Joseph, or know someone who knew him. Someone would recognize the deacon in Chance's charming—no, manipulative—grin and disregard for rules. But if Chance had to rely on Gary Watkins, a basketball coach who neglected his own mother ... she'd failed him. *Manbo* Sivelia and the spirits knew it.

Gary Watkins said something to Chance she didn't catch. Never mind the positive thinking, she had to pay better attention. Chance nodded seriously. The lawyer and Gary exchanged a couple of quick sentences. Everyone stood, and she followed suit. They shook hands. Nadine realized she had no idea what would happen next.

She followed Chance and Gary out of the courthouse, surprised to find the pink and white blossoms still backlit by the afternoon sun. She'd forgotten all about light and air and flowers. She breathed in deeply and sneezed.

"Do you want a ride somewhere?" Gary asked them.

"No, man, thanks," Chance said before Nadine could answer. "Gotta take care of some business. I appreciate you being here. Didn't know how it was all gonna go down."

And he was off toward Cambridge Street and whatever mysterious business he had, crossing the street right in front of a moving car.

"Do you want to get a cup of coffee or something?" Gary Watkins asked. "Café right over there."

"When did he call you?" she asked.

"Last night. He's scared, even though he tries to hide it. He's a good kid. Coffee?"

"What happens to him now?"

"He'll have another court date and end up with probation, as long as he stays out of trouble. You know, I'm surprised we never met while your boys were growing up. You never came to their games?" He put a hand on her back as if to move her toward the restaurant.

She jerked away. "I was working. And working. Taking care of people like your mother. A job with very low pay and not many thanks."

"I'm sorry," he said. "Lots of parents don't make it to games—they're just for fun anyway—intramurals, not like the NBA or anything."

Shame washed over her again. She'd made it to every one of their school conferences and curriculum nights, even early on when she had a harder time understanding the English. How was she to know parents were expected to know about their kids' recreation time as well? Henry and Chance would tell her all about the games afterward, anyway, gobbling fried plantains and bubbling over about this rebound and that steal. Henry had taken her over to see the big painting he'd made on the youth center wall, before work one day.

When she remained silent, Gary went on. "I've been an advocate for lots of kids. It's become a piece of my job, unfortunately—so many kids getting themselves in trouble with the police. Chance, with no previous record, should be okay. So do you want that coffee?"

She didn't know what she wanted. "No. No coffee now. Thank you."

"Have you thought more about helping out with my mother's trailer? We could ride down there next weekend? Or whenever you have time off? I know you're busy."

You're trying too hard, she wanted to say. Just stop. Keep my son out of jail, and I'll do anything you ask.

He took a card from his wallet and scribbled on the back. "Here's my number. Call anytime. No coffee?" He gestured to the curtained café two blocks down.

"I'll check my schedule," she said. "For a time to clean your mother's trailer."

"Ride home?"

She imagined sitting beside him in a car. What *would* they talk about? She had to get ready for work. She needed to get home and call Henry. Her legs hurt. Her back hurt. There was no direct bus line to her house.

"Yes, thank you," she said. "I would appreciate that."

At every red light he turned and smiled at her until the light turned green. Odd. She wanted to ask him about drug dealing and the little notebook, but was embarrassed she'd given it back to Chance. That had not been the right decision.

Cold rain battered the window and made it easy for Henry to hide out in his room for the rest of the weekend. He had two papers to write; he was never so glad to have his own computer. The half a pizza and fried chicken abandoned in the mini fridge by his roommate kept him going. He peed in a paper cup and only went to empty it when he was sure the hall was clear. He'd buried his phone in his laundry bag; then, when he decided he was ready to check his messages, it was dead, and he couldn't find his charger. All for the best. He already had his plane ticket home for summer vacation. Until then, he would think only of his own business.

When he finished his paper for African-American Autobiography on Zora Neale Hurston and her time in Haiti— she'd actually spent time on Lagonav where his mom was born—he jerked off multiple times watching music videos and thinking of Sage, naked under her dress—the fine curve of her ass, his face pressed between her breasts. What an idiot he'd been to leave that night. She'd probably never speak to him again and truth was, no one else around here, other than Tiberius, Mr. Roy and the occasional professor, took the slightest interest in him. He thought again about transferring to UMass Boston. He'd put in an application just in case—Africana Studies with actual Black people and Black teachers. *Keep your options open*, Coach used to say. His mother might be disappointed about his giving up his fancy-ass scholarship, but she'd be glad to have him home. He'd never felt as Haitian as he did here in Minneapolis. He missed his fucked-up brother. If he'd been home, they might still be friends; he might have been able to keep him out of jail. Now that Chance had taken down his Myspace page, there was no way to keep tabs on the situation.

On Monday the rain finally stopped. His roommate had shown up sometime in the night and snored in the other bed. Henry had lunch prep at 10:00. He dug out his phone. Tiberius had the same model; there was a chance he'd have his charger with him. Emerging from the dorm, into the gray light of the overcast day, he squinted at the distant tree—the one he'd danced around with the hippie kids. It hadn't even been two months ago. The brightest thing he'd seen all weekend was his computer screen. He crossed the campus without running into Sage, a small, oddly disappointing miracle, and entered the kitchen at 9:59.

"You're early," Tiberius said.

Henry hung his pack and jacket on a hook. Spared the ridiculous hairnet, thanks to his closely shaved head, he tied on an apron and washed his hands. He pulled out the stack of metal containers for the vegetables he would spend the next hour and a half chopping.

"So?" Tiberius passed on his way to the walk-in.

Henry concentrated on an onion. He knew to cut it, then slice it resting on its flat side. He knew to core and seed the peppers before chopping them, and how to julienne a carrot. The semester hadn't been a waste.

Tiberius returned with a box of apples. "You gonna say how the big date went with the white Rasta girl?"

"You have your phone charger on you?" Henry asked.

"Why? You use up all your juice talking to her?"

Henry brought the knife down hard against the cutting board again and again in an angry rhythm.

"That bad, huh?" Tiberius turned on the faucet, let the water run over the apples, and went to get the charger. "Here you go, man."

Henry wiped his hands on his apron and plugged in his phone. When he finished his shift, he'd call home.

He positioned the full metal containers in the tray of the salad bar and looked up to see Sage approaching, shoulders uncharacteristically slumped. She hesitated as if trying to read his expression. He jammed tongs into the vegetables while trying to figure out how to look at her. A humble smile. An apology for rushing off. A short and vague explanation should do it—I'm overwhelmed by work, life, can't handle a relationship right now. Satisfied he was ready, he straightened, but she was gone.

He hurried to the door of the cafeteria and saw her striding across the quad. Her rigid shoulders and neck revealed no inclination to look back. She was finished with him.

Back in the kitchen his recharged phone rang. "This is really you? Not the machine talking? Henry, where have you been?" His mother's words—a mix of English and *Kreyòl*—poured into his ear. "I've called you more than a hundred times this weekend. I'm sick with worries about your brother and now you too." She was hollering. Tiberius over by the walk-in could hear her. "Your brother is throwing his life away, not only in school, but now he is in trouble with the police. The police! Jail! I should have left him there for all the weekend to feel sorry, but instead I paid money to get him out and he went to court this morning and guess who it was that he called to come help him—your old coach, Gary

Watkins! And I know that man from Riverview. He is the son of one of my patients there. I was so—"

"*Manman! Manman!* Listen! *Tande mwen!*" Henry shouted. "Let me talk to him. Is he there?"

"I don't know where he is..." she trailed off.

Henry flipped an empty bucket and sat on it. He wanted to kick his brother's ass. He wanted to tell his mother to kick his brother's ass.

"But Gary Watkins seems like a nice man," she said, "who knows how to find his way through the courts." She waited, as if hoping for confirmation from Henry.

"What did he do?"

"He talked with the lawyer. He gave me a ride home—"

"Not Coach Watkins—Chance! What did Chance do to get arrested?"

She told him. He'd seen it all coming. He'd tried to tell her. And he'd certainly tried to tell Chance.

"The bondsman said he was a gentleman," she said. "He complimented your brother's manners."

Henry snorted.

"What do you want me to do?" he said. "He doesn't listen to me. Maybe this will teach him a lesson. Let's hope he gets off because what college is going to take a convicted felon?"

"Tomorrow we have a meeting at the high school with the principal."

"Good luck with that." He knew he sounded mean. His shoulders tensed as he waited for his mother to scold him.

"Thank you, Henry. I have to leave for work now. I will call you after the meeting."

Tiberius headed his way with a box of lettuce, eyebrows raised, signaling Henry to talk if he wanted. Henry shook his head and stared at the black rubber floor mat.

"A'ight then," Tiberius said. "Yesterday folks complained about gritty lettuce, so make extra sure you wash this up right, man." He dropped the lettuce on the metal counter next to the sink and patted Henry's shoulder. "That new guy can't wash lettuce for shit."

For the next half hour Henry ripped up heads of romaine as if it were all that mattered.

"**C**hance is a good boy," Nadine whispered. She would have to believe it to help her sleep. She lay in bed, ears straining, praying Chance would come home to sleep and be on time for the morning meeting at school. She had not seen him since he'd walked off in front of the courthouse, but dirty dishes in the sink and clothes on his floor showed he'd been at the house. A siren shrieked past. Her eyelids snapped open and every muscle in her face clenched. Panic flooded her chest. With each new minute displayed on her clock, her stomach ached more. When the hours changed, her heart hurt. "I'm not a bad mother, though I should have beaten him." She certainly wanted to beat him now—his terrible friends too. Henry had never needed a beating, so she hadn't been prepared for a son who did.

Finally, light tinged the sky. Chance had stayed out all night again. If he did not show up at the meeting...she couldn't end the thought. He would be there. He had to be there. She tried calling him and listened to a woman's recorded voice tell her that his phone was out of service.

Yara had suggested looking businesslike to make sure the principal knew she was a mother who commanded respect from her children and from the school officials. They'd gone through her wardrobe together after sharing a bottle of bubbly pink wine and chosen a straight black skirt, yellow blouse, and long black cardigan. Yara insisted she wear an uncomfortable pair of black heels. Businesslike, but sexy, she advised. It never hurts, in a meeting with men, to show off your legs.

Nadine dressed carefully. She squeezed her feet into the shoes, straightened her skirt, and teetered toward the counter where her cup of coffee sat growing cold. As she lifted the cup to her lips, coffee sloshed over the rim of the cup and onto the floor; it missed splashing her.

Whenever liquid spilled, she paused to consider the reason. What message from the *lwa*? Water was *La Sirèn*. Coffee, which her mother loved and never had enough of, meant that her mother had something to tell her. Nadine sat, palms pressed together, rested her forehead on her fingertips and closed her eyes. She saw her mother, seated on the ground, grating ginger for tea, hair wrapped in a red scarf, heard her singing softly to herself. *Manman's* arm stopped. The song and the raspy sound of the grating stopped. The smell of ginger filled Nadine's nose. "Help me, *Manman*," Nadine whispered. "Help me and our boy." *Manman* fixed her deep dark eyes on Nadine and said, *"Chemen long pa touye moun."*

"Yes, I know," Nadine said. "'A long road won't kill anyone.' I have had a very long road and I am not dead. Yet."

"You are strong," *Manman* went on. "The early years in the United States, with Uncle who was not the man we wanted him to be. Then pregnant, hiding from him, though he never troubled himself to look for you. There was always help. I was there. Social service people. Immigration lawyers. You had your boys and work. Always children and work. That is what it means to be a woman."

A long road, and it hadn't killed Nadine because she'd provided herself with a comfortable bed to rest her bones when she was tired and couldn't go on walking. But now worries stole her sleep. She'd rested better as a girl curled up on the dirt floor. She'd slept better as a servant in the house where she'd lived pregnant with Henry.

"*Lè w ap neye, ou kenbe branch ou jwenn,*" her mother said.

"'When you are drowning you hang onto the branch you can find?' What branch is that? Please tell me."

"Find your branch—maybe church, maybe the *manbo*, a trip home. I want to see you at my tomb, my daughter. I want to see the boys at my tomb. Don't tell me you cannot do this." Her mother began to grate the ginger and sing a tune Nadine didn't recognize. The words were neither *Kreyòl* nor English.

"*M pa konprann anyen,*" Nadine said. "I don't understand anything."

C hance arrived with Gary Watkins at the main office of the high school just after she did. He spread his arms to show off his nice blue button down shirt and khaki pants belted almost at his waist. She hardly recognized him.

"Coach took me shopping." Chance kissed her on each cheek. Gary Watkins looked as if he expected her to be upset.

"Hello, Gary Watkins," she said. "Thank you for being here."

"Hello." Gary Watkins brightened and leaned toward her, as if she'd invited him to kiss her cheeks too, but she stepped back. He caught himself, shrugged, and made a face at her that was more amused than sorry.

During the meeting, her feet in the uncomfortable shoes went unnoticed under the table and she half slipped them off. Gary Watkins said Chance was a fine young man. Principal Johnson echoed that. The principal said they never allowed students accused of felonies to attend school while awaiting trial. Chance said he understood. They handed him paperwork for the alternative bad boy school and directed them to go now and enroll. Nadine sucked her teeth. The loud *tuipe* hung in the air as all the men looked at her. She glared at Chance from the corner of her eye. They seemed to want her to say something, but *tuipe* said it all.

Gary stood and thanked everyone, shook hands with the principal.

"Good luck," Mr. Johnson said. "I hope to see you graduate with your class in June. Most kids over there have to pass the MCAS, but you're all set with that. Just finish that English credit and stay out of trouble."

Nadine followed Chance and Gary into the hall, pulled a big handkerchief from her purse, and wiped sweat from her neck. The room hadn't even been hot, but her blouse stuck to her. The sweater hid damp patches under her arms and breasts.

"We can drive over in my car," said Gary. "It's right out front."

"You serious?" Chance loosened his belt, untucked his shirt, tugged his pants down a few inches, and re-buckled the belt around his thighs as he spoke. "It'd take longer to park the whip than walk. You the one always talking about global warming."

Her shoes rubbed against patches of raw skin on the backs of both heels. Beginnings of blisters burned her little toe on one foot and her second toe on her right.

"Let's drive," Nadine said. "We are getting in that car." She limped toward Gary Watkins's station wagon, Chance and Gary a few steps behind.

The high school paperwork, carelessly rolled up, poked out of Chance's pocket. He opened the passenger door and looked about to slide in, when Gary, already opening the driver's side yelled over the roof, "Gentlemanly of you to open the door for your mother."

Chance waved Nadine inside, seating himself in the back. Nadine boiled. This selfish boy was much too pleased with himself. He owed her an explanation as to where he'd been all night. The coach should not have bought him new clothes.

Only the smallest of signs identified the alternative school, as if it were ashamed of itself. They were buzzed into the brick building, an old Catholic elementary school, and climbed three wide, waxed linoleum stairs. A sloppy, handwritten sign on a window of frosted glass read "office." Gary shoved open the door without knocking and gestured Chance and Nadine forward. The principal, a friendly-looking white man about her age, put down the sandwich he was eating, and still chewing, said he'd show them around. In the hallway, a skinny pregnant girl stopped kicking the vending machine. Nadine thought it was because she'd noticed the principal, but no.

"Chance!" The girl ran over to hug him. "What you doing here?"

The girl's hair hung long, stringy and blonde. She had pimples on her face.

"Doreen," the principal said. "You're supposed to be..." He checked his watch. "Where ARE you supposed to be?"

"I'm hungry," she said. "And this machine ate my money."

Chance put a hand on each side of the vending machine, hit it with a knee, and her pack of chips dropped down. He handed them to her—the principal, Gary, and Nadine his audience.

"Thank you!" The girl ripped open the bag and held it out to him. Chance helped himself.

Nadine's purse felt too heavy to carry. Her feet screamed in silent pain. More students wandered in the hallways than sat in the open-door classrooms. One narrow room held a row of computers, and every one had a student in front of it, who greeted Chance by name.

"He could be mayor," Gary whispered to Nadine.

"We do a lot of independent, online learning here," said the principal.

Chance chatted quietly with a Haitian boy who had come over once for *soup joumou* on Independence Day and eaten four bowls of it. The principal leaned against the door frame surveying the classroom with a look of pride. Gary studied Chance with a kind of pride too. None of this was right. This was nothing to be proud of.

"Chance," the principal said. "Come with me to meet Ms. Garcia, the guidance counselor. She'll get you registered."

Everything about Ms. Garcia sparkled or glowed—her long-lashed eyes, her straight white teeth, her smooth dark hair, her gold and silver jewelry, her long purple finger-nails, her confident energy. Chance, clearly dazzled, puffed himself up, preparing to charm her. Ms. Garcia pressed her glossy lips together and rolled her beautiful eyes. The sidelong look of understanding she directed toward Nadine gave rise to a throat-blocking lump of tears. Nadine tried to swallow it while somehow communicating to this lovely person her appreciation.

"Okay, Chance," the guidance counselor said. "We're going to talk about your goals and get you started with the self-directed, online English class right away."

Chance followed her without protest into her little office.

"We'll be in touch," Ms. Garcia told Nadine and, for the first time that day, she felt a shred of hope.

"Bye, Coach," Chance said. "Bye, Ma."

She walked with Gary past four boys pushing through a classroom door.

"Coach Watkins," one of them said. "I got off with a year's probation, but Dashawn's down for a year—Fall River."

"Did he plead out?" Gary asked. "Y'all know which lawyer he got?"

"Nah, don't know, some old white dude."

"They all old white dudes," said his friend. They laughed and high-fived.

"You playing in the game tonight?" Gary asked.

"Hell, yeah! I'm gonna score fitty points."

"Fitty points, my nuts!" said another boy. "Potheads don't be scorin' no fitty points!"

"You smoke before the game, you won't be playing," Gary warned.

"Aw, come on, coach. You know I play better when I'm high," the first boy said.

"I'm a drop fitty points on your mom!" said the friend.

Nadine had no idea what they were talking about, but Gary seemed to understand this strange bad boy language. He listened to their back and forth with a funny little smile and shake of his head as if he could only partly believe what he was hearing.

"We'll see about fifty points," he told them. "I'd be happy with half that!"

"Later, Coach! Hey, that Chance's mother, wit you?"

As Nadine and Gary walked down the hall, Nadine trying not to limp, the boys' laughter swelled. "Chance's mama, yo mama, deez nuts."

"Those guys," Gary said. "Sometimes I think all they can talk about is their genitalia and their mothers. I should make a tape and play it back for them. I don't think they realize how repetitive they are."

Nadine had no response. He shook his head but his lips pressed together in a crooked smile and the spark in his eyes even shone through his glasses. He seemed to like these frustrating boys. He understood their language.

"This school?" she asked. "It doesn't seem like they are studying anything."

He laughed and nudged her toward the exit with a hand

on the back of her arm. "The goal is to get them through any requirements so they graduate."

What kind of people need an education pushed down their throats? Nadine stepped through the heavy doors into the sunshine, her relief at being free of a school full of students who don't want to learn, shadowed by the fact that her son was one of them.

MAY 2005

Verite se tankou lwil nan dlo, li toujou anlè.
Truth is like oil in water,
it always comes to the surface.

A slam and a clatter from the kitchen startled Nadine awake before her alarm buzzed. She sat right up and swung her legs over the side of the bed. In less than a week she'd come to expect a silent, empty house in the morning. Chance might not talk with her, but there would be answers in his eyes and in the set of his shoulders. She hurried in the bathroom and, still in her nightgown and sandals, entered the kitchen where Chance stirred a package of ramen noodles into boiling water.

"Want some?" he asked.

He had on the nice shirt and pants he'd worn at the school meeting. He smiled, waiting for her answer. She looked him up and down. Was he going to school? Spending time with his bad friends? Listening to the pretty counselor?

His smile faded. "*Manman,* you hungry? Dis shit, uh, stuff, only be taking a minute till it's too cooked. You want some, tell me now." He rattled an unopened package in his hand.

"Yes, thank you," she said.

He ripped through the orange wrapper, dropped the block of curly noodles into the pot with the others, and poked it apart with a fork. He tore the flavor packs and sprinkled those in too.

"*Chita*," he said.

Sit? Her son was telling her to sit down as he took bowls from the cabinet and filled them with noodles. She sat, and he set a bowl in front of her. He gathered forks and salt and hot sauce and grabbed the chair across the table.

He lifted his head in a nod and gestured toward her with his full fork. "Eat."

She plunged her fork into the noodles and twirled it. In Haiti she'd never seen a man cook or do laundry. Her sons did both. She struggled to think of something to say that wouldn't start an argument. No asking about school or whether he'd spoken to his lawyer. Her brain flipped between those topics. Soon he would be finished. He'd already eaten his noodles and was lifting the bowl to his mouth to slurp the broth. Gary Watkins. They could laugh about the coincidence that she was taking care of his old mother.

"I was talking with the coach," she said. "Gary Watkins."

"What? What did he say?" She flinched at the edge in Chance's voice.

"Did you know he's been to Haiti?"

"Yeah, he told me about that. He worked in an orphanage. He had a great time except that everyone there kept asking him about his wife and kids and acted shocked when he said he didn't have any, so he started making things up."

Yes, people *would* ask. How's your mother? Your father? Your cousin's uncle? What had Gary said when they'd asked about Hazel? What would Nadine say in the village when they asked about Maxim, about her boys' fathers, about—

"Are you ever going to go back?" Chance asked.

"Me?" She filled her mouth with noodles to give herself time to think. She could tell him now about the *manbo*, tell him they would all go this summer.

"Roots and all that," he went on. "Relatives. Maybe..."

Nadine squirted more hot sauce into her soup and waited for him to finish his sentence. Her last contact with her siblings had been before the boys were born, to send money for her father's funeral and the tomb where both parents now rested. People there needed so much, asked so much of her. Even if she had the money for three tickets, she'd need a lot more to go home with her head held high.

Her family had no idea how much each day cost her in the US. When she sent money, people whispered that it wasn't enough or she'd given too much to a less deserving brother or niece. It wasn't easy to communicate with people on the island with no regular mail and no cell phone tower. Port-au-Prince would have been different, but she wanted nothing to do with Uncle and the rest of her father's family.

"Maybe we could holla at our father," Chance said.

She hid behind her lifted bowl and gulped broth to avoid his gaze, but the hot sauce burned her tongue and throat, and she came up spluttering, teary-eyed.

Since the visit to Sivelia, she'd been missing her brothers, aching to pray at her parents' tomb, daring to imagine she could handle the brutal *tripotay,* gossip, about Maxim and her life in the US. But the father question. She should have known the day would come when the boys would press her. She wouldn't mind telling them about Lucien—continuing the pretense he fathered both of them. Maybe she could find his family. Maybe they could stop in Florida en route.

Chance leaned forward with a long, considered look, the exact sort of look she'd expected to be giving him this morning, as if trying to see her mind, her heart. "You okay?" She had to tell him who his father was, of course, but not now, not in the middle of all this mess.

She swallowed a mouthful of noodles and forked in another. He wouldn't expect her to talk with her mouth full.

She swallowed. "I don't know if it's time to make a trip. There is a lot to think about. We'd need money."

"Well, I would like to go," said Chance. "I would love to go."

Chance sat still and serious, chin resting in his hand. Nadine hadn't seen this side of him in months. She'd almost forgotten it existed and wanted it to last. The soup he'd made for her warmed and filled her belly.

"Let's do it," she said.

"Really?" He straightened, eyes wide with wanting. She had to look away.

"You have to meet your uncles." Her voice caught.

"How about our father? Someone would know where he is, right?"

"We'd need money," she repeated.

"Oh, don't be sweating that," he said in his puffed up voice. "I got that covered."

"What? No!" she said. Then, forcing a calming breath she added, "Gary Watkins is hiring me to help with his mother's house. I'll get the money. And there's court. You have to finish up there." His face hardened, and she had to bite her lip to keep from saying more.

He shoved back his chair and collected their bowls. "I'm outta here," he said.

She wondered where he was going so early, two hours before school started, but if she asked him, he'd snap back or not tell her. He had on his respectable clothes so she decided not to worry.

☆

"**M**rs. Watkins says she wants to eat breakfast in the dining room," Ronnie filled her in. "But she wants you to help her dress."

"She's told me ten times or more," he said. "You're looking good today, *chica*. Want to see my new tat?"

"Depends on where it is."

"What? You don't want to admire my ass?"

Nadine sucked her teeth.

"I'm kidding!" He pulled down the neck of his shirt and showed her a hummingbird on the front of his right shoulder. She couldn't see a hummingbird without thinking of Uncle's lap and moist lips on her neck.

"Symbol of joy, baby!" Ronnie swaggered. "And working hard, finding joy in the work. In this place, we all need reminding of that! Should probably get another one tattooed on my face. What? You don't like it? Who doesn't like a hummingbird?"

"It's beautiful," said Nadine. "But no tattoo for me. Enough pain in the world without giving yourself more."

"Suffer for beauty, baby," he said. "No pain. No gain. All that. I gotta do my notes. Mr. Singer had a BM last night so big, I should have christened it!"

Nadine laughed. "I better go see Hazel Watkins before she changes her mind."

"That lady doesn't change her mind," Ronnie said. "She's the most stubborn-ass resident we've ever had."

"She just changed her mind! For four months she's eaten alone in her room."

"That's not really changing her mind. It's called recovery." Ronnie had an endearing smile. "Have a good day."

A good day. Heading to Hazel Watkins's room, Nadine wondered again where Chance had been going this morning in those nice clothes.

"Mrs. Watkins!" Nadine rushed to the bed. Hazel had somehow kicked the covers off, scooted herself down to the bottom to elude the bed rail, her legs stuck through the gap between it and the foot of the bed. She gripped the top of the rail with her unaffected hand and struggled to sit. "You should not be trying to get up by yourself yet!"

Focused on her task, Mrs. Watkins didn't look at her. She was so close to succeeding that Nadine had to stop and watch. Hazel sat up, breathing hard, her toothless mouth in a lopsided grin of triumph. Nadine clapped her hands, all while knowing that any other staff person witnessing this would see that, with this action, Mrs. Watkins had just shown herself to be a fall risk. They'd alarm her johnny, so that whenever she tried to get out of bed, loud beeping would alert them.

"I hear you are going out to breakfast today," Nadine said. "Let's get you ready." She held up two shirts to give the woman a choice. But Mrs. Watkins shook her head until Nadine held up the soft, flowered one. She probably knew that the pattern of small brown and yellow flowers would be forgiving when it came to breakfast spills. Nadine should have thought of that herself. Yes, Hazel Watkins was no fool.

Nadine laid out her clothes on the bed, within reach of the chair, in the order she would put them on. Mrs. Watkins showed motivation this morning. "It is a good thing you are going to the dining room," Nadine said. "Too much time in bed is not healthy for you. Much better to stay active. You can join the craft activity this afternoon. I think they are going to make flowers out of paper."

Mrs. Watkins tensed and glared and pointed at her computer sitting open on the table next to the bed. "Eed."

"You want me to read what you wrote?"

Hazel nodded.

It would take me more time than I have left to write about everything the young don't know—how the body becomes a liability, the ruination and decay. Talk talk talk about menopause, but people are still young when the ovaries stop working. Wait until they put you back in diapers—then you have a change of life worth talking about.

"Well, you're right about that," Nadine said.

Why? Why? Why!!! Why do I forget the things I want to remember and remember the things I want to forget?

Why am I so full of regret? Why didn't I talk while I still could? Why didn't I talk to my son while I could explain?

The words stopped on the page but reverberated in Nadine's head. Choices, losses, secrets. Chance's voice, "How about our father?" Uncle Maxim and hummingbirds.

"You're right about all that, too, Mrs. Watkins. I think you have a best seller here."

Mrs. Watkins indicated she wanted the computer. She typed, *Don't patronize me.* Nadine nodded and moved the tray table, arranged the shirt so Hazel Watkins could best use her unaffected arm to help slide the other into its sleeve. She stood ready to help, but Hazel Watkins seemed to have forgotten she was getting dressed and sat stiff and bare legged, on the edge of the chair staring at the floor.

"Om-m-m," Hazel said.

"I know," Nadine said. "If you want to go home, you have to be active." Her words seemed to shake Hazel Watkins into full cooperation. Nadine helped with the shirt and the brown velour track pants, heavy with the knowledge that Mrs. Watkins was not going back to her mobile home, no matter how hard she worked in OT or PT, even if she went to the dining room for every meal and took advantage of every activity.

Nadine could certainly use that five hundred dollars for airplane tickets or gifts, or groceries, and if she didn't clean the trailer, Gary would hire someone else. She might as well be the one to earn the money. But with each of Mrs. Watkins's slow, forced steps toward a dining room she didn't even want to sit in, guilt tightened its squeeze on Nadine's heart. Hazel Watkins's birdlike bones pressed against her arm, as they waited for the elevator that would bring the old woman to her breakfast. There was nothing wrong with encouraging her to spend time with others. Nothing. She'd seen many patients insist they were going home, only to settle in at Riverview once they found their bingo game or regular mealtime companion. It was for her own good.

E venings, after his cafeteria shift, Henry ran around the track in the fading light of the long May days, and sweated out his loneliness. He pretended he was pounding through the streets of Cambridge. He had to make it through three more weeks. His phone rang. He slowed his pace and answered.

"What's good with you?" said Chance.

Henry couldn't help it. When he heard his brother's voice, he smiled.

"Started at the alternative school. Should see my guidance counselor. She's sexy."

"Alternative? How's that? Is she guiding you? Counseling you?"

"Guiding deez nuts!"

Henry laughed. "Seriously bro. She helping you apply to school?"

"I told you. I don't know if I want to go to school. School ain't the only thing."

Henry picked up his pace to keep from saying something he'd regret, sounding like the father he wasn't. "Okay, yeah, right. Job then. She helping you think about a job? Graduation's coming. You trying to be broke?"

"I'm hip. I ain't even sweatin' that. I don't be calling you to tell me how to live my life. I got something going. I'm doing my thing already. You'll see. Just want you to know I got something big going on. Me and my team—"

"Chance, be serious. Your music's fine and all, but you not be making any money trying to be the Haitian Jay Z—"

"Whoa! Who said I'm talking about music? We got a whole thing happening. That's why I'm calling—wanted you to know I got everything figured out. You'll be borrowing money from me."

"Whoa. Wait. Not something illegal. You know, right, if you get caught for anything right now they'll give you sixty days? You better not be doing anything stupid."

"I'm smarter than you think. How's that computer working out?"

"It's fine. It's great. Bro, you better graduate. You're killing Mom."

"No. You got that all wrong. When I finish with this, I'll have enough gwop to take all three of us to Haiti in style. She said she wants to go."

"Haiti? Since when you want to go to Haiti?" The Haitian kids forced to go hated it. After a couple days Chance would be wanting to come home for Mickey D's and electricity that worked and good showers.

"Don't you want to meet our father?"

"If you fuck up and get yourself put away—besides how you know we could even find our father—I'm done. I can't—" Henry stopped, bent over panting and pressed the phone against his cheek.

"Done? Done? I'm your brother. You can't be done with me!" Chance's voice sounded screechy. "You like that computer, right? Well, I got something going that's way bigger than a truckload of laptops. You want a piece of it?"

Henry paced up and down the sidelines. "I'll be home in just a few weeks. Mom says you'll have two graduations— the regular and the alternative school. I'll sit through both. We'll hang out. Play ball." He sounded desperate. He was desperate. Chance doing anything illegal right now was risking too much.

"Henry, you worry like an old lady. We know what we're doing. We wouldn't be trying anything with no gangsters. Only Harvard students who think they big dealers. We wouldn't do anything without scoping it out. They're a bunch of pussies."

Henry, aware of another person on the other side of the track, slowed his frenzied pacing and held his arm to his side to keep from gesturing. "Chance, you do not want to go to jail. You really don't."

"I'm not going to jail! I'm too smart for that. In fact I have my own plan after me and my boys do the one thing together, part two—all mine."

Henry squeezed his forehead and squinted across the field. His glasses rested on the pile of clothes and books he left on the bleachers, so he couldn't be sure, but the girl who stepped onto the track sure looked like Sage. Every girl looked like Sage. He saw her everywhere, until he got close enough and saw she was someone else.

"Henry, you having any fun?"

"Be safe," Henry said. "I gotta go."

He stuck the phone back in the pocket of his shorts and let his anxiety push him. He would finish his five miles, head back to the dorm, shower, prepare his oral presentation on

Piri Thomas, and go to bed. Maybe he'd try giving Rosie a call, see what she'd heard about Chance and his friends, try to enlist her help. She still cared about Chance no matter what had gone down between them.

He overtook the girl and realized it was, in fact, Sage. She didn't look at him as he passed. The sky burned orange in the west and glowed violet overhead. They were the only people on the track. Had someone told her he'd been running here every night? He ran faster, suddenly aware of his pounding heart and ragged breath. She jogged slow and steady. Her ass in black spandex was as fine as he remembered it. Her locs, pulled together with some kind of white band, bounced against her back. He passed her again. She still didn't acknowledge him. Her belly was bare and muscled and as fine as her ass. She glowed in the evening light. He wished he had his glasses on so he could read the expression on her face. Her hair. Locs on a white girl were not beautiful. They were affected and ugly. He approached the bleachers. Four more laps, but maybe he should quit, grab his stuff, and get out. He stopped long enough to slip on his glasses and kept running. He passed her again and this time, scanned her face. She didn't smile. He slowed to give her a chance to say something, but she regarded him with a long unreadable look.

"Fuck this," he muttered and sped up.

What did he want to tell her? If he could figure that out, he'd say it. His glasses slid on his sweaty face. He wiped his forehead with the bottom of his shirt. He caught up to her again. "Sage," he panted. "I'm sorry."

She stared at him, waiting.

Honest but unacceptable apologies rattled in brain. I'm sorry we didn't fuck. I'm sorry I ever came to this nowhere school. I'm sorry you only like me cause I'm exotic to you. I'm sorry my brother's fucking up his life and my mother can't deal with it. I'm sorry all I can think of is putting my hands on your beautiful spandexed ass. I'm sorry the world is so fucked up. I'm sorry this is all so weird.

"I'm sorry," he said. "For everything."

"Me too," she said.

He matched her easy pace. "Where've you been?"

"Around. I've been thinking about you a lot. Your family stuff. Are things okay?"

"Don't worry about it. Sorry I ran off like that. I had fun with you that night."

"You know," she said. "You can talk to me. You can tell me what's going on."

She really thought he could. But he couldn't. He wanted to. He talked plenty to her when he was alone, in that way he talked to Chance, to his mother, to George Bush, Malcolm X, Karl Marx, and Bob Marley. But when he was with her, the words stuck in his head with no way out. That was the problem. That was the problem, right there.

"That day, right after, in the cafeteria, when you came in?" he said. "I didn't know what to say and then you left and...I don't know. I felt like an asshole."

"How do you think I felt?"

He stopped to seriously consider the question. "Like an asshole?"

"Exactly!" She laughed.

He pushed his steamed up glasses onto his head, wrapped his arms around her, hands cupping her butt, and kissed her hard with a lot of tongue, right there in the middle of the track under the wide purple sky. She smelled like summer rain on the streets of Cambridge. She tasted like licorice. She pressed herself against him. Happiness swelled in his chest. He'd forgotten what it felt like. He was happy. Somehow they moved toward the bleachers and his pile of things.

"You're cold," he said. He wrapped his sweatpants around her like a shawl.

"Stars are nice," she said. "Sit down."

He sat and leaned back. She sat on his lap on the bleachers and picked up where they'd left off weeks ago. Henry unwound the pants from her shoulders and pushed up her shirt or bra or whatever it was. The weight of her gorgeous breasts rested in his hands. He sucked her nipples and his dick strained against his shorts. She rubbed herself against him and moaned. They satisfied each other right through their clothes. Imagine how it would be when they could get naked. Suddenly three weeks seemed short.

Just after noon on Sunday, Henry woke up next to Sage, the light of a perfect spring day splashing over the pale green walls of her aunt's guest room. He'd never slept all night with a girl before. Strange to come to consciousness with somebody breathing right there in the bed beside him. He wanted to touch her closed eyelids—delicate, like eggshell—with his tongue, but it might wake her. He was glad he'd opened his eyes first; he loved watching her sleep and didn't so much like the idea of her watching him.

Last night they'd gone downtown to hear John-o's band. His roommate had been playing late on Saturday nights all year long, urging him to check it out. Why hadn't he gone until now, with the year almost over? Sage had forced him to dance, and he actually enjoyed it. Maybe this school wouldn't be so bad if he got off campus more. He hadn't explored Minneapolis or even St. Paul.

He wasn't sure about touching a sleeping girl. He didn't want to startle her, but just then she rolled onto her side and nestled her back and beautiful ass against him, like an invitation to wrap around her. Henry carefully positioned an arm over her and rested a hand on her breast. He began playing with the nipple, and it didn't take long before her whole body wriggled awake. If her aunt had been home, he would have been more self-conscious. He knew that whatever happened, for the rest of his life, when he saw that honeydew melon shade of green, he'd think of this room, this day, when he'd first woken up in a bed next to a girl and fell so naturally, so deliciously, into making love.

Afterward, they were in no hurry to get up. A sunny spring day in Minnesota lured most everyone outside, but Henry, and Sage, too, it seemed, didn't need any more light and warmth than was right there in the house. The long cold lonely winter faded, irrelevant now.

Sage drew a line along his arm with her finger. She was so white. "You're beautiful," she said.

He looked away from her to hide his pleasure.

"Do you think I'm beautiful?" she asked.

He did, he really did. "Yes. Very."

"I've been wondering about your animal spirit," she said.

Should he say he didn't believe in that kind of thing, or would that ruin everything?

"Yours is moose, right?"

"You remembered! I dream about moose all the time. Moose energy is powerful—full of contradictions. My book says that people with Moose as a totem find that they stir up contradictory feelings in other people about them."

Who doesn't? Henry thought. Propped on her elbow, face animated—she really loved this stuff. "So what do you think? What animal do you dream about?"

"I don't remember ever dreaming about an animal. Sorry."

"Did you ever go to the zoo? What animal were you drawn to?"

"My mother took me to the Franklin Park Zoo in Boston

once, and I spent the whole time climbing on a backhoe parked in the lot. She couldn't get me to go in. I guess I like heavy machinery more than animals. What does that say about me?"

She laughed.

Suddenly he remembered the youth center mural. "Wait a minute! There's one thing. When I was about eleven, yeah, sixth grade, we did a mural project at the youth center near my house. For some reason, I insisted on including a panther. I drew it and painted it myself. That little piece of the mural was all mine. It's still there. I could show you if you ever come to Cambridge." He stopped, embarrassed in his sudden enthusiasm. But she loved it.

"The panther is all about reclaiming one's true power!" she said. "They're loners. That fits! Oh, I wish I had my book here. Later, I'll read you the whole thing, but I'm telling you, it says a lot about power and sexual energy and overcoming suffering. It makes sense, doesn't it?" She rubbed his chest. Whatever made her happy right now, made him happy.

"What do you remember about choosing to paint that?" she persisted.

"Oh, I don't know." He tried to think back. "I think I'd studied it in third grade for my animal research project."

"What made you choose it then?"

"Sage," he laughed. "I really don't know. Come here!" He pulled her close again.

"Do you think maybe it had something to do with the Black Panthers?"

"Come on!" He released her. "My mother is Haitian. You white people have no idea how different that is from African-American. Caribbean Black. I didn't learn about the Panthers until high school. Should've learned sooner. They taught us about the KKK in elementary school and I didn't sleep for a month. Knowing about the Black Panthers might have helped."

"You white people?" She sat up and moved out of his reach.

"Yeah, you white people. You're white."

She wouldn't look at him.

"Come on, Sage." He put his arm around her. "This is ridiculous. You act ashamed of being white." He stopped short of asking what was wrong with her own smooth reddish hair. "I mean, I guess I can see it. White people as oppressors, white people are oppressors, but that's not us, right now. Right at this moment, I can honestly say, this Black man does not feel oppressed by you."

"But you feel oppressed at school."

"True dat!" But her saying it, her acknowledgement, lifted the weight of it somehow. He could let her know. It would make her happy, but he wasn't ready to give her that, to go that far.

"When does your aunt get back?"

"She said around 4:00."

"That gives us time."

"I'm hungry."

"Me too. First we eat each other, then breakfast." Henry couldn't believe he'd just said a line like that. He sounded more like Chance than himself. And it worked. She took his earlobe between her teeth.

Dressed and in the kitchen, they fried up some vegan bacon, for BLTs. It smelled pretty good. Henry checked his phone—messages and twelve missed calls, all from his mother, or the home phone anyway, all from the morning. He slipped the phone back into his pocket. Sage plucked toast from the toaster. He sliced into a plump tomato, its disappointing insides nothing like his mother's homegrown crop. Sage arranged bacon on the bread. He washed the lettuce and spun it dry. His phone vibrated in his pocket. He spun the lettuce again. "I'm sorry," he said. "I have to answer this."

"Your brother?" Sage opened the salad spinner. "I can put these together."

He answered the phone while walking to the nearest door which put him on the stairs to the basement. He closed the door behind him. "Henry!" his mother wailed. "*M pa konn sa pou m fè! Ede m!* Now he has a gun!"

"How do you know?" Shit! This dude was half cooked. And what did their mom expect him to do from so far away?

"He left his coat on the floor. I picked it up and felt something in the pocket—heavier than a wallet. *Mezanmi!* I put my hand in. What does he need with a gun, Henry? What kind of trouble is he in? What kind of trouble is he making?"

"Calm down," Henry said. He rubbed his head and tried to think. He strode down a step or two, needing to move, but the stairs only descended into Sage's aunt's basement where he had no business going.

"I was afraid I might shoot it by accident. How do I know if it has bullets in it?" His mother's loud sobs distorted her words.

"I gave him back his drug dealing notebook. I shouldn't have. I'm sorry, Henry. I'm sorry *Jezi!* I will get rid of this gun, but I don't know how. Should I bury it? Should I throw it in the river? I'm afraid to pick it up."

Sage tapped on the door to ask if he was okay. He cracked it open wide enough to shake his head at her. She retreated, clicked the door shut behind her, and Henry fell back against it. What did his mother expect him to do?

"Call Gary Watkins," Henry said finally. "He knows

everyone in Cambridge. He knows guns enough to tell you if it's loaded. Don't call the police. Whatever you do. Don't call the police. Of course you're right to take it away. That boy needs saving from himself. *Se pa lè yon moun ap neye pou w montre l naje.* It's not when someone's drowning that it's time to show him how to swim; it's time to just do what you gotta do to save his ass."

The gun, snub-nosed and gleaming, rested next to the salt shaker. She could almost pretend that it was a toy, except it wasn't. Now that she'd spoken with Henry the energy that had her pacing and crying and calling him over and over had drained from her body. If Chance came home now, she had nothing left for him. *Sak vid pa kanpe.* How long had this gun been in her house? On TV, if someone was arrested with a gun, it was a lot worse for them than being arrested without one.

She opened her purse to look for Gary's business card. It had probably slipped to the bottom. She felt pens and loose change, a pamphlet from Yara that explained how to attain every desire through chanting some phrase over and over. She laid it on the table near the gun and rummaged deeper. Where was that card? Finally, she dumped the bag, and picked through the messy heap of all she carried with her just because she might need it, because her boys might need something.

She spread the pile, leaving a wide zone of safety around the gun. She should have put the card in her wallet, but she hadn't thought she'd come to need it like this. A gun in her house! She swept the contents back into her purse, leaving only the gun and Yara's pamphlet, a smiling Asian man on the cover with a glow around his head, on the table. She opened the pamphlet, and Gary Watkins's card fluttered to the floor near her feet.

When she stooped to grab it, she wrenched her back. Ignoring the pain, she dialed his number.

"Please, not a message. Please," she prayed. She tried to sit while it rang, but when a muscle in her lower back screamed, she leaned her belly over the back of a chair, her rear end jutting out. It seemed to help.

"Hello?" A real person. Gary Watkins. The panic in her throat and chest liquefied. She did not want him to hear her tears. "Hello?"

"This is Nadine Antoine. I need—I—I—I found a gun in Chance's room."

"No! What kind of gun?"

"*M pa konnen.* I don't know. A small gun. Just a small gun. With tape around the handle. It's small. But I don't know what to do. I don't want to call any police. I called Henry. He said you would know."

"Chance isn't there, is he?"

She'd been waiting to confront Chance, but now realized she wanted to get rid of the gun before he came home. She had not raised her sons to be criminals. "No."

"I'll come right over." The steady calm of his voice settled her a little. "I can take care of this. I'll be there in a few minutes."

"*Mèsi.*" She moved carefully around the pain in her back and plucked the bottle of ibuprofen from the pile on the table. She swallowed two without water and then two more. When the doorbell rang, she hobbled over to buzz Gary Watkins in.

Hand on her back, she waited, listening to his unfamiliar footsteps climb the stairs. There he was, Red Sox cap on his head, no jacket, just a sweat-soaked t-shirt and shorts, a towel around his neck. "Got here as fast as I could." He wiped his glasses on the end of the towel. "Hey, it's going to be okay. Are you hurt?"

"My back. I hurt my back." She leaned against the open door. "It's okay. The gun is in the kitchen. That way."

She limped behind him. He looked from side to side as if memorizing her house.

"Ah, a twenty-two. Let's make sure it's not loaded." He picked up the gun, released a cartridge into his hand and placed it on the table. A bullet glinted at the top of the cartridge, and she thought she might be sick. He slid back the top of the gun somehow, as easily as if he were opening a stapler, and popped out another bullet.

Gary Watkins checked the gun one more time and put it along with the bullet and cartridge—magazine, he called it—in the center of his grubby towel, then wrapped it all up. You wouldn't know what was in there. She dropped to a chair.

"I'll get rid of all this for you. I'll get it to the police. I'll tell them I found it out behind the center." Gary Watkins looked thoughtful and serious.

"I don't know what I will say to Chance," she said. "He's crazy. I'm scared. He's..." She rested her head on the table and pressed her thumb and forefinger against the inside corners of her eyes.

"You know," Gary said, "most times these wannabe G's just think they gotta pack heat to be somebody—makes them feel big.

"Gangsters," he said in response to her confused look. "They think they should have a gun. I'll talk to him. Try to anyway."

Chance, a gangster? All that music. She shouldn't have let him hear any of it. She shouldn't have let it in the house. Even as the thoughts spun in her head, she knew she had no control of his music or anything else.

"He shouldn't have this, obviously," Gary said. "The fact that it was loaded is bad. No kid should have a gun."

Gary talked on. "You know, my mother has one—a rifle. She shot gophers right out the window of her trailer. Good aim too."

Nadine needed to lie down flat. "I'm tired," she said.

"I'm sorry." He put his hand on her arm. "You should ice your back. Let me help you." He opened her freezer and took out a bag of frozen mixed vegetables—the kind she kept to cook with rice when she was too tired and hungry to use fresh. "Where are you going to lie down?"

She wasn't going to allow him into her bedroom, though that was where she'd choose to be. "The couch."

She staggered to her feet, and he followed her into the living room. "Nice tomato plants," he said. "You know, my mother is quite a gardener. That's why she hates the gophers. If she were still at home, she'd have plants started, just like this."

She wished he would stop talking. And why so much about his mother? He'd seemed comfortable dealing with the gun, but now he seemed nervous, as if he'd drunk too much coffee. If Gary were still in the house when Chance came home, it might help. But she couldn't take much more of this chatter.

"Lie down," he said. "I'm an expert on back trouble."

She tried to lower herself to the couch without folding into a seated position.

"Where would I find some pillows?" he asked.

She directed him to the boys' room.

Gary arranged and rearranged the pillows around and under her and positioned the package of frozen vegetables against her back. She'd never liked beards—they reminded her of animals, but today his was neatly shaven. As he leaned close to adjust the vegetables, she breathed in the grassy smell of his sweat. He was old, probably fifty—with wrinkles—wrinkles around his eyes and on his forehead, wrinkles of concern for her. "How's that?" he asked.

Strange. It was all strange. Every day, she adjusted pillows for people, yet no one, ever, after she'd lost her mother, had ever put this much effort into making her comfortable. Well, sometimes Yara took care of her.

"Can I get you a blanket?" Gary stood over her.

She nodded, closing her eyes to hide whatever was showing there.

He brought the fleecy brown blanket from Chance's bed and covered her, tucking it over her feet and shoulder. His face loomed close. "Phone. Remote for the TV. Water." He set them within reach on the coffee table. "Your carrots and peas are already thawing. You really need one of those ice packs. I can bring you one later, after work."

"You've done enough already."

"It's no problem. I can swing right by here on my way home."

"Thank you, no." She stopped herself from telling him to visit his mother instead.

"Okay, then. Should I stop by tomorrow? See how you're doing?"

Tomorrow. Tomorrow she had to work. How could she work?

He answered himself. "I'll call you," he said. "Now I've got your number in my phone. To see if you need anything." He bent over her, almost as if to kiss her on the head, but gave her hair an odd little pat instead.

This man was making himself too at home in her life.

"Don't forget to take that gun," she said.

"Call me anytime," said Gary. "Even in the middle of the night. I don't sleep much." She thought she saw him wink.

After he left, Nadine drifted into fragmented dreams. Uncle, riding a *taptap* in Port-au-Prince. She pulled a gun from her purse, but the *taptap* drove off before she took aim. Painted across the back, along with a portrait of Michael Jackson clutching a microphone, was *Chance se yon bon gason*. She faced the same words scrawled in that writing the boys called tagging across her parents' tomb. Chance's lawyer stood beside her rubbing her back, and Gary Watkins peeked from behind the tomb, maaing like a goat.

Chance's clomping feet on the stairs woke her, but she pretended sleep as he banged his way into the house and passed through the living room. He closed his bedroom door. She dozed.

"My shit's gone! The deuce-deuce. Who else knows I gots it?"

He was yelling, talking to someone on his phone. Her back spasmed. Next thing he'd be asking her about it.

"*Manman,* you okay?" Chance bent over her, worry in his eyes.

The instinct to reassure him asserted itself. "*Wi, pa pi mal.*"

"Not too bad? Really? You don't look so good."

"My back is telling me to rest for a little while." She handed him the bag of thawed vegetables.

"What? What am I supposed to do with these?"

"Cook them. Eat them."

"Ma, I'm not hungry and don't have time to cook that shi— to cook them. I gotta talk to Razz about something important. I gotta go."

I'm not hungry. She would not have believed that one day she would have a son who could say those words and not be lying. "Chance, these vegetables are very small pieces and already thawed. In only five minutes they will be cooked."

"Ma! I gotta go. Now. I got bidness."

"We cannot waste this food."

"So, I'll put it back in the freezer. You need anything before I leave?"

"What is this business?" When she lifted her head, pain ripped through her.

"Do you need anything?" He sounded angry.

"I need you to..." Behave? Appreciate all she'd done for him? Be safe? Graduate? "... cook those vegetables with some noodles. That is not too much to ask."

"You don't understand!" he shouted. "I gotta deal with something. It's serious! Who came by today?"

"What do you mean?"

"Junior? Razz? Anybody? Anybody go in my room? Did you go in my room?"

"Bring me the ibuprofen and some water please, before you go."

"Someone came over. Right? Who? Yara?"

"I should call Yara now. To cook these vegetables. Stop by and see if she's down there. Chance, I can't get up. I can't go to work. I won't be paid. I have serious business myself." As she said it out loud, the truth of it hung heavy in the air.

"*Tande, Manman*," Chance's voice softened. "I can help out with some cash. Don't worry. You rest. Your back will feel better."

"No!" Nadine shouted. "I don't want your drug dealing, criminal money. I want you to be a good boy."

"Too late for all that." He bobbed his head and poked his chest with his thumbs. "Time for you to see that I'm a man."

Nadine closed her eyes, unable to bear the aching of her back and the rest of her waking life, yet dreading the dreams that waited to take her when she sunk into sleep.

☆

I n the glittering sunshine of May in Minneapolis, Henry's bleak winter faded. So far he had A's in all his classes, his final papers were underway, and he was having fun worthy of reporting to Tiberius and Mr. Roy Washburn.

He and Sage stood at the edge of a pond in the sculpture garden regarding the Spoonbridge and Cherry fountain. "I love it," Sage said. "So totally whimsical. Don't you love it, Henry?"

He did. He loved the whole thing. Every weekend a new experience. Why not love a fifty-two foot long white spoon with a giant gleaming cherry in the bowl? "Pose over here," Sage pulled him away from the pond toward the sidewalk. "Stick out your tongue. Way over here. In the photo it'll look like you're licking the cherry."

Henry didn't understand.

"It's an illusion." Sage handed him the camera, directed him back still further, stuck out her tongue and tilted her head. "Check and see how it looks," she managed to lisp around her protruding tongue.

Sure enough, there she was on the little screen licking a cherry the size of her head. "How do you know these things?" he marveled, taking the shot.

"I told you. I grew up visiting my aunt here," she said. "We have all kinds of pictures of this spoonbridge. From every angle and with me and my sister pretending to hold it. I'll show the next time we're at her house. Your turn. Tongue?"

"You never talk about your sister."

"Yeah, well..." She wandered farther back, shifting the camera. Henry stood with his tongue stretched out, people passing by; everyone in the city thronged outside on these bright days, desperate for sun against their pasty white skin. He was the only Black person in sight. The old Henry, Henry before Sage, Henry of the long Minnesota winter, would have felt embarrassed posing like this, and yes, maybe, he felt some of that, but mostly he felt happy to be a guy indulging his girlfriend by being silly.

Finally satisfied, Sage clicked and walked toward him. He met her halfway and took her hand. She showed him the picture.

"I should send that to my mother." He tried to imagine her response.

They wandered around with the rest of the crowd, taking pictures of each other, posed and candid. Henry preferred the sculptures made of sticks or stones. He studied a big wooden frame that looked like it might walk away on three legs made of tree branches. How could a piece of wood have so much personality? "Weird how a frame around something automatically makes what's inside different from what's outside, even if it's just blue sky. Look," he said.

"Yes! Exactly. That's by David Nash. I love his work."

How did she know these things? His phone vibrated. He checked the number.

"My brother. I better see what he wants."

She shrugged and looked away as he answered. "Yo!"

"Hey, my dude, what's poppin'?"

"Not much. Just walking around, enjoying the fact that it's warm enough my balls aren't shriveling."

Sage raised her eyebrows and smiled.

"Yo, listen, Henry, I was holding heat. Me, June, and Razz have this all worked out, but my deuce-deuce went missing. I gotta tell them. We got this punk-ass Harvard kid with more bud than he deserve. We gonna help ourselves. But I don't think we can convince him without a little heat, you know?"

"Whoa!" Henry stopped in the middle of the path. Someone behind stepped on his heels. Sage nudged him onto the grass, out of the flow of pedestrians. "You're awaiting trial. I thought you had the sense not to be messing with anything illegal."

Their mother must have listened to Henry and taken the gun. Or asked Coach Watkins to take it. Chance was better off without it. Junior and Razz too—punk-ass kids.

"Yo! This a come-up. No way we could fuck this up 'cept not to do it."

Sage hovered nearby, trying to act like she wasn't listening, idly aiming her camera at the sky.

"But what the fuck happened to my gun?"

"You got no business messing with guns!" Sage looked up, startled, and Henry realized he'd shouted. He lowered his voice. "Don't talk with me about that shit. I'm not visiting you in jail. You'll get a lot more than sixty days if you get caught."

"I told you, I'm not messing with gangsters. Just a pussy-ass student. But come on, why I'm calling you is to ask what you think happened to my heat?"

"Be glad you can't find it. It's the universe saving your ass."

"I don't need saving. I need my gun so we's can do this thing. Just this one thing and I'd have gwop for—whatever we need. Mom be wanting to go to Haiti. How she going to do that on her hourly rate? We'll all go. I might even stay down there awhile."

Since when had his brother wanted to travel so hard? The silly spoonbridge arced over the little pond, just as it had minutes ago. Sage snapped pictures of the puffy clouds. The day still sparkled. Nothing made sense.

"You and that gun got nothing to do with anything! I don't know where you be getting these ideas. You got what? A month until graduation? One fucking English credit. Finish high school. Get done with court."

"Sorry I called, bro. Just thought you might have heard something."

"Forget about the gun. Stay away from Junior and Razz. They're not awaiting trial. You can't be taking any chances."

"You don't get it! This is cake. I'm not stupid."

"You're stupid if you do this!"

Sage looked bored.

"Don't fucking do it." Henry hung up.

Sage approached as soon as he slipped the phone into his pocket. "Everything okay?"

He couldn't answer.

"Everything's not okay," she said and took his hand.

They walked along in silence, chatty people passing them in both directions. "My brother's a knucklehead," Henry said.

Sage laughed, then when Henry didn't, grew serious. "It's hard. I don't know what he did, I don't need to know, but he's him and you're you. My sister, Lisa? The one I don't talk about? She's an addict. Coke, meth mostly, but she's done it all. My parents have spent more money on rehab for her than on college for me, and it never works." Sage didn't look at him. "We were close when we were small. She's only a year and a half older than I am." She stared purposefully ahead and walked faster.

"I hate addicts," she said. "They take and take. They ruin their lives and everyone else's. You just have to distance yourself as much as possible."

"My brother's not an addict," said Henry. "He's an idiot." He'd pictured Sage's family wealthy and self-satisfied in a house like the aunt's but more glamorous because it was in California. When he thought about her sister, he'd pictured a girl like Sage, upbeat and persistent, but without the locs. He'd seen pictures of her at Sage's aunt's house, but they were all from when the girls were little.

"Well, it sounds like he's got plenty of problems," Sage said.

A flash of rage jolted him. But she wasn't saying anything that wasn't true.

"Everybody has problems," he said, and fought the urge to drop her hand.

"Yes," Sage said. "That's why people need to focus on their own."

"My brother's problems are my problems," Henry said. "Can't you see that?"

"They're really not," Sage said. "Know how much therapy I've gone through to understand that? Save yourself some money and hours of time. Listen to me, your brother's problems are not yours!" She pulled her hand from his and pressed her forehead between her palms.

She looked so upset, so sad and angry and confused, that Henry felt sorry for her; instead of storming off as he'd been about to do, he moved close and wrapped his arms around her.

"We were having fun!" she said. "We're always having fun and then your brother calls." Her back shook. She was trying not to cry. Her hair rubbed against his cheek as she squeezed her face into his shoulder.

He held her close. Tears dampened his shirt. He looked up for a moment. Passersby either stared or deliberately didn't. No one gave him any indication of what to do when holding a sobbing girl in a public place. "Come on," he said. "Don't cry."

If he tried to explain that his family's problems were his, that he didn't understand how she could see it any other way, would it make things worse? How would she feel right now, if he walked off, leaving her weeping right there on the sidewalk, saying her problem wasn't his? You helped your friends and family. Wasn't that the whole point of being a person?

Sage sniffled and wiped her eyes. "Can I visit you this summer?" she asked.

"What?"

"I've always wanted to see Boston," she said. "This is the farthest East I've ever been. I have a friend there from high school who goes to Harvard, and she'll be traveling. She said I could use her apartment."

Chance on the phone while Henry stood in a Minneapolis sculpture garden or hung out in Sage's aunt's rich-ass house was one thing. Sage in her dreadlocked white flesh in his mom's house in Cambridge was another. Chance would laugh his ass off.

But the thing about Cambridge, even though it was small, worlds didn't have to overlap. Usually they didn't. He could hang out with Sage at her friend's place.

"What'll you do, though?" he asked.

"My aunt said she'd pay for a class at Harvard summer school," Sage said. "She felt sorry for me having to go home. She knows what it's like there."

"I'll be working," he said.

"You don't want me to come?"

"You've been planning all this?"

"I was thinking how much I'll miss you. The rest just fell into place this week."

"Well, I don't own the Boston area," Henry said. He laughed to cancel out his strangely sneering tone. "I mean, of course you can visit."

"You don't really want me to."

"I was surprised—it feels weird you made these plans without talking about them." That was the truth.

"Well, if I come, we'll hang out, right?"

If he spent time weighing his answer she'd feel hurt. "Yes," he said.

"You can show me around," she said. "Like I've been showing you the Twin Cities. Then we'll be even."

"Okay." Henry made himself smile. "Want to get some food?"

Sage winced and recovered. "There's a really good falafel place over there." She pointed with one hand and grabbed his arm with the other.

He hesitated. She'd gone along too easily with his attempt to change the subject.

"They have meat too!" she said. "Kababs, gyros." She released her grip and looked at him questioningly.

Better to keep the peace for now—enough drama going on. Food. Sex. A warm spring day. No point in ruining it. "Okay," he said. "Let's go. Sage—" He wrapped her in a hug and whispered in her ear. "I don't always have to be eating meat, you know. I like vegetables too."

She pressed her whole body against his and right there at the edge of the sculpture garden, people all around, they shared a long kiss. Someone clapped.

Nadine worried the zipper pull of her purse, as Gary's beat up station wagon peeled over the curvy Connecticut roads. She'd heard about countryside in the United States but had only experienced cities and big roads like numbered interstates. This narrow road twisted and flowed like a satin gray ribbon through trees, past lakes, along a river. At home, roads this width were always rough and rutted. Nadine enjoyed the new green on the trees, the moist warm air wafting in through partly open windows, though she wished he drove more gently. A furry animal darted into the road in front of the car, he slowed and swerved. It zigzagged to the other side in a blur. Her stomach lurched, and her back spasmed.

"Not much farther." Gary looked at her over his glasses. The car drifted toward the shoulder; she gasped, and he jerked the steering wheel, eyes on the road once again.

Her sharp inhale seemed to embarrass him. She hugged her bag close to her belly and took a long silent breath.

Gary leaned forward to peer through the windshield as if he weren't sure exactly where he was. "Thanks for doing this."

"We are going to the house you grew up in?" Nadine asked.

"No. My mother moved after I went to college. She visited me up here, decided she liked the area, bought a piece of land, put a trailer on it, and stayed. I think the turn is coming up on the left. I remember a barn right across from it."

"Do you ever go home?" Nadine asked.

"Home?"

"That place you grew up. Is it far from here?"

"Cambridge is home to me. Thirty years. Home is where you're happy, right? Not where you come from."

"Happy?"

"Here we are." Gary slowed looking for the turn, giving Nadine plenty of time to study the homes they passed— sweet little houses with shutters and porches and lawns, some in need of paint. "Are you?" Gary asked. "Happy?"

Chance was still in trouble, but Henry was coming home soon for the summer. *You are only as happy as your unhappiest child,* Yara said. Gary didn't have children. He was free to make his own happiness.

They turned onto a poorly surfaced road and bounced along through the woods, finally pulling up to a neat tan rectangle of a building. "This is it," Gary announced. "Her trailer. She's got a huge garden out back. Life in the country!"

With the bright day still in her eyes, it was hard to see

in the dimness of Mrs. Watkins's home. Nadine breathed in the air of a long closed up space, no spices, cooking oil or leaves, no dampness or mildew, no trace of anything that had once been alive. Someone had taken care of any leftover food or trash. Hazel Watkins would be pleased.

"I'll get the boxes from the back of the car," Gary said. "I was hoping that today we could empty cabinets and drawers. The movers will deal with the furniture and whatever we've boxed up."

"When are they coming?"

"Haven't called anyone yet," Gary said. "I've got to do that."

Nadine's knees wobbled and, full of a sudden sadness, she sat on the couch. "With enough help, she could be home."

"Okay," Gary said suddenly. "Do you want the job?"

Nadine had all she could do to take care of the boys and herself. She couldn't say yes. She wouldn't survive out here alone with Hazel Watkins. She knew her own limits.

"Where will you put her things?"

"Have to figure that out too. Storage facility in Cambridge, I was thinking." He stood in the middle of the tidy space, hands on hips, looking around, businesslike.

Nadine imagined Chance and Henry standing in her bedroom, discussing what to do with her framed GED certificate, the photo of her parents' tomb, and her *drapo vodou* of *La Sirèn*. She could see them arguing about who got her bed. That was a very nice mattress. Neither of them would want her purple curtains. Hazel Watkins was not dead. She would die if she saw Nadine sitting on her couch preparing to ransack her closets.

"It isn't my business," Nadine said. "But I have to ask, why can't she come home with someone to help her?"

Gary sat on the edge of a huge reclining chair; Nadine imagined it was where Mrs. Watkins would have sat too.

She looked around. There was no TV. Balls of yarn pierced by knitting needles rested on the floor at one side of the chair. On the other stood a table with drawers underneath and a radio/tape player on top just like her own—the one Chance and Henry teased her about because it was so old fashioned.

"The staff at Riverview says she won't be able to live independently. I have to sell the trailer to cover her expenses."

"Who said that? How do they know?"

"They're the professionals. And her lawyer, another professional, says it's time for me to manage her assets. This is a health emergency. She's a very old woman who had a stroke. And I have Power of Attorney."

Nadine shut her mouth. She didn't know anything about all that. The law was a mystery to her. She'd trusted the lawyer who helped make her a citizen. Diana Klein seemed to know how to help Chance. Mrs. Watkins's lawyer probably knew what was best for her right now.

"I'll get the boxes from the car," she said.

Gary didn't answer, already rummaging through drawers.

Pale gray clouds massed overhead. Nadine breathed in the thickening air and took her time walking the short path to the station wagon.

She dragged a stack of flattened cardboard from the back of the car and grabbed the roll of packing tape. It looked like a weapon with its handle and metal blade.

Gary shaped and taped the boxes with a sticky ratcheting sound.

"I can start to fill those," Nadine said. "Kitchen or the bedrooms first?"

"Doesn't matter," Gary flopped himself back into the chair as if in folding the boxes he had used all his energy for the day. "Whatever you like."

Nadine began work in the kitchen where Gary could see

her and realize he should be helping. She slammed drawers and cabinets, clattered dishes, pans, and silverware, and groaned as she squatted and stretched to reach and pack, but he paid no attention to her except to demand, every few minutes, that she listen to him read from the diaries he'd found in one of the drawers.

"Can you believe this? Every day, the weather, what she ate, time she woke up, time she went to bed? Every year my birthday in red—son, Gary and my age. And then as I'm reading along, bored out of my head, something a little different. 'Slept well. Dreamed of Edwin. Woke happy.' 'Told that ignorant spic lady bagging at Stop and Shop to make sure the bananas were on top. Didn't understand me. Bananas bruised and brown—good for banana bread only.'"

Nadine didn't want to hear Mrs. Watkins's inner thoughts. She wanted to finish this job and rest her back.

"Banana bread," said Gary. "She was a great cook. I'll say that for her. When you find her recipe file, don't pack it. I was thinking I'd try making a few things. Maybe I'll invite you over for a meal."

Nadine laughed over the ache in her back. "I'm almost done in here." Three full boxes stood under the small kitchen table, and she'd stacked three more on top. She handed Gary a covered shoebox labeled recipes. He thumbed through the cards, and she regretted giving him yet another distraction. Well, he'd helped with the gun. Now with all this work, maybe she could consider them even.

"It's getting late already," she said. "*Men anpil, chay pa lou.* With many hands, the load is not heavy. I know you are paying me a lot of money for this work, but if you work with me, we may finish. If you sit reading and talking, we won't."

She sat on the couch to rest for a moment. Her whole back, upper and lower, felt stiff and tired. "Let your mother come home. Once more. To say goodbye."

He looked up from the recipe file. "Stuffed cabbage," he said. "She made the best stuffed cabbage. I can try to make that for you sometime." She squeezed her shoulders, first one, then the other, then the first one again, pressing deep into the stiff muscle.

"I haven't been helping much, have I?" Outside the sky darkened suddenly. He stood and peered through the Venetian blind. "Looks like rain. A thunderstorm I think." He turned toward her. She couldn't understand his complicated expression. She felt her mother's breath in her ear, whispering advice Nadine knew was important, in a wordless language she could almost recognize. Gary switched on the lamp, then turned it off.

Nadine considered standing up, grabbing an empty box, and heading for the other room before he came any closer, but that fiery pain in her lower back and a curiosity about what would happen next kept her seated, waiting. She massaged the base of her spine where the pain was worst. Gary paused, and she realized that by pulling her shoulders back to touch her sore spot, she'd thrust her chest out like a prostitute on a street corner. She crossed her arms over her chest.

Lightning flashed, followed by window-rattling thunder. Raindrops ricocheted off the metal roof, then drummed down, louder and louder, a pounding flood cloaking the trailer. Nadine hadn't heard such rain since she was a girl, roaring rain that made conversation impossible.

Gary sat beside her on the couch. "That back acting up again?" He had to shout to be heard. She nodded.

"Lie down," he mouthed and gestured to a small round couch pillow they'd yet to pack.

Nadine took up the pillow. Made by Hazel, she was sure. Crocheted flower-shaped patches of leftover acrylic yarn, sewn together—Hazel Watkins hated waste as much as Nadine did. Gary slid it from her arms and reached over her to place it carefully at the end of the couch. His shoulder rubbed against hers, his neck stretched centimeters from her lips. The smell of rain-soaked earth wafted in from partly open the kitchen window. She would have to make sure no rain had damaged the walls and floor.

She couldn't get up unless she pushed him out of the way. One small twist of his body and he would be facing her. His lips, very close to hers, moved.

"We'll have to come back anyway," he said. "I didn't realize how long all this would take. Put your head on the pillow, face down. You've done all the work. The least I can do is take care of that back." His matter-of-fact tone reassured her. He perched on the edge of the couch cushion, his hip warm against her thigh. Her nose pressed against Mrs. Watkins's pillow. She wouldn't be able to relax. The ridges of the crocheted pattern tickled her face. She pushed the pillow onto the floor.

Rain beat down, less forcefully. One time, before her uncle had taken her to Port-au-Prince, she and her mother had walked to the waterfall in Gran Sous. A child had drowned there so *Manman* had not allowed Nadine in the deep pool, but showed her the small ledge under and behind the veil of falling water. They'd stood there together, holding hands, looking and listening to the splashing music. Gary placed his hands on her neck where hers had been. She talked to herself the way she talked to old people. Breathe. Easy. *Rilaks. Poze w.*

Every day she touched, calmed, and comforted. *Sak vid pa kanpe.* Lovely to be an empty sack lying down, relieved of the need to try to stand. Where had Gary learned this?

"Feel okay?" he asked.

"Mmmm."

"After you showed me how to rub my mother's feet, I took a couple books out of the library and looked online. Haven't practiced on anyone though. How am I doing?"

"Mmmm."

He pressed his fingers along a muscle under her shoulder blades, discovering tight places that actually crunched under his touch. She let the sofa hold her and the earth hold the sofa. The rain slowed to a lullaby. His thumbs pressed into the stiffened tendons of her neck and the skin over her skull, warming and loosening all the strained and frozen places. His hands moved over her back, steady and strong. He located that gnawing pain just above the curve of her bottom and dug in.

The rain stopped. She drifted in that lovely place just beside sleep. His hands stopped. He was straddling her thighs, his erection nudging her ass, undeniable, unmistakable even through his pants and the folds of her soft green dress. Instantly tense, she rose on her elbows, startling him. He leaped up with an apologetic groan.

Nadine couldn't look at him. Hummingbirds beat their wings in her throat. She bolted barefoot across the short distance to the door, flung it open, and ran across the wet grass. She stopped at the back corner of the trailer to breathe in steadying gulps of damp evening air, thick with the smell of flowers. When enough minutes had passed and she trusted Gary had decided not to follow, she wandered through Hazel Watkins's yard, putting distance between herself and the couch. His need-filled cry stuck in her ears. She should not have let him touch her, she heard her mother say, he was a lonely man, what did she expect? Nothing happened—Yara's voice now. *This is not the biggest deal! Your back ached from helping him fill his mother's boxes. A massage is nice. You're acting like a child.*

Lilac bushes, heavy with blossoms—dark purple, lavender,

and white—brushed her shoulders on the path to the garden. Nadine lifted the wire loop that held the gate shut and walked to the center of the untended plot. She crouched and pushed her fingers into the dirt. It crumbled in her hands, dark and moist, ready to give a seed everything it needed. This garden could feed a big family. She brought a handful to her face and smelled. She tasted it with the tip of her tongue. Nadine was not hungry now, but this rich soil started her mouth watering.

What would Hazel Watkins say if she knew that Nadine knelt in her garden avoiding the attentions of her son? Nothing compared to what she would say about Nadine taking part in the plan to remove her from her home.

She would cut a bouquet of lilacs, some sprigs of mint for Mrs. Watkins. Gary could bring them to her. Nadine didn't have to be involved. And for this long day of work she would be paid well, enough for one plane ticket, maybe two.

She stood under the purpling sky and looked toward the trailer just in time to see Gary emerge from the path between the bushes.

"I am cutting some mint to take back to your mother," she called and turned away from him.

"Yes," he called back. "I thought she might enjoy some of her lilacs. I have some scissors with me. Do you want them?"

She nodded, neck relaxed.

The last of the sun glinted off the shears he waved at her. Leave it to Hazel Watkins to have a beautiful pair of scissors. Were they gold plated like her nail clippers? Gary snipped blossoms from the bushes, feigning unawareness of Nadine standing beside him. The scissors cut easily through the lilacs' woody stems.

When he'd clipped all he could clutch in one hand, Gary stopped. His face, over the lopsided bouquet, looked sober. *Wont pi lou pase sak sèl.* Shame is heavier than a sack of salt. He held the closed blades of the scissors, presenting her with the handles, the way Hazel had undoubtedly taught him. Nadine knew suddenly and for sure that he would never presume to touch her again. If she decided she needed another massage, she would have to ask.

"I put a box of her jams and relishes in the car already," Gary said. "We should get going."

She cut the mint, reluctant to leave the garden. She cut enough for Mrs. Watkins and for herself, enough for tea and a bath when she got home. As Gary moved through the trailer a final time, she wrapped the stems in a wet paper towel and a plastic bag.

The ride home was not as awkward as she'd feared. Gary popped in a CD of the *kompa* she loved. She regarded his hands resting on the steering wheel; who would have suspected such magic lived in those thumbs? It hadn't been there when she'd tried to teach him to rub his mother's feet, or had it?

Gary turned the music down. "Will you help me bring her home. Just for a visit?"

"She won't like it that we've moved her things," Nadine said. "But maybe that will help her to understand that she isn't going home and begin to adjust to Riverview."

Home. Henry would be home soon, for the whole summer. Nadine thought of Lucien home somewhere in the world—Port-au-Prince? Miami? Fort Pierce? Queens?—unaware that he had a son with a rare smile and a gap between his teeth that matched his own.

"I like this song," she said and turned it up loud so there was no possibility of conversation. Breathing mint and lilac, she danced a little in her seat, rolling and shimmying her loose shoulders as much as she could, given the restraint of the seatbelt.

*H*azel made slow progress toward the community room with Ronnie beside her. Heaps of flower arrangements hid the nurse's station. She paused and leaned on her walker.

"Almost there," Ronnie said. "A little further."

She knew they were almost there. She could see the door right in front of her. She tilted her head toward the flowers and raised her eyebrows in a question. Though her speech was constantly improving, it took too much effort to talk and walk at the same time.

"Mother's Day," Ronnie said. "Soon as I get you settled, I'll start delivering them to rooms."

Mother's Day. Hazel hated it. Edwin had died on Mother's Day. She had to sit down.

"Mrs. Watkins?" Ronnie touched her arm.

She should ask to go back to bed, but the door to the community room stood open and her room was a long way behind her. Hazel forced herself forward, through the door, to a chair, just inside it. A young woman stood in front, where the piano player usually sat, letting a squirrel run up her arm and over her shoulders. Hazel shuddered. The squirrel lady again. Other residents loved her.

"Bed," she said to Ronnie.

"But you only just got here." He laughed. "Let me take those flowers around real quick, and I'll escort you back."

What could she do? There was a time she would have made a fuss, but she didn't want to waste her energy. The squirrel lady shared her squirrel facts. Mother's Day at Riverview Manor. Could there be anything sadder? Mothers took care of people. Mothers spent their whole darn lives taking care of people until they couldn't anymore, and then who took care of them? This godforsaken place was full of mothers who couldn't take care of anyone, including themselves. She'd gone fishing with Edwin, one of those last times you didn't *know enough to appreciate. Fifty years ago! They'd driven farther than usual, to the state park. The day was hot. She fished while Edwin stood beside her, his hand on her pregnant belly. She hooked a gigantic rainbow trout. Edwin helped her reel it in and they grilled it for supper.*

"So you're enjoying yourself now?" Ronnie said.

Where had he come from?

"You're smiling!" he said. "You gonna hold the squirrel?"

The woman squatted next to Mr. Singer and placed the squirrel on his lap while feeding it a nut.

"Heavens, no!" Hazel blurted before she even thought about forming the words.

Ronnie laughed. "You want to go back now?"

She wasn't ready to make the trip yet. She shook her head.

"Check with you in a little while?"

She nodded. Where had she been a moment ago? So happy. Yes. Eating trout with Edwin. That wet fish thrashed and glittered in the sun, solid muscle, striped rosy pink. Her fish. Her day. Mother's Day. The baby moving under Edwin's calloused hand.

Edwin wasn't moving. They described him lying on the ground at the foot of a ladder whispering her name, but by the time she arrived at the hospital he wasn't whispering anymore. He was dead, and she was going to be a mother, the baby reeling inside.

A service was organized. People spoke. She didn't. "Easy to like," they said. "Easy to love." "Mild demeanor with a ferocious heart." If she'd allowed herself to feel the storm of grief that threatened her functioning, she would have drowned. She had practiced not feeling for much of her life. She was good at it. She could have her baby, manage insurance salesmen, keep house, if she paid no attention to people's pitying looks and sorrow-soaked words. The Mother's Day roses he'd given her, still gorgeous in their vase, mocked her until she stuffed them into the trash.

"Ready?" Ronnie asked.

He stood by as Hazel clung to the walker and lifted herself out of the chair. Every day she grew stronger. She only hoped they noticed.

The squirrel lady had finished her rounds and was shutting the twitchy animal into what looked like a big bird cage. Home.

Nadine filled large pots with dirt and transplanted her baby tomato plants to their new outside home in the sun of her back porch. Mother's Day. When the boys were young they'd observed both American Mother's Day and Haitian Mother's Day, that's how much they loved her. Henry must have been ten and Chance, eight, when they dressed up in their little jackets and ties to bring her breakfast in bed—*ji sitron* and *pen manba*. Henry carried the glass of juice, so careful not to spill, and Chance followed with the plate. Few foods pleased her as much as Haitian peanut butter—a hot pepper ground right in with the peanuts. Her boys knew that, loved to make it themselves. Henry would call today.

As she patted soil around the stems of her plants, she thought about her own mother's life, so different from hers. Chilove had never left Lagonav, even to go to Port-au-Prince. She'd worked hard from the moment she could push a broom across the yard or grate a coconut or wash a dish. She'd given birth to seven children, four of whom grew up, Nadine the only one who left home. Her three brothers still lived on the island—Onaldo made furniture and coffins, Kervens taxied people around on the motorcycle he'd bought with money she'd sent, Jonas spent his time playing dominoes and flirting with other men's wives. She thought more often of her dead parents than her living brothers. Chance and Henry's uncles whom they'd never met.

She filled a bottle with water at the kitchen sink and soaked her plants, making several trips. She'd have more tomatoes than ever and still no relatives here to share them with. She'd be bringing them into the break room at Riverview for the staff. She'd have to make sure to feed one to Mrs. Watkins, nicely salted. That lady would appreciate a good tomato.

Manbo Sivelia had told her to make the trip. If she'd been able to take them right away, Chance might not be in this trouble. He'd feel part of a real family. She had to go home. She'd never even met her nieces and nephews or one of her sisters-in-law. The gifts she'd have to buy, the money she'd have to bring! All those reaching hands. But Chance said he'd like to go. He would understand better all he had, all she'd made possible for him. But then what if her sons insisted on finding their father—fathers?

The plants looked happy soaking up the water and the May sun—green and perky. Birds chirped conversationally on the power line. Nadine wrapped her sweater tightly around herself, air still a little cold for her taste. Another reason to go to Haiti. She'd almost forgotten what it was like to spend days, weeks, months being warm all the way to her bones.

The phone rang deep in the house. She rose to answer it, eyes adjusting the dim indoors. It would be Henry calling to wish her well.

"Yo! *Manman.*"

"Chance?"

"Wassup?"

She prepared herself for bad news. Maybe Gary Watkins had told him she took his gun, and Chance was calling to yell at her. "Why do you ask me what's up?" she said. "You're the one who is calling. Where are you? Why don't you come home at night?"

"Be easy, Mom!" Chance said. "It's Mother's Day, right? I'm your son. I'm calling you. To invite you out to eat. You want to check out one of those Mother's Day brunches somewhere? How 'bout I take you to Legal Seafood?"

"I told them I would work today—at 3:00." It was 1:30. "I have to get ready."

"What about dinner then? When you get home?"

"At midnight? How about you be sure you are home then, where you belong at night, and how about you wake up tomorrow and go to school? How about that? That is the present I want. You—safe in bed in the next room. You—getting an education."

"Aight then. Forget it. Happy Mother's Day."

The dial tone droned loud in her ear. Better she yelled at him than the other way around. Good that he hadn't mentioned the gun. When she unclenched her fingers to put down the phone, they ached.

Nadine prepared for work in a daze, no call from Henry.

"Smells like a funeral home in here," Ronnie greeted her in the hallway, pushing an empty wheelchair. "All these flowers."

She managed a smile and moved to maneuver the laundry cart past him and the chair.

"Busy Sunday—church services and the squirrel lady. Mrs. Watkins was asking for you. Son's there now."

"I have no problem with missing church," said Nadine. "Or the squirrel lady."

"What about Gary Watkins? Would you mind missing him? Cause he's asking about you more than his mother's asking. What's going on with you two, anyway? Should I be jealous?"

"What?" Nadine flushed. "What are you talking about? Shut your busy mouth."

"Oh!" Ronnie smirked. "So the old lady's right. You two are scheming. What? You plan to run off together, right? Isn't he a little old for you?"

Nadine wondered if it were against some nursing home rule for Gary to hire her to clean out the trailer, so she decided not to mention it.

"I'm telling you, lady," Ronnie said. "That guy has got a thing for you. Think about it, and you'll put two and two together. He never used to visit. Now he comes every couple days. When you're not here, disappointment drips down his face like soup on Mr. Singer's when he feeds himself, and he be asking me, what shift is Nadine working today? What shift is Nadine working tomorrow?" He broke into song and clasped his hands in front of his heart. "Nadine. Nadine. Nadine. My Haitian queen."

She swatted him with a chuck pad. "Go do your notes."

Ronnie pushed the wheelchair around in a circle. "Give the guy a break. I like him."

"Then *you* give him a break!"

She made her way down the hall with her stacked cart, room by room restocking closets with diapers, chuck pads, johnnies, sheets, and pillowcases. Hazel Watkins emerged from her bathroom, with only her quad cane for support, too focused on progressing toward her chair to acknowledge Nadine's entrance. Gary beamed hello. Nadine's face burned so hot it hurt, echoes of Ronnie's teasing in her head.

An extravagant bouquet of varied flowers dwarfed the bedside table. "Lovely," Nadine said.

"Nothing but the best for my mother," said Gary. Was he

saying that sarcastically? He must be, but it didn't sound like it. She couldn't tell. "How's your back?"

"Fine." Nadine shoved a pile of diapers onto a shelf and turned to grab a tower of chuck pads from the cart.

Hazel stopped in her slow trek across the room, right in front of Gary as if she might be considering whacking him with her cane. Maybe Nadine was reading too much into the pause. Maybe Hazel needed a rest. Maybe Nadine herself was the one who would like to hit him, playfully, of course.

She rearranged the pillowcases and sheets, lining up the edges. By the time she closed the closet door, Hazel was lowering herself into the chair. Gary hovered nearby, not touching her.

"Hah!" Hazel said and glared at Gary, then Nadine.

"You did it!" Gary said. "I'm impressed."

"Home," said Hazel. "I...can...go...home. Now."

Gary widened his eyes at Nadine and raised his eyebrows. He wanted her to say something. Mrs. Watkins was her responsibility while she was here at Riverview. Nadine was the professional. But Gary was the woman's son. Whose job it was to tell her she wasn't going anywhere. If Gary were a really good son, he would take her home and hire a home health aide.

"The flowers are beautiful, Mrs. Watkins," Nadine said.

"Hmmph." Hazel looked beyond her, out the window.

Gary broke a big white and purple many-petaled blossom from the bouquet. "Mother," he said. "I know you have a safety pin somewhere." He opened the top dresser drawer.

"In the little box there," Nadine said. She nudged the cart toward the door.

"Wait," Gary said. He touched Nadine's shoulder, and she turned toward him. They stood eye to eye. He bit his lip. Slowly, as if giving her time to step away, he grasped the top edge of her smock drawing it away from her body. The backs of his fingers brushed her collarbone. Peering over his glasses, he attempted to jab the pin through the stem of the flower and the fabric of her top. He closed the safety pin, his breath uneven, warm and smelling of mint, then moved back to consider his efforts. The blossom not only drooped, but hung straight down toward the floor. He grinned an apology, but remained where he was, hands at his sides. Finally, she fixed it herself while he watched. He couldn't have known that on Haitian Mother's Day you wore a red flower if your mother was living, purple or white if she'd passed on. He didn't know, unless the boys had mentioned it, that her mother was dead. It was just a coincidence he'd chosen that color flower, yet she appreciated the gesture, more than she wanted to. Hazel made a disapproving, growling sound.

"You're a mother too," Gary said. "Happy Mother's Day. Sometimes it must feel like a thankless job."

"R-r-r-right," said Hazel. "T-r-r-rue."

Nadine had the rest of the supplies to deliver. She had people to toilet and feed. She couldn't remain in Mrs. Watkins's room all day.

Gary's phone rang—a perfect moment to make her exit.

"Hello? Henry!"

She froze right in the doorway, cart already in the hall. Her Henry hadn't even called her today, and he was calling Gary Watkins? She heard her own son's agitated voice through the phone, but couldn't make out the words.

"Yeah. I'll talk to him," Gary was saying.

Henry again—a long, long string of words.

"Okay, okay. Thanks for filling me in." Gary said. He'd turned his back on the questions in her eyes. "No. What can you do from there? True dat. Think about yourself, hear me? Finish those papers and exams. You'll be here, in what? A couple weeks. Man, calm down. Yeah, your mother and I took care of that. Yeah. Listen, we'll talk later, okay?"

Nadine grabbed Gary's arm and reached for the phone. Gary shook his head and hung up.

"What?" Nadine yelled before remembering she was at work. "If that was my son, you have no right to hang up when I am standing right here. What is happening?"

"I'm sorry," Gary said. "I didn't think it was a good time."

"If my son is in trouble, then it's a good time, I am his mother!"

"Henry's fine. He's worried about Chance. So are we."

We. A quick stab of resentment—what right did he have to say we?—followed by a soothing wash of gratitude. Worry shared felt easier to bear somehow.

"Here." Gary held out his phone. "You want to call him? Go ahead."

"In a minute," Nadine said. "What did he say? Please tell me."

Hazel groaned. "Home!"

"Nothing we don't know. Chance has to take his situation more seriously if he's going to stay out of jail. I'll track him down later and try to talk some sense into him. Can't promise anything, obviously. But I'll do my best."

Hazel pounded the floor with her quad stick. Across the hall Mr. Singer began shouting. "I need a good woman! I have natural urges. Natural urges. I may be old but I can still get it up."

Gary laughed.

"I've got to quiet him down," Nadine said. "Or at least shut his door."

"Lawyer," said Hazel clearly. "Need lawyer."

"I've talked with your lawyer, Mother," Gary said. "Remember you gave me Power of Attorney."

"Noooo."

Nadine breathed in the sweet smell of her flower. She would call Henry during her break.

"Mrs. Watkins." Nadine leaned close to Hazel. "I'll be back in a little while. Enjoy your bouquet. Enjoy your son." She would persuade Gary to bring his mother back to the trailer for a visit, even next weekend. Anything is possible, Nadine thought. The woman needed to see her garden again. People had the right to feel home around them—the ground against the soles of your feet, the particular air in your lungs—all the things you took for granted until you'd landed somewhere else.

*T*hey turned into the park entrance. Hazel's pulse quickened and pounded in her forehead. She would get to her mobile home and go right to the garden. She'd be sure to find rhubarb—the gophers left that alone. Strawberries—a few might be ripe—if they hadn't been eaten by birds or squirrels or those damn gophers. She would pick some, Nadine could help her—Black people were good at that kind of thing. She would make a pie. She could feel the ball of dough in her hands—she'd never understood why anyone would buy a pre-made crust—pie crust was so easy to make, so inexpensive— some people swore by lard, others by butter, but for the best crust, only Crisco worked. Her rolling pin—how many pies had she made in her lifetime—now that would be something to figure out—at least two pies a week for most of her years, even when working full time at Travelers—that rolling pin bore the shape of her hands—like her favorite slippers held the shape of her feet.

Gary always loved her strawberry rhubarb pie. Edwin had loved her apple. She'd never taught Gary how to roll pie crust, how you have to use white vinegar. If he'd been a girl, she would have. Was it too late now? Another mistake. Come to think of it, vinegar made almost any food taste better. Hazel believed in vinegar—for cooking, cleaning, gardening. Pickling. Oh, how she wished for a homemade pickle right now. She swallowed the saliva filling her mouth, but some trickled out anyway. The indignity of drooling. She swiped at her lips with the back of her hand.

Gary stopped the car. She was home. Home. Gary got out and Nadine too. They stood outside talking as if they'd forgotten her. The dashboard loomed over her, and her feet barely skimmed the floor. She was so small, so weak. She couldn't open a car door by herself. Hazel began to cry, sobs so huge and heaving that they hurt.

She slapped at her tears and tried to catch her breath. Why cry? She was home where everything was cool and quiet, clean and well cared for. Oh, how she had missed her garden. She would check the garden first while she tried to remember where she'd put the key. Nadine opened the car door and leaned over her to unbuckle the seatbelt.

"Shh now, Mrs. Watkins. Shh."

She had to stop crying in order to stand. She wanted to stand. But tears had taken over. Nadine rubbed her shoulder and hummed. Gary disappeared into the house. Had she left the door unlocked? No, Gary had the key all along. He hated the mobile home, yet he was inside it and she was not. Hazel would ask Nadine about the key, why he had it, why he went into the house without her.

Years in business had taught her plenty about agendas—conflicting agendas and the more dangerous hidden kind. She leaned on the quad stick, Nadine beside her. The pavement felt solid under her feet, but dirt would feel even better.

"Garden," she said.

"Before you go inside?" Nadine asked. "You don't want to go in the house first?"

"*Garden,*" Hazel said again, even more clearly, and they began to make slow progress around the mobile home, past the leafy, blossomless lilac bushes.

"*I will yell for Gary to bring a chair,*" Nadine said.

"*No!*" No Gary interfering or overhearing. The garden was both terribly overgrown and dry, but she had to get closer to see if there were strawberries. Bees buzzed and the smell of mint crushed under their feet filled the air.

"*St-ay here,*" Hazel said. She held Nadine's arm and tried to squeeze it. She wanted to explain about picking fruit for pies and never going back to Riverview. She remembered that May was too early for strawberries.

Hazel leaned into Nadine's steadying shoulder and planned her next step forward.

A sudden flash of pain ripped through her chest, then settled and spread—she wanted to clutch Nadine, but her arms wouldn't move and her cold fingers wouldn't close. Nadine yelled something, sinking to the earth right beside her.

It was the end of May, too late for lilacs and not yet the season for chrysanthemums, but the thick spiced smell of the fall flower filled Hazel's nose and throat. She leaned into the breathing cushion of Nadine's body, the buzz of bees in her ears and the sun rosy and warm on her closed eyes. Edwin reached for Hazel's hands, uncurled her closed fists, and pulled her up. He handed her a fishing pole. Her line unfurled through the air in a perfect cast rippling the surface of the sky.

Henry liked the more peaceful Sunday hours in the cafeteria. He peeled pesky little fruit stickers off the last few dirty plates. "These things should be illegal. Or at least we should put up signs warning people not to put them on their dishes. Wonder how many hours it adds to my job. Wonder if it's humans or machines sticking them to every apple and pear."

"Stupid either way," Tiberius laughed. "But what do you care? You're getting paid."

Henry slid the plates into the rack and shoved the rack into the dishwasher.

"How's your shorty?" Tiberius asked. "You gonna be missing her over the summer?"

"No." Henry rinsed the soapy dishes with the hose, splattering water.

"You be careful with that," Tiberius said. "I got to go to my mother's after this, and I got to look fresh and make up for missing Mother's Day."

"I forgot about it too," Henry said. "Lucky Haitian Mother's Day always comes later. American Mother's Day is my reminder."

Henry's jacket hung by the door, cell phone jangling in the pocket. He thought about not answering, but dried his hands on his apron. If it stopped ringing before he got there, so be it.

"You telling me you won't be missing that pretty lady?" Tiberius prompted. "You're full of shit."

"I won't be missing her because she's coming to Cambridge!" Hearing the words aloud, even from his own mouth sent a prickly shiver across his back.

"Hah!" Tiberius slapped his thigh. "You smarter than I thought. You taking her home to meet your mama?"

The phone stopped ringing, only to start up again moments later.

Since Sage had sprung her plans, Henry had tried many

times to picture her and his mother meeting, and drew only a blank. He couldn't see it—couldn't imagine any of it—the how, the where, the conversation, the reactions—theirs and his. He got as far as *Manman* offering her *fritay* and *pikliz* and Sage politely trying to figure out whether it was vegan.

He retrieved his ringing phone and read the number—Riverview Manor. Speaking of his mama. He'd better answer—if she was calling from work, it could be another emergency.

"Yo, *Manman*. How's everything? I was about to call you."

"Oh really?" she said. "When?"

Her loud tooth-sucking sounded through the phone. Tiberius, who had been pretending not to listen, laughed.

"Did Chance bring you breakfast in bed on Mother's Day?"

Another loud scorn-filled *tuipe*.

"When I get home, I'll do something nice for you. *M ap la pou jou fèt manman.*

You always said Haitian Mother's Day is the one that counts."

"Henry, you know Coach Watkins's mother died? Have you talked to him?"

Henry said he'd give the coach a call.

"Right in my arms, she died!"

"Whoa!"

"In her garden. Better for her than dying in her bed, but I'm worried the trip home killed her, and I was the one that pushed on Gary Watkins to do it."

"The director of nursing said I'm not in trouble. Gary had signed some papers ... but I'm scared."

At least she had something to worry about other than Chance.

"And I miss her."

"She was old. She had a long life." Henry didn't know what to say. Maybe he'd wait and talk to the coach when he got home.

"Henry, your brother—"

"What?"

Tiberius looked up. Henry waved away his friend's concern, and Tiberius went back to wiping the counter. "Listen, *Manman*, I'm not there. I'm here. If Chance is playing the fool, there's nothing I can do. Talk to Coach. Helping you might be good for him if he's upset about his mother. Take care of yourself. Remember *Sak vid pa kanpe*." He hung up.

"What'd you say, right then?" Tiberius asked after Henry put his phone away. "You giving your own mama advice? You hanging up on her?"

"Huh?" Henry didn't care that Tiberius was in his business. What difference did anything make? "Haitian saying," he said. "An empty sack can't stand up."

"True dat," Tiberius said. "I'm about empty myself, right now." He hung the rag over the edge of the sink. "Hey, your mama gonna care your girl's white?"

"Don't think so," Henry said. "But she's going to hate the hair."

Tiberius laughed and untied his apron.

"I don't like it much either," Henry said. "And I didn't invite her. She's coming to take a class. I'll be working. Might not see much of her, really."

"That would be a shame," Tiberius said. "A real big shame."

"I don't know," said Henry. "I've got enough going on without pressure from her. That girl can be relentless. She wants something, she won't stop until she gets it. She's kind of scary."

Henry stuffed his down comforter into a box. Maybe he should just throw it out. He folded a blanket and his sheets and put them in the box too. His pillow wouldn't fit, so he started another box.

"Henry?" Sage knocked on his door. "Henry?"

He checked the time. His plane left in two and a half hours. He had to leave for the airport. He didn't really need any of this anyway. Was he even coming back here? He'd known for a week that he was accepted into the honors program at UMass Boston.

"Henry?" The doorknob rattled.

It was Sunday. The post office was closed so he couldn't mail these boxes to himself. The little dorm room really was awful—100 square feet, beige walls, cold linoleum floor tiles neither he nor John-o had thought to cover with a rug.

"Just a minute," he hollered as he swept the junk off his desk into the box with the pillow and pressed it down with a football and a fedora. He considered the small stuffed panther Sage had given him after all that spirit animal talk and tucked that in next to the football. Why was he even packing these things? If he left them here, he'd probably never even think of them again.

The door handle rattled again. "Henry. Let me in. I thought you wanted a ride to the airport. It's pouring out there."

He opened the door, and the small room filled with the licorice sunshiny smell of her. The fennel seeds she chewed explained the licorice, but after all these weeks, he still couldn't figure out how she smelled like a sunny day even in the rain.

"How can you even see what you're doing?" she asked. "It's so dark in here."

He hadn't even noticed. The gray light coming in through the rain-streaked window was plenty for tossing things in boxes.

"And it doesn't smell very good." She opened the window a bit and breathed deeply. "Better!"

She dropped her bag on the floor among his boxes and hugged him. He let himself relax into her, his cheek against her wet hair. He'd gotten used to the texture. He breathed in. That was it! Hair product that smelled like a beautiful day even in a poorly ventilated dorm room full of dirty laundry.

"I wish we could have slept together last night," Sage said. "But we'll have time in Cambridge. It'll be like having my own apartment. Our own apartment."

"We don't have to leave right this minute." He palmed the warm skin of her back and pulled her even closer. Only the fabric of their clothes separated them. She lifted his shirt; he lifted hers, and they fell onto his mattress. Her skin shone in the rainy gray light. With the sweet ache of their naked bodies moving, sweating, dissolving, he thought he might love her. And while their breathing steadied and their sweat cooled, he still thought he might love her. And then they'd start talking. Why couldn't that might-love feeling last? Why couldn't sex last? He reached for her arm to pull her back beside him and missed, fingers just brushing her elbow. He put on his glasses.

She slipped into her clothes, rescued the small panther from the box, and stroked its back, holding it like a kitten against her breasts that showed through the gap in her unbuttoned shirt. "Aww," she said to it. "He thought he could leave you behind."

"Sage," Henry said. He didn't know how to say that he wasn't leaving anything behind except things he planned to ask her to sell or toss. He looked at the boxes—two full of things and two still standing empty.

"Why don't I put them in my aunt's basement? She won't mind," Sage said. "That way, your stuff will be here when you come back. I'm happy to hang onto this guy for you." She kissed the panther on its fuzzy little face.

"What's wrong?" Sage asked.

"Nothing. Thanks, but I'm going to bring all this shit with me."

"My aunt wouldn't mind. She loves you. She thinks it's great I'm going to be in Cambridge this summer instead of working in my dad's office. She's always telling me to keep a healthy distance from my family. They're so crazy." She put the panther back in the box and picked up the fedora, pushing out the dents he'd made when he crammed it into the box. "I never saw you wear this." She put it on and posed in front of the mirror John-o had attached to the back of the door.

"Looks fly on you," Henry said. "I'm not the hat type." He stood close behind her. She looked more beautiful than ever as she tilted her head one way, then another, angling the hat, considering herself. Her shirt draped open, revealing different views of her breasts and glimpses of her nipples as she positioned and repositioned herself. He watched her in the mirror, then noticed his own face staring back from over her shoulder—the familiar shaved head and Malcolm X glasses, sharp chin and angular cheekbones, unsmiling lips in a tight line, all recognizable, but the odd expression in his eyes was not. He looked scared and needy and deceitful. What the fuck was up with that? He narrowed his eyes and glared that loser of a chump down. He wrapped his arms around Sage and pressed hard against her softness.

Henry slouched in his seat on the T, backpack on his lap, box and two duffle bags stacked on the floor by his feet. He'd left his box of bedding in the trunk of Sage's car.

A late spring, end of semester, Saturday night on the red line, the crowded train car full of perfume, aftershave, beer breath, body contact, and conversations that didn't include him. His mother hadn't made it to the airport. When he called, she was in the middle of preparing food and said it would be ready when he arrived. They'd eat and she'd tell him all about her interesting day. She'd sounded happy, delighted even. He had a lot to carry and did not look forward to lugging it the rest of the way home from the Central Square stop. He steadied his box as the train accelerated out of Charles/MGH. A very drunk and pretty girl clung to the pole near him to keep from falling onto his pile of luggage.

"Sorry." She laughed, as if she were on an amusement park ride instead of the subway. Her boyfriend slid an arm around her to keep her upright and kissed her on the neck. When Chance and he were little, they always wanted to stand on the T without holding on and try not to fall. Their mother always made them sit down.

Henry liked the view as they crossed the river into Cambridge. The last flush of sunset colored the sky over the shiny Hancock Tower, the glittering Prudential, and the flashing Citgo sign. He pushed his glasses up on his sweaty nose and sat straighter, stabilizing his bags with his knees and the box with the flat of his hand. He realized for the first time that he lived in a place that people wanted to visit, and a funny feeling of pride swelled in his chest, as if he were personally responsible for the beauty out the window. The girl and her boyfriend were entwined and kissing hard now. Two weeks before Sage came. Two weeks to come up with sightseeing ideas. Two weeks to prepare his mother and brother. He'd introduce her to Coach Watkins—that, at least, would be easy—and knowing Sage, she'd have her own list of places she wanted to go. She already asked him about the swan boats and the glass flowers at the Harvard Museum, which he'd been to once on a fourth grade school trip—boring—but maybe he'd been too young to appreciate them.

The train squealed to a stop at Kendall/MIT, and the couple, attached to the pole and each other, didn't even notice. Henry tried to ignore them, though the girl's bare leg wobbled just inches from his knee. He focused on his possessions. Central Square was next. How would he get everything off the train before the doors closed? How would he get it through the gate and up the stairs? He began loading himself up, shrugged on the knapsack, strapped on the duffels, one over each shoulder, and sat forward on the seat prepared to lift the box the moment the train stopped moving.

He shoved past the couple and wrestled his way out the door. The smell of hot metal and grime and piss hit his nose. The dirty stairs stretched up, and the box cut into his arms and strained his back. On the sidewalk he allowed himself to put it down, lifted the bags off his shoulders, and stood, sucking in gulps of warm night air. People streamed by, zigzagging around him. He should have unloaded closer to the curb.

"We 'bout to come up! This gonna be easy!" Henry recognized Chance's voice and turned. Of course, he'd be holding forth in his regular territory near the corner. It was a beautiful evening.

"As long as none of you bitch out," Razz said.

Four guys with lowslung pants, oversized sports jerseys, and caps sauntered past.

Chance, Junior, Razz, and a white guy Henry didn't recognize from the back.

"Yo! Bro!" Henry called. "Chance!"

They turned together, as a pack, and identical looks of annoyance flashed across their faces. Then Chance recognized Henry and beamed, grabbed his hand, pulled him close and thumped his back. The others fidgeted and bounced and glanced over their shoulders.

"Didn't know you was coming tonight," Chance said.

"What's poppin'?" Henry said.

Chance released him and stood at arm's length.

"Henry," Razz said. "Good to see you man, but we got bidness—time sensitive bidness—going down."

"Yeah, we'll catch you later." Junior patted a lump under his shirt, about where the waistband of his shorts would be. Another gun?

"Chance," Henry said and stopped.

The skinny white guy adjusted the angle of his cap and moved to leave.

"Catch you later, bro," Chance said. He gave Henry a what-am-I-supposed-to-do-got-no-choice look before turning away.

"You're my fucking brother!" The words exploded in the air between them shocking them both. Henry lowered his voice. "You can't help me carry my shit home?"

"We gotta do this thing!" the white guy said.

"Chance, man," said Junior. "We gotta dip. Sorry, Henry. You hauled all that in from half way cross the country, you can make the last few blocks to the crib."

"Want me to hit up Coach Watkins?" Chance waved his phone. "You could put all them bags in the whip."

"Bro, I just got back, and Ma's cooking."

"Coach loves your mother's cooking." Razz raised his eyebrows and Junior laughed.

Henry glared. "What's that supposed to mean?"

"Just that he wouldn't mind helping you out, especially with a good Haitian meal afterward," Junior said, smirking. "Let's go, my dude, we ain't got time for all this."

"Nad-i-i-i-i-n-n-n-ne!" Razz called out. Junior and the shifty white boy laughed at the joke.

Chance's lips tightened. An angry wrinkle crumpled his

forehead and drew his eyebrows together. He bounced a couple of times in his perfect sneakers, ran a hand across his face and smoothed it out, but Henry knew his brother—Chance's eyes glittered with deepening irritation.

The white kid whined some more about being late.

"So, you helping me or what?" Henry asked. "You can catch up with these clowns after we get all this shit into the house. I haven't seen you since March."

If Junior and Razz hadn't continued to smirk about his mom—Nadine and Coach Watkins—ridiculous!—Chance might have gone ahead with his friends, but before Henry had to push any harder, Chance hefted Henry's box to his shoulder and grabbed the larger duffle.

"What the fuck, Chance?" the white kid said.

"You really dippin' right now? When we 'bout to get it poppin'?" Junior asked.

"Yo check this out. I gotta take care of my fam. But I'm a be right over there. Hit me up when y'all 'bout to be there. I'm a snatch up a bike and come through."

"We 'bout to be there *now*," Razz responded.

"Why you bitchin' up on us? We 'bout to get this come up!"

"What you think? I ain't tryna come up with y'all? I'm a be right there. This shit is heavy. Henry, let's hurry the fuck up." Chance ended the conversation with a decisive nod and with long strides began walking away from his friends.

Henry rushed to catch up. "What's that all about?"

"Don't worry 'bout it. Just that thing we been working on for the past few weeks. Everybody been sleeping on me... They 'bout to see how I get down."

"Like what? That Harvard guy you were telling me about? You're not really doing that dumb-ass shit!"

Chance smiled, studying the sidewalk, while he set down the duffle and readjusted the box on his shoulder. "Those guys are dumb as rocks," he said.

"You are, too, for hanging out with them. Look, if you get locked up, don't expect me to be taking care of you."

"Bro, don't be telling me what I already know." Chance's long legs kept him well ahead of Henry as he turned onto their street, or maybe it was the urgent business waiting for him, or maybe he was fed up with Henry coming home and telling him what to do.

"You need to be doing better, graduation is in a fucking week!" Henry cringed inside as the words leaped from his mouth. He should shut up. Chance wasn't going to listen anyway. They climbed the steps to the house. "Thanks for helping with all this."

Chance grinned from behind the carton. "You get wit any of those cold-ass girls in Minnesota yet? You got your key or do I gotta put this shit down?"

Henry groped for the key. Shit. Somehow he would have to finesse the summer so that Sage and Chance never crossed paths. "Bro, women hear you talk like that, you won't be getting anything, anywhere," Henry said.

"You see any women around here?"

Henry shouldered open the door, and Chance stepped through. The smell of *fritay* filled the stairwell.

"I guess you want me to be taking this shit all the way up for you," Chance whispered.

"That'd be brotherly of you."

"Shh. Mom's gonna try to get me to stay and eat. I can't be doing that. I'm gonna drop all this right outside the door and you gonna go in alone. My boys are counting on me." Henry had never seen Chance walk so lightly up the stairs. His stomach ached. How would he be able to eat the food his mother had waiting?

"*Manman!*" Henry hollered. "I'm home." She'd open the door, see Chance, and good luck to him getting away without at least a fried plantain. Every moment those guys did their thing without Chance was a moment his brother wasn't yet in deep shit.

"Fuck you, asshole!" Chance dropped the duffle and box in the middle of the stairs, leaped over the duffle, and followed the box as it crashed to the bottom and broke apart. As Chance barreled out the door, he turned his head just long enough to skewer Henry with a poisonous look.

"Henry?" His mother's head appeared above, over the rail of the landing. "What's going on?" She noticed the wrecked box and the avalanche of books, a broken lamp, and all the rest of it on the stairs.

"So much to carry! I should have come to the airport to help." She hurried down and folded her arms around him.

He stiffened. She had no clue. He tolerated her hug until he couldn't stand it, then ducked away from her and scrambled to collect his things.

"Henry, I'll help you," she said. "But I need to turn off the stove first."

"I'm fine, *Manman*," he said. He hoped she hadn't heard the catch in his voice. He swallowed and tried again. "I'm fine."

"I'll carry this in." She lifted the duffle bag that Henry had set by the door. "So heavy! I'm sorry I didn't come to the airport. I should have asked Gary Watkins to pick you up. I think he would have been happy to do that."

Coach loves your mother's cookin'. Razz's voice. Junior's smirk.

"I managed," Henry said. He sat on a step, in the dim light of the stairwell, holding his copy of Malcolm X. How was he going to make it through this summer? The stuffed panther lay on its side by his foot. Sage must have shoved it in the box when he wasn't looking. He thought she'd kept it.

☆

202

Nadine found Henry at home, awake but still in bed, shades pulled down. Maybe she was worrying about the wrong son.

"Would you like some food?" she asked. His face looked young and naked without his glasses. He shook his head. "A soda?"

"No!"

"Are you sick?"

Henry rolled away from her and faced the wall, wrapping the sheet tight around him. "I'm fine," he said.

"A person who is fine doesn't spend the day in bed."

"I'm tired, okay? I worked hard these last couple weeks and flew halfway across the country, and I'm tired!"

"You make it sound like you"—halfway through her feeble joke, she knew she should swallow the rest but said it anyway—"had to flap your wings to get here."

Henry groaned. On the floor by the bed, his phone rang. He stretched out an arm and grabbed it, checking the number. "Yeah, hey Coach." He sat up at full attention. "No, he's not. Okay. Shit! Okay. Yeah. Later."

Nadine's tired legs threatened to give out on her. She sat on the edge of the bed. "What happened? Chance?"

"Mom! Nothing. Coach just wondering if he was here."

"I am not an idiot. Tell me what Gary Watkins said."

"Mom, nothing okay? Ask him yourself. You're such good friends all of a sudden."

"What is going on? Don't you start being rude to me now, Henry."

Henry reached for his glasses and put them on. "Mom, you mind? I need to put some clothes on."

He was sleeping naked now? Nadine sucked her teeth and forced herself to stand.

"Tell me what Gary Watkins said!"

"Okay. All right! Coach was looking for him because his friends got arrested last night—both Junior and Razz."

"But not Chance?" Nadine pressed a hand to her heart and breathed a thank you to her mother and *La Sirèn* and whoever had intervened on behalf of her son. "Come to the kitchen when you're dressed. You need to eat."

She made *espageti* with a lot of onion and extra meat, the way Henry liked it, humming to herself as she pounded the spices and chopped the hotdogs. By the time he appeared showered and dressed, it was ready. She served him, then sat down with a plate of her own, tiredness gone. She bowed her head and gave another silent prayer of thanks. Henry poked a piece of hotdog with his fork and raised it to his mouth in slow motion. At least he was eating.

"Do you think we should all go to Haiti?" she asked. "Chance wants to go, and it might do him good to get away."

Henry lifted one shoulder and chewed. He needed a haircut.

"I think we should make a trip. I have never seen my parents' tomb." She willed herself to be quiet and concentrated on her food, thinking about home—the bright red blossoms of the flamboyant tree in the *lakou*, the funny sound of donkeys braying, the summer rain pounding on the metal roof. She pictured Chance and Henry scrambling up trunks of palm trees to grab coconuts, hacking them open with one sharp blow of a machete, pounding ripe mangoes against a rock and sucking out the juicy pulp, and dancing late into the night to *rara*.

"You know why he wants to go?" Henry's sharp tone startled her. "He wants to meet our father. Are you ready for that to happen? Could you even find him?"

Nadine carefully laid down her fork. Why suddenly did everyone want to know everything? Lucien. Deacon Joseph.

Yara would have pushed and bothered her to tell them the truth, had she known. Hazel's writing haunted her. *Why didn't I talk while I still could? Why didn't I talk to my son while I could explain—myself, my choices, the losses that drove me to wrap myself in a blanket of secrets that no longer keeps me warm.*

She could find Deacon Joseph at the church she no longer attended in Mattapan. Lucien would take more time to track, but someone would know where he was. "I could find them," she said.

"What?" Henry half-stood, leaning closer to her, over the table and the food still heaped on his plate. "What did you say?"

"I could find—" Had she said "them?" She had. Panic tightened her voice. "Hem," she coughed out. "I could find him if I had to, but I don't want to right now. Henry, I have enough on my mind. After we get your brother through graduation, I'll think about it some more."

Henry slammed the table with the flat of his hand. The dishes clattered. "We? No one can get him 'through graduation' but his own self. He's a fool."

She stood up. "I need to think."

"You think. I'm outta here." He grabbed his sneakers and left in his socks, slamming the door hard.

Nadine couldn't move. If Yara were here...but she was always at her daughter's now. And if Yara were here, all she'd say would be, *you should have told them sooner.* Well, she hadn't. Another mistake in a long list. She couldn't look at Henry's half-finished spaghetti, and she couldn't throw it away so even though she felt sick to her stomach, she sat down in his chair and ate every bite.

Henry laced up his sneakers and pounded down the stairs. He knew from long experience that he couldn't outrun his confusions or fears, but he could put some distance between himself and his mother until he could figure out what to say to her. He could sweat out that angry adrenaline ripping through his body. He could track down his brother, his half-brother, he'd known it all along in some unarticulated way. Them. Two fathers. Did it matter? Undoubtedly they each had other half siblings out in the world.

In the light of early evening he sprinted down traffic-free side streets to get to the river. Henry would run for a while, then, calmer in his exhaustion, head back toward Central Square to look for Chance. What else didn't he know about his mother? It would be cool to see where she'd grown up, meet some relatives, but she had a whole life after that, in the US, that he knew nothing about. He'd never thought to ask her about any of it. Even now, he had no idea what went on with her. These rumors about her and Coach Watkins. She was his mother. Their mother. Feeding them, worrying about their education, answering the phone when he called. He liked her that way. What was up with this father thing? Them? He would make her tell the truth. The whole story. As soon as the three of them were together in the house long enough.

He ran along the Cambridge side of the river and crossed the same bridge he'd ridden over on the T just the day before. It seemed like months ago. He ran down the stairs to the Esplanade and stopped, bent over, hands on his knees, gulping air. Strains of classical music floated from the Hatch Shell, like the soundtrack to a movie. He walked now, toward the concert, past the boat house—he'd often thought about doing that community boating, had heard it only cost one dollar for the whole summer. Maybe he and

Sage could try it. Sailboats filled the river basin, lit by the sun low in the sky. He meandered over the footbridge to the island where he began running again. Toward the Mass Ave bridge, and across it, back to Cambridge, past MIT to Central Square where he was sure to run into Chance on his corner or in Wendy's or Mickey D's depending.

Sure enough, half a block ahead of him, near the bus stop bench danced his brother, acting the fool in front of three girls who were feeding his ravenous ego with their appreciative laughs. Henry had never made a girl laugh that way. Even if he figured out what to say and how to say it, he'd never have the audacity to pull it off. He stopped running and wiped the sweat off his face with the bottom of his soaked Wu-Tang shirt. Chance spotted him. "Henry, bro!" he called.

Cars and buses and pedestrians pulsed in Henry's peripheral vision like an incipient migraine, his brother in too-sharp focus in front of him. His half-brother.

Maybe Chance's father was a tall dude. That would explain the unfortunate difference in their heights. Maybe Chance's father wasn't even Haitian. *Manman* had told enough stories about Lucien, her Haitian man, with dimples like Henry's that he figured that piece of history was real. But Chance's father could be anyone. Some kind of player, most likely, if he was anything like his son. But that would mean their mother...no...he couldn't think of his mother falling for that kind of guy.

Chance elbowed Henry and laughed. "You hear 'bout last night?"

"Coach called. What happened?"

"Some neighbor called the cops when the Harvard kid chased my boys out the back of the apartment. I couldn't find the bike I'd stashed so by the time I hiked over, they were cuffed and sitting in the back of a police car. I kept on walking." Chance rocked back on his heels and eyed the girls.

Henry let the words echo in his head before he understood. "You're lucky you weren't there!" he said.

"Lucky someone stole that bike," Chance said. "My bike karma. I take a bike. Next someone who takes it takes it from me. Or maybe it's my nice guy karma. I helped you carry all your shit home."

"I heard they got caught with a lot of weed," one of the girls chimed in. "They gonna have big charges against them."

"Waiting to see if the cops try talking to me," said Chance. "I ain't no snitch."

"You might not be a snitch," Henry said in a low voice. "But you're standing on Mass Ave. running your mouth. Where were you last night anyway?"

"Stayed over in Everett with Razz's cousin." Chance shook his head. "We were all hoping this deal would work out. Would have meant a summer of easy living."

"We were waiting on our Coach purses," the blonde girl said. "You promised us, Chance."

"Hey," he said. "Could still happen."

"I don't need your shit," Henry said. "I don't need any of this shit." Every tired muscle in his body twitched and burned.

"What shit?" Chance asked. "You ladies see any shit?" All three girls laughed. Chance shrugged. "Relax, brother. You gonna give yourself a heart attack."

"Fuck you!"

"Henry, come on."

"No, really. Fuck you and your fucked up schemes and your wanna be gangster thing!" Henry no longer felt small and ridiculous. He felt right. "You're a bigger asshole than I thought."

Chance's smirk crumpled a little at the edges before he could secure it. They stood, breathing hard, looking at each other. Chance glanced at the girls, moving just his eyes.

"This isn't a show," Henry said.

Chance puffed himself up and adjusted his pants.

"Or maybe it is," Henry added. "But it's over now." He took off down the sidewalk, no idea where he was headed.

His phone rang. The knucklehead apologizing, ready to talk some sense? No, of course not. Sage. Sage bubbling over with her plan to see him soon.

He waited, until it stopped ringing, walked a block to calm down enough to call her back.

"A week from today I'll be there," she said. "I can't wait."

"That's cool," said Henry. "I already thought of some things we could do."

"Like what?"

The white kid who had been with Chance and Razz and Junior the night before gave Henry a nod as he passed him. Henry's head filled with questions.

"Henry?"

"I'm here," he said.

"What things are we going to do?"

He couldn't think of anything right now. "You'll see."

"Mostly I just want to be there with you. You can stay over at the apartment whenever you want. And I'm excited to meet your mom and your brother."

The reality of Sage in Cambridge silenced him.

"I miss you, Henry."

"Miss you too."

"Really?"

She sounded so eager. He said he missed her. He said he'd been thinking of things they could do. Fuck all these people. She exhaled into the phone, and he felt instantly sorry.

"Yes. Really. I'm glad you're coming. I can't wait."

JUNE 2005

Wont pi lou pase sak sèl.
Shame is heavier than a sack of salt.

H enry waited in the Coach's office. Everything looked
fresh since they'd renovated the center—all the shabby
wooden furniture carved with the names of his friends
replaced by colorful molded plastic. Haitian metal works
hung on the walls—a tree of life, a lady with a wide smile
riding a bicycle, and a colorful *taptap* loaded with people,
their baggage on the roof. He sat in the Coach's big black
chair, swiveling a bit from side to side as he surveyed the
messy desk. It didn't bother him that Coach was late.

A vaguely familiar Asian guy with long hair and a worried
expression looked in. "You seen Coach? I need the keys for
the supply closet." Henry shook his head and the guy rushed
off, and that was only the beginning.

"You seen Coach? Anthony's mother lost the permission
slip for the field trip to Canobie Lake and wants another."

"Hey, where Coach at? I supposed to be interviewing him
for my oral history project."

"Coach Watkins! Oh. Where is he?"

A middle school kid headed straight for the desk. "Where's Coach? Them basketballs are all flat." He reached over Henry to open a drawer and began rummaging around. "He's got a pin in here somewhere." Henry would never be the kind of person whose drawers were open territory. The kid was sifting through everything. "Got one!"

A small girl, knees scraped and bleeding, wailed, escorted into the office by Rosie. If Henry had to deal with that mess, he'd be all flustered. "Need some first aid," Rosie said. "Hi, Henry. You're back! Here for the Mother Tongue Book meeting?" She plucked a pair of gloves, some Band-Aids, and antiseptic wipes from a box in front of him and kneeled down next to the girl.

"It's gonna hurt!" the kid screamed.

Rosie reassured her and patched her up. Henry watched in awe. "Was that so bad?" she asked.

Henry realized, just in time, that she was talking to her patient, not to him. He almost embarrassed himself by saying, "No, that was amazing."

The little girl inspected her Band-Aids and sniffled.

"You're really good with kids," he said.

Rosie ignored his compliment and unearthed a free hardware store calendar full of scribbled appointments. "Might say on this where Coach is," she said. "You go on now," she told the little girl. "Get back on that scooter and show it who's boss."

She pointed to the date. "He's supposed to be here. Two o'clock Mother Tongue Book Meeting with Professor Edmond." Henry leaned in close, trying to read Coach's tiny scrawl, and breathed in the peppermint of Rosie's gum.

"Ro-Z, I'm sorry for asking, but I need to know. It's important," Henry said. "I should have called you. Do you know what's going on with Chance?"

She actually growled, stamped her foot, and glared at him with narrowed eyes, but he wouldn't let this small person intimidate him. "If you know what's going on with him, tell me. Come on!"

She whirled around and slammed the door. He thought for a moment that she'd stormed out, but instead she'd closed them in together. He looked over his shoulder out the window, then back at Ro-Z. Trapped. Her palms flat on the desk, stiff arms trembling she angled her face close to his. Her eyes flashed.

"I loved you guys," she whispered, then pressed her lips together, and shook her head. Her nostrils flared. "You were my friends. Chance messed that up."

"What do you mean?" He fought the urge to put a hand on hers. "What did he do?"

She turned her face away. "Last summer he knew I loved him. He also knew he didn't love me back, but he fucked me anyway."

Henry's head ached. You guys? Fucked me? What was she talking about?

"You mean, literally, fucked you? Like sex?"

She hugged herself. "Henry, yes. I'm embarrassed about it, okay? I wanted to, but he shouldn't have done it if he didn't want to be with me like that."

"But we're practically siblings. Or cousins. We grew up together. That's weird."

"Well, we're not siblings or cousins and now Chance and I aren't even friends. So I'm not all up in his business. I don't care what foolishness he's got going on."

Something didn't add up. Lots of people had relationships that soured. "What else happened?" Henry heard himself ask.

They stared at each other like little kids waiting to see who would blink first.

"I had an abortion," she said. "And no one, I mean no one, knows about this except Chance and me and now you. So keep your mouth shut. My parents would kill me. My friends only know that your brother treated me real bad. If he'd come with me to the clinic, I might have forgiven him. But the second I found out I was pregnant, it was all my problem."

Someone banged on the door, but they ignored it. Rosie shrugged one shoulder and bit her lip. She'd had Chance's dick inside her. She'd had the beginnings of Chance's baby inside her. She should look different somehow, but she didn't.

The knocking on the door grew louder, and Rosie cracked it open. *All my problem.* Henry stared at the coach's messy desk and thought about fathers—fathers who have never met their sons, fathers who don't go to clinics.

"Oh, Professor Edmund," Rosie sing-songed. "Coach Watkins isn't back yet."

On Coach's calendar Henry spotted the word, "Nadine." He looked more closely. Yes, Nadine, written in more than one place. She'd mentioned helping with the trailer, and Coach had helped her with court and the gun, but Junior and Razz's jeering "Nadiiiine," buzzed loud in his ears.

All business, Rosie arranged three chairs close to the desk. "We'll be meeting here." She looked at the clock. Henry could almost convince himself he'd made that abortion up.

Professor Edmond, silk scarf around his neck, stepped through the doorway of the office looking stately, elegant, out of place even in a recently renovated youth center.

Rosie, like Sage, enviably at home in her body and in the world, introduced them. "Professor Edmond, this is Henry Antoine." How could she be so smooth after what just happened? But then she'd been living with this story for months. Henry was the one who had just found out. What else could he find out today?

Professor Edmond frowned, studying Henry with a confused do-I-know-you look.

"You visited Professor Kim's linguistics class last spring. I enjoyed your talk."

"Ah!" Professor Edmond's smile softened his stern face. Henry relaxed. "Yes! I remember. You are a fellow Cantabrigian?"

Cantabrigian? Not a word Henry heard very often. Sage would love it. He nodded. He'd have to remind Chance and his friends they were Cantabrigians.

"You will be working with Rosie and Gary on this project. I hear you will help with the initial translating of the children's books into Haitian Creole. I have offered to do the final edits. Translation is a tricky business. It is very important we do this right." Henry wondered what the word for abortion was in *Kreyòl*. There were countless words he didn't know.

Professor Edmund pulled a laptop from his briefcase. "This project is vital for the future of Haiti. When children are forced to learn in a language that is not their own, they cannot learn to think. They are so busy trying to understand. Imagine it!" Professor Edmond challenged Henry. "Imagine you had to learn in the language of your oppressors, a language that even the teachers cannot speak fluently or write correctly. How is a country supposed to make any progress with such a system?"

He seemed to be waiting for an answer. Henry struggled to find a response while maintaining an intelligent expression.

"I've already started brainstorming topics with the kids," Rosie jumped in, saving his ass. "I've got a group that's interested."

"I'd like to do most of the work this summer. Come September I'm very busy." Professor Edmond studied his laptop screen. Henry couldn't see what was on it—maybe a calendar. "I'll be traveling."

"To Haiti?" Henry asked.

"Oh, no!" Forehead wrinkled, he regarded Henry as if he'd said something ridiculous.

The guy was Haitian and specialized in studying Haitian Creole. Assuming the man traveled to Haiti wasn't so dumb, yet Henry regretted opening his mouth. "It's dangerous there these days. Kidnappings. Violence. I haven't been back in years. The government isn't stable enough yet. The news is bad."

"My mother is going this summer," Rosie said.

"Yes, well—"

Coach Watkins, sweaty and disheveled, charged in, breathing hard. "Glad you started without me." He shook Professor Edmond's hand and nodded at Rosie and Henry before seating himself behind his desk. He grabbed an old t-shirt from a messy pile, removed his glasses, and wiped his dripping face. They watched him.

"Sorry. Sorry. Already hot as hell out there. Funny, the one white guy in the meeting operating on Haitian time! Ha!"

Professor Edmond winced. Rosie frowned. Henry felt momentary pity for the sweaty awkward coach. A dutiful laugh formed in his throat, then he remembered his mother's name on the calendar and swallowed it.

"Okay, yeah." Coach replaced his glasses and flipped through some papers.

They created a timeline for the project—Rosie and Professor Edmond did most of the talking. He recommended a good Creole dictionary that cost seventy-five dollars. Henry had made it through his freshman year of college without buying required books. "Do you know where I can borrow one?" he asked.

"You will want to own a good dictionary," Professor Edmond said. He shook his head as if Henry had disappointed him.

"We'll get you one," Coach said. "Don't worry. There's money in the grant for something like that."

Henry nodded. He hoped he was, in fact, the right person for this job. He hoped he wouldn't disappoint anybody. He stiffened his neck and shoulders to better bear the familiar weight of that worry.

"My dance class is waiting in the gym," Rosie said. "We're finished here, right?"

"I look forward to working with you, young lady." Professor Edmond packed up his laptop. He shook hands with Henry and Coach Watkins. "We will make a difference in education in Haiti."

"You're at UMass?" Henry blurted. "I'm thinking about transferring."

The professor paused. Henry squirmed under his silent questioning attention and tried to frame a sentence of explanation.

"If you do," the Professor said, "you be sure to let me know. I could use a TA."

Henry flushed. "I will!" Coach beamed at him. Through the window they watched the professor stride across the park, their silence neither companionable nor awkward. Where were all the kids and counselors now that Coach was back?

"Uh, Henry?" Coach began.

Henry's whole being tensed. No. No. No. Do not talk with me about my mother. Do NOT.

"Don't let Professor Edmond intimidate you. This is a real opportunity. Who knows where it will lead?"

Henry exhaled long and loud.

"He's a great guy. We're going to have fun with this. And Rosie is one organized, creative, and energetic young lady— the kids love her. They'll do anything she wants them to— we're going make some good books here." He glanced toward the window. "Is that your brother?"

Chance, standing on a bike way too small for him—Henry wondered if he'd snatched it from a child—pedaled across the grass toward the center. His shorts flapped as his legs pumped up and down. His pristine white t-shirt clung to his upper body and gleamed in the light. He bought new ones almost daily. His mirrored aviator glasses glittered. The guy radiated love for himself. Coach grinned at the sight of him, and Henry felt the same indulgent smile at the edges of his own lips until he thought of Rosie going to the clinic by herself.

"That's him," Henry said. His half-brother. Chance dropped the bike near the door and rearranged himself.

"'Sup?" Chance filled the open doorway, reached high to grasp the top of the doorframe with his fingertips, and swung-stepped into the room. In middle school, during a pick-up basketball game, Chance realized he'd grown taller than Henry. Of course, he crowed about it, pulling Henry close to prove it over and over, until Henry stormed off.

"Bro! What you doing here?" Chance seemed surprised, and Henry realized the doorway grab wasn't for his benefit, but just Chance being Chance. "Coach, man, my lawyer wants me to go for a CWOF. Says it's the best way for me to keep on with my life. What you think? I want a trial. If I had a jury, I could get off. I didn't even do nothing except be standing there."

"In the wrong place at the wrong time with the wrong person," Coach said.

"CWOF?" asked Henry.

"Continuance Without a Finding." Coach Watkins taped up a crumpled paper with "Do Not Disterb" crayoned on it by some kid and closed the door. "A deal where you're admitting there's evidence against you—enough to find you guilty—so you agree to probation. If you make it through probation with no new charges, case dismissed. Given what I've heard, I'd say you should listen to the lawyer."

"But that's whack! They didn't even catch me doing nothing."

"Chance," Coach said. "She's a decent lawyer. You should go for it."

"She don't want to be bothered with a trial."

"I see why you might say that. If it were a different lawyer, I can think of a few, I'd be saying the same thing. But this lady knows her stuff and she cares. She must trust you can handle probation without any fuck ups?" Henry heard the question mark at the end of Coach's words. Chance paid no attention to it.

"Everyone knows a Black man can't get a fair trial in this country. Come on Henry, you the one throwing all your statistics around all the time. You the one memorized Malcolm's autobiography." Had Chance finally read it? Maybe he'd seen the movie.

"Coach, you the one always saying there's one legal system for the rich and another for the poor. You know it be mostly Black guys ending up in jail. You don't see rich folks sitting around on death row."

Chance slumped into the chair Professor Edmond had been sitting in. "I don't trust no court-appointed lawyer." A note of fear sounded through his bluster.

Coach Watkins rested a hand on Chance's shoulder. "There's good reason not to trust the system. No one's arguing about that. But Diana Klein knows her stuff. She's done right by lots of guys. Get through this, graduate, figure out what you're going to do to be part of the change this fucked up world needs."

"Be serious, Coach. You think the world really want to hear from me?"

Henry fought the urge to laugh. "This is Cambridge, Massachusetts!" he said. "Not the Deep South. Give me a fucking break. If you went to class or took one of these Mayor's program jobs, with all you got going for you, you'd have colleges fighting with each other to give you scholarships. Don't blame the system because you want to act the fool." He stopped, though he could have gone on about impregnating old friends and tormenting their mother and being an asshole of a brother.

Chance sat straight, eyes hidden behind his mirrored glasses. Henry waited to hear what his brother would throw back.

"Fuck you, Henry. Cambridge ain't all that. Racist courts and cops here too. You think you're so smart. You don't know shit. I have plans. I have my own shit happening. You ain't the only one who can go to college and all that."

"You're the one don't know shit," Henry said. "You don't know nothing."

Chance turned away with a disgusted shrug.

"You know we got different dads?" Henry said. He hadn't planned to say it right then.

The glasses hid Chance's reaction, but Coach stiffened and hugged the basketball, mouth hanging open.

"Yeah," Chance said. "That's why I'm beautiful and you're ugly."

"I'm serious," Henry said.

"I'm serious too. That's why I'm big and Black and you're

little and yellow. You got more white blood in you than I do."
Chance made a big show of admiring his biceps.

"Ain't no one can talk to you!" Henry shouted. He grabbed
at Chance's sunglasses, but Chance slapped his arm out of
the way. Chance shoved Henry away again—this time with
a lightning quick, kung fu move that ended in Henry's arm
twisted painfully behind his back—one of Chance's hands
gripping his wrist, the other pushing on his elbow.

"Guys!" Coach yelled.

Henry ducked, jerked, and kicked, trying to free himself,
but Chance held tight and pushed him down to the ground.
Henry's glasses pressed into the linoleum. His whole body
shook with rage.

"No fighting here!" Coach Watkins sounded far away.

"Fucking door's shut," Chance said. He wasn't even
breathing hard.

"Closed doors make no difference," Coach said.

"He's my brother," Henry hollered. "I have the right to
beat the shit out of him."

"As if you could," Chance laughed.

"Let him go, Chance," said Coach. "Now."

As soon as Chance released him, Henry sprang to his feet,
punching.

Chance's mocking grin urged Henry on. His easy sidestep-
ping mocked him further.

"Henry! You work here!" Coach yelled. "Be a role model!"

Henry slammed the desk and swept Coach's fucking
calendar and pencils and all his other shit onto the floor,
before falling into a chair. Chance perched on the edge of
the cleared desk.

No one moved. Shouts and chatter of happy kids filtered
in from the hallway. Henry breathed hard. Chance sat,
unreadable behind his sunglasses and his deliberately
arranged posture.

"What you saying about different dads?" Chance asked finally.

"I'm not talking to you with those glasses hiding your eyes," Henry said.

"Chance," said Coach Watkins. "Take the glasses off."

Chance opened his mouth, then closed it. After another stretched out, silent moment, he slid the shades off, snapped down the earpieces, and set them on the desk beside him with a final-sounding clack. He crossed his arms over his chest and gave Henry an "All right, you got what you asked for, now you owe me" stare.

Henry kept the squirmy feeling in his stomach from showing in his face. Sweat dripped down his neck. He fiddled with a bent hinge on his own glasses, settled them on his face and rubbed his forehead. He looked Chance in the eye.

"We'll have to talk with *Manman* about it," he said. "I don't really know anything except that she let it slip—fathers-s-s."

"You know anything about this?" Chance turned on Coach Watkins. "You been talking with our Mom. She say anything to you?"

"Well ..." Coach cleared his throat.

"What the fuck?" said Chance.

"Yeah," Henry said. "What the fuck?"

"When I go to Haiti I'll find them," Chance said.

"We don't even know they're in Haiti. We don't know where they are. Why all this time, she be lying?" Henry asked.

Chance cracked his knuckles. "What else she not saying? When we going to talk to her?"

Coach motioned to a kid outside the door to wait a minute. "Give your mom a break," he said. "She must have her reasons."

Anger flared up again in Henry's chest. What right did Coach Watkins have to defend their mother?

"You know more than you're saying?" Chance asked.

"Okay. Okay. I do know that one is in Haiti—Henry's father—and yours is closer to home. In Mattapan. He's a deacon there. Wouldn't have looked good for him to have gotten a parishioner pregnant so your mom—"

"Henry, let's go," said Chance. "You think Mom be home now?"

"Should be," said Henry. "Unless she's working a double."

"She's not," Coach said.

Henry and Chance exchanged glances.

They left Coach Watkins standing behind his desk.

"Get on the bike, bro," Chance said. "On the seat. I'll ride you to the house."

"That little thing! No."

"Get on," Chance said. "Trust me. And fuck old Coach Watkins be thinking he knows everything about everything."

Chance pedaled, standing up. Henry, legs dragging, arm still sore, clung to the back of the seat. He had to lean and turn sideways to avoid Chance's ass, inches from his face. He tried to imagine the conversation unfolding and plan what he would say, but came up blank. He felt like a clown on that little bike. They were both clowns. "Clowns in the circus of life," he said.

"What?" Chance looked back at him.

"Watch where the fuck we're going."

Chance threaded the bike between two parked cars, hopped a low curb, and pedaled steadily across the playing field toward home.

On her way home from the bus stop, Nadine stopped at the corner market to pick up *malanga*, black eyed peas, and peppers. She would make *akra* fritters tonight to go with the fried chicken and *pikliz*. Chance loved them. *Akra* fritters would show him without words how happy she was. *Mèsi Bondye!*

When the beautiful counselor called her at work, Nadine had assumed bad news. She wished she had a recording of the conversation because her happy shock blurred her memory. "Financial aid, interested schools, Lesley University. Just in time to fill out last-minute applications. Fantastic essay. Inspiration to other students. You have a lovely son Ms. Antoine, so respectful, so smart, I look forward to his speech at graduation."

She unpacked her groceries, turned the radio to a music station, her favorite *kompa* and *zouk*, and realized she felt something bubbling up inside that might be happiness. Perhaps things would be okay for Chance. Henry seemed sad, but he had a summer job. And Gary Watkins—he had given Henry that job. He was helping Chance in court and had taken away the horrible gun. He was her friend. Those were all good things.

Before she began to grate the *malanga* and season the chicken, while her hands were still clean, maybe she'd call Gary Watkins and invite him for dinner, as a thank you. Nothing needed to be discussed; her invitation and her food would say every necessary thing—to Gary and to Chance, and to Henry too—he was a good brother and a good son. With all her worrying about Chance, she hadn't done enough to show Henry how glad she was to have him back home for the summer.

This delicious meal would be a celebration of everything good. The weight of the day lifted from her bones as she pressed Gary's number into the phone. She left her invitation in response to his recorded message. "If you are hungry, come over to eat with us. Remember, I told you about *akra* fritters and you said you'd never tasted them? Come when you're done working."

She peeled the rough skin from the *malanga* exposing the white insides. As she grated and grated, one vegetable after the other, milky white *malanga* juice spilled over her fingers. She grated in time to the music, feet and hips moving too. Maybe she should have bought some wine. Maybe Gary Watkins would bring some.

Nadine mixed the *akra* batter and heated the oil. She would fry the chicken first and cook the fritters just before eating. What a pleasure to cook when there was so much to cook with! In the village, only the neighbors ate chicken, she was lucky if she tasted a bite. The only birds she ate were the ones she was fast enough and lucky enough to catch—small birds with so little meat on them that after singeing off the feathers in the fire, it took only minutes to roast the meat all the way through, even less time to chew the meager flesh and suck the bones. She dropped a plump chicken thigh into the oil, satisfied with the sizzle. There was more meat on one of these legs than she'd eaten in a year on the island or in a month in the city.

Henry and Chance burst into the kitchen together—united somehow, in a way Nadine hadn't seen since before Henry left for college. They shared a look that left her out, and neither one of them announced he was hungry or exclaimed over the feast she'd prepared.

"The food is ready," she said. She placed a *kouvrepla* over the plate of chicken and fussed with the fritters.

Another look passed between them. Trouble. Chance was in trouble. Her heart raced and her lower back spasmed. She clung to the edge of the counter. "What happened?"

Again, that look. Neither one willing to talk. Brothers together, leaving her out of whatever knowledge they shared. *Chay soti sou tèt, tonbe sou zèpòl.* A load falls from the head onto the shoulder. Things go from bad to worse.

"*Di mwen!* Tell me!" Yara accused her of being too quick to assume the worst. Maybe they had good news. Maybe Chance was going to tell her about the speech.

A very long minute passed. The lazy ceiling fan did nothing to lift the heavy, grease-soaked air of the kitchen, yet Nadine shivered under its rotating blades. Chance looked at Henry. Henry looked at Chance.

"*Di nou.*" Even as she said it, she wished she could hold on to this moment of not knowing.

She picked her way across the room, toward a chair, trying not to wobble, and reminded herself that she was a survivor, a strong Haitian woman. She could handle whatever news these two boys had to give her. The solidity of the chair beneath her gave her strength. "*Chita!*" she ordered them, and they obeyed. Each of them grabbed a seat at the table.

She folded her hands to keep them from shaking. Chance glanced toward Henry who studied the table. "I'm ready," she said. "Chance, what have you done now?"

Chance jerked his head toward her. "What?"

"Henry, what has your brother done?"

"You tripping, Mom!" Chance said. "I ain't done nothing. You always thinking I be doing shit."

Because you are always doing... shit! Nadine thought, letting herself think the bad word. But he was speaking at graduation. Should she mention it now?

"This isn't about me," Chance said. "It's about—"

"You." Henry said.

"Me?"

Chance nodded, his lips trembled as if he might be trying not to cry.

"Me?" She laughed—a confused, relieved gurgle in her chest and throat. "Me?"

Both boys glared at her in strange silent accusation.

"What is it about me?" A flutter filled her chest. "Should we eat while we have this conversation? The food is getting cold." Her hands shook as she lifted the *kouvrepla* from the chicken and speared a piece with a fork. She put a piece on Henry's plate and another on Chance's. Why wouldn't they smile? She squeezed the fork handle and knew. They were going to ask about fathers.

They paid no attention to the food. She leaned back in her chair without serving herself. Her plate sat empty in front of her. She would have to tell them the truth.

"Why didn't you tell us we have different fathers?" Henry pounded the table with his fist. "That's something we have a right to know. Why would you keep that a secret all these years? When were you going to tell us?"

"And mine lives across the river! In Boston! Does he know about me?"

Nadine closed her eyes, rested her forehead on her folded hands, and prayed to *Bondye* and *La Sirèn* and *Èzili* and her mother to put the right words in this mother's mouth—she'd worked so hard to give a good life to these angry boys sitting in front of her. Good boys, bad boys. Mixed up boys. Long silent moments passed. She kept her eyes closed. How did Chance learn that his father lived nearby?

"It's a long story," she said into her hands.

"We got time," Henry said.

"*Bon*." Where to begin? What to tell? What to leave out? No story was ever complete. Where to begin? When her mother died? Before she was born? Before her mother was born? When she came to the US? If they went to Haiti, heard more of the stories, they could put them together and understand for themselves.

Slurping, swallowing, and lip smacking melded into an

encouraging music. She blinked and saw Chance sucking a chicken bone and Henry reaching for another piece of meat.

"It is a long story," she said again. "A big story I don't like to think about. A story I don't like to tell. But it's true that you should hear it."

"It's our story too," Henry said.

Where does one person's story end and another's begin, especially the story of a mother and child, child and mother?

How were the nights she risked Uncle Maxim's beatings and slipped out to meet Lucien anyone's business but hers? Nadine had never had a problem keeping a secret. Her survival had depended on it. A habit of silence was not easy to break.

"I don't know where to begin," she said.

"Just get right to it," Chance said. "Who are these guys? Where are they? Have they ever tried to find us? You can fill in the rest later, right Henry?"

"Tell it however you want." Henry's flat voice lacked any trace of encouragement.

"I don't know exactly where your father is, Henry. Haiti, I think."

"But you know how to find mine." Chance said. "In church. In Mattapan. I could hop on the T and find my father, right?"

She looked from one son to the other. "Who told you that?"

"Doesn't matter," Chance said. "I want you to tell me."

She began to explain that his father was the deacon of the church she'd attended, but the words stuck in her throat. It sounded too ugly. A church deacon, a one-night stand, a naive and foolish woman. There was no excuse for that lapse in judgment. But there was Chance—the product of that union—his life depended on it.

"Henry, your father was my high school sweetheart. We were so inexperienced. My uncle kept me in the house except for school and told me nothing. I met this boy, Lucien, at the bakery in Little Haiti where he swept the floors and washed the trays and gave me the day-old sweets. When you smile, you look like him." Her favorite moments in Miami were spent sitting beside Lucien in the thin strip of shade outside the bakery's back door, throwing crumbs to the birds in the parking lot, crumbs he'd collected from the bread slicer. Once a bright green bird appeared, scattering the pigeons. Awed by the unexpected beauty of that bird, some escaped parrot, they thought, she and Lucien found themselves kissing, then twined together with hands fumbling beneath each other's clothes. His skin tasted like sugar. But this story belonged only to her. And Lucien. Wherever he was, did he remember it?

Henry took off his glasses and rubbed them with a napkin. Chance looked grim. Nadine realized her mistake. "Chance, your father was—is—a powerful man. He helps many people with his influence and money—but I didn't want him to know about you. I didn't want my life tied up with his. He had a wife. She would have cursed me. Her friends would have cursed me."

"So he doesn't know I exist." Chance sounded disbelieving. "I don't think so. I stopped going to that church. Or even to that side of the river. So that people wouldn't talk." It had been painfully easy to disappear. "Henry's father doesn't know about him either," she added, hoping that would help.

"Who talked to you about this?" she asked. "Gary Watkins?"

Their expressions told her she'd guessed right. Gary Watkins and his big mouth! These boys were all she had. They were so angry. If they looked for their fathers, what trouble would they unleash? She resolved to pray and go back to *Manbo* Sivelia for advice on what to do next.

Henry sat silent and still. Chance played with the bones on his plate. All three of them watched his fingers move.

"You never told him about me?" Chance said as the small stack of bones collapsed and fell. Nadine, forehead resting in her hand, focused on Chance's fidgety fingers.

"No," she said.

Footsteps on the stairs broke the silence. Gary Watkins. She'd invited him for dinner, this celebration in honor of Chance, who sat across from her with clenched jaw and blinking eyes. She'd invited him before she knew he'd spilled her secrets. But she herself had slipped, and Henry was on his way to finding out anyway. Maybe Gary would know what to say. Chance and Henry liked him. He knew how to deal with teenagers. She stood to answer the door, hope straightening her shoulders.

"Who the fuck is that?" Henry said. "Chance, who is it?"

"Didn't invite nobody," Chance muttered.

"I invited Coach Watkins," Nadine said.

Chance stood suddenly; his chair crashed to the floor behind him. Nadine flinched, and Chance pushed past her, Henry right behind him. They barged through the door of the apartment, past Gary Watkins, who waited with a bottle-shaped bag. Gary's expectant smile dropped as Chance and Henry thundered down the stairs and out the front door.

"You might as well come in," Nadine said into the silence.

"I brought you this." Gary handed her the bottle. "It's pink. Ronnie over at Riverview told me you liked pink wine."

"Why did you talk about their fathers?" she asked. "That was not for you to tell."

"They pushed me. They needed to know. If you told them the truth long ago, it wouldn't be so hard right now."

"For twenty years I held this secret close. I trusted you," she said. "Don't judge me." She stepped away from him, out of his reach, muscles in her back seizing.

"Nadine, I'm sorry. I—"

"Go away." Why had she ever thought for even a moment this man, this white man, this white American man, this old, white American man, would understand? She was so tired. So angry. So disappointed. "Leave my house."

He stood like a fool. His lips moved, but no words came out.

"I am going to my room now," Nadine said. "Goodbye."

She left him without looking back, passed the uncleared kitchen table, and banged her bedroom door shut behind her with a finality she hoped was loud and clear. Moments later his footsteps sounded on the floor, then stopped. She prepared for his knock, but heard him go into the bathroom instead. The toilet flushed, water ran, more footsteps. If he did tap on the door, would she let him in? No. But if he said good night, she would say good night too. Silence. Footsteps again, and the door to the stairs opened and closed.

She sat on the edge of her bed, clenching and unclenching her fists, haunted by her own story. She had learned early to keep quiet no matter what it cost her. She had lost her family on Lagonav, Lucien in Miami, and an entire church full of kind people in Mattapan by keeping secrets. Her father had died without meeting his American grandsons in the flesh—all because Nadine didn't want him to know about his brother's treachery. Her own brothers had plenty of sons and daughters close by to joke with and scold. The cousins would show Chance and Henry how to slaughter a goat and make her favorite creamy *ji kowosòl*—soursop juice they called it here. She didn't think they'd ever tasted it.

Leftover food waited for her to put it away. Dishes needed her attention. She took a few pills for her back pain, turned the radio on loud, and lay down in bed, unable to face clearing the kitchen of the party that never happened.

C hance stormed ahead of Henry, down the sidewalk, toward Central Square. After a couple blocks he turned another corner and then another, back in the direction of the river. "Yo!" Henry called after him. "Hey!" Chance forged on without responding. Henry's phone rang in his pocket. He fumbled to switch it off as he raced after Chance. It could only be Sage or his mother, or maybe Coach. He wanted to talk with each of them, had to, but not now. The phone continued ringing. All his running had paid off, the distance between them narrowed. Close enough to hear Chance's ragged, smoke-impaired breathing, Henry spoke again. "Where you going?"

Chance stared straight ahead. They approached Mem Drive at a slower jog. Cars whipped past. Chance stopped on the sidewalk, hands on his knees, head down, sucking air. Henry stopped himself from resting a hand on his brother's shoulder. Chance would just shrug it off.

"Want to run along the river?" Henry asked. "We can cross over there at the light."

Chance straightened up and wiped at his cheeks with his shirt. Sweat, not tears. No. They'd run and sweat some more. And maybe they'd talk.

They ran east side by side, toward Mass Ave and MIT and the salt and pepper bridge. It wasn't clear who set the pace. Henry's phone rang again. He didn't answer. Chance's phone played its tune. He didn't answer.

"Want to cross the river?" Henry asked.

"Nah. I'm done," Chance said. "And I'm thirsty. Let's cut back through the streets and find some water. And speaking of finding—you want to find that dude?"

"You mean my father?" The words sounded so strange. "Yours is closer." They crossed Mem Drive again and walked along Main Street for a few blocks, until they reached the dry fountain, the one with the big metal globe in the middle. Chance stopped, as if waiting for the water to shoot from the jets.

"Yours sounds like a better guy. Don't you want to go to Haiti and meet him?"

Henry's mind played with possibilities, a smiling father with arms spread wide, a serious father with an appraising nod, or one of those "deadbeat dads" who refused to recognize Henry and never paid child support. But how could a father give anything to a son he didn't know existed?

"I don't know," Henry said, finally. "You hear those stories about people being all disappointed and shit. Might be better to keep my own idea about him." He realized what he wanted to know was not what he thought of his father but what his father thought of him. "What about you? You gonna track yours down?"

"I want to kick his ass," Chance said. "I want to kick his fucking ass."

"Yeah."

"She loved yours. Mine sounds like a rapist."

"Nah," Henry said.

"Sounds like an asshole," Chance said. "Fucking church guy acting like that."

"She should've told us long before this," Henry said.

"I thought our father was in Haiti." Chance set his foot on the edge of the fountain and stretched his leg. "I liked thinking of him down there, doing his thing."

A father in Haiti had less choice about finding a son. There were visas to consider, and money. But if a man lived in the States, or in the same damn metropolitan area, he could've been around.

"It's her fault," Henry said. "She should've told him. Both of them. It should've been their decision—whether or not to see us. They didn't even have a choice."

"Us!" Chance banged his fist against his thigh. "She should've told us!"

"Well, she didn't." Henry sat on a bench and kicked at an empty soda can. It rolled across the concrete with a lonely sounding rattle. A police car drove past, but didn't slow to check them out. Chance didn't even seem to notice. The sad slump of his shoulders called out for an encouraging brotherly shove or a joke. Henry couldn't gather energy for that. Point was neither of them knew their fathers, and their mother had lied to them about everything but Henry's father's name and smile. And who could say she wasn't lying about that?

"I don't feel like going to the crib," Chance said. "Dealing with mom."

"Let's see who's hanging at Mickey D's. Get us a big ass drink."

"Burgers are better at Wendy's," Chance said.

Henry stood. "Wendy's. McDonald's. Same shit."

"No, no! How can you be saying that?" Chance bumped Henry with his shoulder. "Wendy's burgers be square. They got chili and baked potatoes. Better milkshakes."

"Wendy's got bad service," Henry said.

"No it don't!" Chance laughed. "Slow ain't necessarily bad."

"Aight—Wendy's." As they approached Central Square, more people filled the sidewalks. Chance nodded and smiled at folks Henry didn't know.

"I'd help you kick his ass," Henry said.

"I'd help you kick the other guy's ass," said Chance. "When we go to Haiti."

They crossed the street just before the light changed.

"Take'em one at a time," Chance went on. "The two of us."

"Yeah," said Henry. "If we could find them."

"You know who's ass really needs kicking?" Chance asked.

"You can't kick your mother's ass," Henry said.

Chance stopped. "You shitting me? Mom's? No way. I wasn't thinking about her. Nah. Bro! What you think I am? Shit!"

"Who then?"

"Coach Watkins."

"Maybe, except he's my boss."

"I gots court tomorrow."

"What? Why didn't you say something?

"Saying something now."

"What's supposed to happen?"

"Don't know. Might finish things up." Chance didn't seem too worried.

Henry hesitated. "I'll go with you. Don't have work till afternoon." He waited for Chance's refusal.

"Coach said he'd be there, but I don't know. I don't trust him. Everything be different now he be trying to get with Moms."

"You think he really is?"

Chance gave a *tuipe* as eloquent as any they ever heard from Nadine.

"He's too old for her," Henry said.

"He's too white for her!" Chance said. "Sometimes he bothers me—thinking he's all down with everybody."

Court tomorrow—Chance seemed to have accepted his offer of company—and Sage's arrival the day after that. What would Chance think of her? White hippie girl from California. With locs.

"You buying?" Chance asked.

"No, you are."

"Aight," Chance said. "But I's only buying soda."

"Lots of food at home," Henry said. "Unless Coach ate it all."

"Better not've," Chance said. "If he did, all this ass kicking we be talking 'bout gonna be more than just talk. It gonna be for real. Henry?"

"Yeah."

"Come with me to Mattapan."

"Now?"

"No. Soon. I want to see that guy. We don't have to talk to him if we don't want to, but I want to see him. See his whip, how he dresses. Maybe we can hit him up for some gwop. We could use it to go to Haiti and find yours."

"Why not? Let's get through this court shit first."

The next morning Henry followed Chance out of the courthouse elevator into a dingy lobby. The fluorescent lights buzzed, their artificial glow illuminated buckled paneling, scratched plastic chairs and scuffed floors, a bank of broken pay phones, and bulletin boards stapled with ripped notices. When he'd dressed this morning in his white button down shirt, gray dress pants, tie, and shiny shoes, he'd expected something grand and marble, dim and echoing.

Chance strode down a hallway past a few doors, then stopped abruptly. Henry almost bumped him. "Wrong way," Chance mumbled. They tried another corridor, Chance checking the room numbers and notices on the bulletin boards. Henry considered making a joke but couldn't think of one. It couldn't be a good thing to be late to court.

Back in the lobby, Chance stopped and looked around.

"We should ask somebody," Henry said. People streamed around them.

"Chance!" An efficient-looking woman with an armful of manila folders approached, eyed Chance up and down and seemed to be satisfied with his polo shirt and khakis. "We're going to plead our case today. I need to talk with you." So this was Diana Klein, Chance's lawyer. She looked past Henry. "Where's Mr. Watkins?"

"Uh, he couldn't come."

"I told you that if you didn't want your mother here, he was the next best thing." She muttered something under her breath. Henry thought she said shit. "I want to move on this. Today's judge is the right one to make this happen." She leafed through a folder, her glasses slipping down her nose.

Chance rubbed the back of his head and looked worried.

A spark of fear made their anger at Coach seemed childish. "He can come," Henry said. "We didn't want him to."

The lawyer peered at Henry over her glasses. "My brother," said Chance. "Henry."

She barely nodded before turning to Chance. "Call Gary Watkins now," she said. "Right now. I fail to understand why you wouldn't want your advocate with you. We're trying to convince the court that you're in a position to fulfill the conditions of your probation should you receive a CWOF. Any community support looks good. I've got some character statements here I want to summarize for you before we go in, but the presence of a responsible adult is—"

"My brother's responsible," Chance said.

The lawyer sighed. "Do you have a phone on you?" She turned to Henry, "Do you? If not, use mine." She shoved the folders under her chin contorting to search her purse while anchoring the folders with her arm.

"We can call him," Henry said before the lawyer's folders could fall and scatter important papers across the floor. "On my phone. Can we sit over there?" An empty bench filled an alcove a few steps away. Diana Klein led the way. Behind her back Chance widened his eyes at Henry and shook his head. "You think I like asking him for help?" Henry whispered. "But I'm going to because this is serious shit."

"We ask him here, he'll act like we's asking him to move in, marry our Mom, and be our father."

"Forget that till later," Henry said. He didn't want to talk to Coach Watkins right now. But Chance would be better off if he learned that in this fucked up world it was helpful to have the white man on your side, even a white man who wanted to sleep with—he wouldn't say fuck—your mother. And clearly who your mother slept with, okay, who your mother fucked, was her business, wasn't it? Just like who he fucked, was his. If/when his mother didn't like Sage, he wasn't going to let that stop him. Coach's phone rang and rang. Chance and Diana Klein sat close together on the bench, heads bent over the paper she pointed at with her pen. Coach's message clicked on, and Henry hung up.

"Look here," Diana Klein said. "Your English teacher says you have a lot of talent and in group work are always supportive of classmates who have learning challenges. Your feedback to others is consistently thoughtful. Vice Principal Johnson says that for three years you were a good student who stayed clear of any trouble. Your supervisor from last summer's job says you received an award for being the most reliable worker."

Chance *tuiped*. "Most reliable, compared to those guys? In the land of the blind, a one-eyed man is king." Quoting the Bible? Must be a lyric from a rap. "They had us painting a school and sealing a parking lot. Boss said the most important thing was to learn how to slack and not get caught. He actually passed out copies of the *Herald*, had us sit down in the shade and read until we heard the supervisor's truck. We'd leap up and grab our brushes. Told us to practice listening for the exact sound so we don't waste energy jumping up for the wrong truck. I gots a good ear. A reliable ear." For a moment Chance seemed like his careless, carefree, genuinely happy self, grinning at Henry.

Chance hadn't always been a wannabe G. He'd been a good kid for a long time.

"Well, you don't need to share all that with the judge." Diana Klein frowned and waved a paper from the folder. "And, most important, we have the victim's statement saying that you didn't do anything but stand there, which lends a bit of credibility to your story that you didn't know Clarence James was going to attack the man."

"I didn't know!" Chance said. "I've told you and told you. I'm not guilty."

"You're guilty of bad judgment, which I hope is improving. You made it this far without more trouble. Congratulations. You'll have to continue to stay out of all trouble while on probation."

Henry searched Chance's face for a sign that his brother was taking his lawyer's words seriously instead of cooperating with the government's desire to keep the prison industrial system in business. His phone rang.

Henry checked the number. "Coach," he said.

"Let me talk to him," Diana Klein grabbed the phone.

"Henry?" Coach's voice sounded small and far away.

Chance mumbled something and kicked the floor.

"What?" Henry asked.

Chance pressed his lips together and shook his head.

"He's on his way." Diana Klein handed the phone back to Henry.

They followed her into the courtroom.

After all the worry and waiting, the whole thing was over in five minutes. Gary Watkins hustled in as they stood to leave. He nodded at Chance and Henry and talked with the lawyer a few yards down the hall.

"I still think if we'd gone to trial I could've gotten off," Chance said. "Look at him over there. Look at the two of them."

Chance didn't need to say more. Diana Klein and Gary Watkins chatted like old friends. Two old white people, cronies, good old boys, even though one was a woman, working the system, fuck—they were the system, patting themselves on the back for helping the Black boy. Fuck that. Henry clenched his jaw to keep from saying things he might end up regretting.

"Guess I should be glad it's over," Chance said.

Diana Klein shook Chance's hand, directed him toward the probation department, and hurried off. Chance slipped away without acknowledging Coach Watkins, leaving Henry standing there alone with the guy, a stew of feelings about to boil over.

"That went as well as it could've," Coach said. "She's the best defense attorney around. Chance was lucky."

A sound escaped Henry's nose.

Coach raised his eyebrows. "She is."

Henry said nothing.

"What do you say when Chance gets back, we swing by the nursing home to tell your mother the good news," Coach said. "She'll be relieved."

Henry wanted to smack him for his presumption. Chance might have. But Coach was right. Going to tell her would be a nice thing to do. Coach Watkins knew his mother and cared about her. Coach Watkins cared about their family. He'd even put on a sloppily knotted tie for court. It didn't look right.

As if reading Henry's mind, Coach loosened the tie and ducked his head through it. A tuft of hair stuck out crazy. He looked like a little boy who just woke up, until he stuffed the tie in a pocket and put his worn-out baseball cap back on his head.

☆

Henry, out of breath from running, checked the address on the huge brown-shingled house. He'd walked by it before, one of many buildings he passed without seeing, and never imagined that one day his girlfriend from college would be living there. Third floor, Sage had said—tucked in under the eaves, great view from the dormer windows.

Before he could figure out which bell to ring, he heard his name. He backed off the porch and looked up. There she was—head and shoulders emerging from one of those windows, way above. "Henry!" she shouted. "I'll be right down."

Her voice made him smile all over. Even his knees were smiling. He wiped his glasses with the edge of his shirt and hoped he smelled okay.

Sage flung open the door and hugged him. He closed his eyes and curved his hands around her ass, no underwear beneath her flowy skirt. There was nothing better to hold. He could lose himself in her body, be free of everything else. Every curve and hollow of their bodies fit into each other, and the heat and sweat only made it better.

"I've missed you so much," she whispered. "I want you, Henry, now. I need you."

Need—this kind of need he could handle.

They stumbled up three long flights of stairs, pressed together. "I'm really here!" she said. The apartment door hung open. A mattress covered in a pale blue sheet filled most of the space. She pulled him onto it before he had a chance to look around. She confiscated his glasses and tugged at his belt. Her gauzy dress slipped off easily, and her breasts rose toward his mouth. Her fingers pressed the back of his neck as he sucked her nipples and thumbed the damp folds between her legs. This sexy girl had flown halfway across the country to be with him, and he would make it worth her while.

After, they lay side by side on the rumpled sheet, staring up at the slanted white ceiling, only their fingers touching.

"That was good," she said.

"True dat." What now? Would she expect him to show her some sights? Introduce her to his mother and Chance? He lifted himself onto his elbow and kissed her deep and hard. Maybe they could fuck again.

She arched her back, pressing her nipples into his chest, good sign. But then she pulled away. "I'm hungry."

Henry had plenty of cash in his wallet. He tried to think of nearby vegan-friendly restaurants.

"Let's cook," Sage said. "It can't get any hotter in here than it already is. Our kitchen debut has to involve using the stove."

Our kitchen? Our bed, okay. But "our kitchen" sounded full of expectations. His mother's kitchen was all he needed.

Sage stood and picked her dress off the floor. "I heard the store where Julia Child shopped is right down the block. Let's go."

"You don't want to go to that bougie place. It's known for exotic meat. You want to support a place that sells zebra steaks?" Henry said. He'd take her to Market Basket, where the food was affordable.

Sage maneuvered the cart through the crowded aisles to the produce section. Henry had never been in Market Basket without his mother. It felt strange to be shopping for himself. Sage approved of the tofu selection and tossed four containers of firm organic into the cart. She grabbed two bags of cashews. "Wait'll you taste the cashew cream I'm going to make. You'll love it."

He trailed her through the mounded fruits and vegetables. She knew what she wanted. "Avocados! I never saw them this cheap outside of California. Pick out four, Henry."

She examined some local strawberries, popped one in her mouth, and closed her eyes. "Mmm!" She held one to his lips, but afraid of being accused of stealing, he kept them pressed shut. She ate it herself.

Henry had no idea how to judge an avocado for ripeness. He pulled a plastic bag off the roll and tried to pull it open, but the sides clung together. When they shopped with their mother, Chance opened them. Some people had the knack. Sage was probably one of those people. He moved to hand her the bag, when over near the sweet potatoes, he spotted his mother. Henry ducked behind a man loading his cart with melons. It couldn't be. He lost sight of the woman, told himself he imagined the resemblance, his mother was at work, but he moved away, just in case. They'd barely spoken since he'd learned about the fathers. And the universe could not expect him to introduce his mother to Sage on her first day in Cambridge. He hadn't even decided that he would introduce them at all.

Sage set two pints of strawberries into the seat of their cart. "Okay, just soy sauce and vinegar and what else? Ginger. Back there by the potatoes and plantains."

The unopened bag dangled from Henry's clenched fist.

"You didn't choose avocadoes yet?" Sage sounded frustrated. "I'll do it." She took the bag. "You go get some chips."

Henry hid in the chip aisle, trying to prepare himself for making introductions, if necessary. He studied the chips. So many choices. He didn't know what Sage preferred. This feeling of incompetence wore him down—first at work with Rosie and the kids, and now with Sage and shopping. Then he remembered Sage's moaning in bed less than an hour before and figured he was good at something.

"Henry?" Sage said. "Why are you just standing there smiling? Is everything okay?" She chose a bag of tortilla chips and nudged him with her elbow. "I think I've got everything. Let's go."

She moved toward the checkout lines, and he followed in her wake. When they reached the front of the store, he scanned left and right.

"Down here," Sage said. "I always find the fastest cashier."

She charged through the winding lines of carts and people toward the one farthest on the right. He should've agreed to go to the fancy little grocery store. This place was packed. They'd be waiting forever. At least it was air conditioned. Sage jerked the cart into a tight space behind a mother with two whiny kids. Two lines over stood his own mother, her cart full of yams, chicken, juice, rice, greens, melon.

Sage turned toward him and right there in a grocery line held his chin and stroked it with her thumb and fingers. "You're sweet, Henry."

If *Manman* turned now and saw her son with this girl rubbing his face—

"I'm really glad to be here," Sage said.

Henry told himself to focus on her, forget about his mother. There were lots of people milling around. She wouldn't expect to see him here, especially not with a strange white girl. She'd put her bags in her rolling cart and head home without looking back. Only two more customers in front of her and three in front of him and Sage.

"Henry," Sage said. He wanted to tell her to stop saying his name.

His mother looked over her shoulder and spotted him. A warm smile brightened her face for a moment before her forehead furrowed into a question.

"Henry, *ki sa w ap fè?*" she asked across checkout lines. There was nothing accusatory in her tone. It sounded like a real question.

What was he doing? Buying food to cook with my girl-friend I just spent the afternoon getting it on with. Oh, and you know nothing about her.

"Who's that?" Sage asked.

His mother squeezed past her own cart, heading their way.

"My mother," he said.

"Your mother? Really? Wow! What are the chances of that?" Sage beamed and stepped forward to meet Nadine.

"Hi! I'm so glad to meet you. I'm Henry's ... friend from school, here for the summer."

His mother ignored Sage's extended hand and stared past her, at Henry. "Mom. This is Sage. She just got to town today."

His mother gave Sage a long unreadable look, taking her in—from locs to the jewel in her nose to bony knees to Tevas, silver toe ring, and unpainted nails, then nodded and smiled. "I'm happy to meet you."

"Henry's told me a lot about you," Sage said.

His mother frowned.

"Good things," Sage said.

His mother was wondering why she hadn't heard about Sage.

The man in the next line yelled for Nadine to put her groceries on the belt, and she returned to her line.

"Your mother's so young," Sage said. "Cool we ran into her. Now I just have to meet your brother. Where does he hang out?"

Nadine, groceries packed in her wire rolling cart, waited for them at the end of their checkout line. Sage insisted on paying for the groceries, and Henry knew that his mother, though chatting with the pretty Haitian bagger, took note of that and every other thing happening between Sage and him. They'd walk together until their routes split. He'd be polite and so would she, though she'd hammer him with questions later.

He and Sage each carried a bag in their arms. Nadine rolled her cart along behind her. They cut through the busy parking lot. Nadine and Sage chatted about the steamy weather and how different it was from California and Lagonav.

"We're going to cook dinner," Sage said. "Do you want to eat with us?"

Henry tripped on an uneven crack in the pavement and caught himself. It was okay. *Manman* wouldn't accept the invitation. The meat in her cart would go bad in this heat.

"We can put the perishables in my refrigerator. I'm staying right up there."

When Henry had pictured Sage and his mother meeting, he'd always imagined *Manman* cooking for Sage, not the other way around. He'd worried about Sage rejecting his mother's chicken, not his mother refusing Sage's tofu.

When they entered the apartment, Henry saw it through his mother's eyes. She regarded the tangled sheets on the mattress.

"You live here by yourself?" she asked.

Sage stowed the package of chicken legs in the refrigerator without comment. She told Nadine to sit down and poured her a big glass of water.

The early evening light slanted across the wood floor and the unfamiliar room glowed orange, like in a movie or even a painting—*Manman* and Sage together, on this long June day, voices blending. Sage brought her a knife, cutting board and vegetables. His mother chopped while Sage began to fry tofu, garlic, and ginger. Henry opened and closed drawers until he found a knife for himself.

"It's nice to have someone else do the cooking," Nadine said.

"It's easy when there's help with the prep," said Sage.

Knives hit the cutting boards. Tofu sizzled. "What was Henry like when he was a little boy?" Sage scraped the vegetables into the pan, and Henry set the table.

"Oh no!" he said. "Don't get her going on that."

"He was serious, and when he was little, he was sickly. All the time, asthma. So skinny. And even though he wasn't quite two years older than his brother, he took care of Chance. I could always count on Henry."

That was it? That his mother saw him this way was no surprise, but tonight it pissed him off to be this predictable a character in his mother's story. They ate quickly.

"That was very good," *Manman* said. "I always like the taste of ginger."

"Me too!" said Sage.

"Did your mother cook like this?" Nadine asked. "Is this California food?"

"My mother didn't cook at all." Sage's tone kept Henry from saying anything even though he felt the pressure of his mother waiting for more.

"I'll go now," said Nadine finally. "It's almost dark. Henry, you're coming?"

Sage glanced at him, eyebrows raised. She handed Nadine the package of chicken.

"I'll carry the groceries down." A slight lift of his head told Sage he'd be back.

He set the cart down on the sidewalk and hugged his mother. "Don't wait up."

Disappointment crossed her face, but she didn't argue. "In the grocery store, Henry," she said. "Were you hiding from me?"

"No!" he answered quickly.

"I hope you're not ashamed of me," she said.

"No." He smoothed his voice. "No—I ..."

His mother waited, her expression hurt, then skeptical, then hurt again.

Finally, when he said nothing, she said, "What a pretty girl. But why does she do that to her hair?"

"There's nothing wrong with her hair." Henry realized he'd stopped being bothered by it.

"She never eats meat?"

"Nope."

"Do you like tofu, Henry?"

"I do, actually."

"What kind of a mother doesn't cook?" His mother sucked her teeth. "Well, good night. Be careful."

Of what?

"Good night." Henry kissed her on each cheek. A rush of freedom propelled him up the stairs. Sage waited at the top.

"Your mother didn't like me," she said.

"I like you." He wrapped his arms around her.

She wriggled free. "But your mother didn't."

"She said you were a pretty girl."

"But she didn't like me."

"She doesn't know you yet," Henry said. His kiss ended the pointless conversation. He was a good kisser.

N adine stood on *Manbo* Sivelia's front walk and watched Gary Watkins drive away. He'd asked to come in, but she'd ordered him off, the only words they'd exchanged during the forty minute ride. Thank goodness they both liked *kompa*. If Yara had been around, she would not have asked him to bring her.

She took three steadying breaths as Yara always recommended, and the thick summer air calmed her. She rang the bell.

Sivelia flung the door open as if she'd been standing right behind it waiting. She pressed a hand against each of Nadine's cheeks and studied her for a moment. "I thought I would see you long before this," the *manbo* said. "You look very tired."

She ushered Nadine ahead of her into the house, a firm hand against the small of Nadine's back, right where it tended to hurt, right where Gary Watson pressed his fingers. A shiver flared up her spine and through her shoulders.

Nadine dropped her rolled up dollars into the open lunch box and followed Sivelia down the stairs into the cool basement. They poured libations in the four directions, lit the string-wrapped white candle, and sat knee to knee on the folding chairs, in flower-scented candlelight, *pànye* resting between them.

"Yes." Sivelia studied the cards she cast. "I hear the same message. You have not made plans yet to return to Haiti."

Guilt burned Nadine's cheeks. "It's not easy to find money for that."

Manbo Sivelia pointed to a ten of diamonds. "Money is coming."

She took Nadine's hands over the cards and peered into her face. "Your son, as you know, he needs male energy. Without the right kind, he will seek out the wrong kind. This energy does not have to come from a father. Better a cousin, an uncle, a teacher, than the wrong kind of father. Men and women love differently. People need more than one kind of love."

A coach! Nadine thought. She pulled her hands free, tipping the *pànye,* but Sivelia caught it before the cards shifted.

Sivelia touched a red card—a heart, a jack.

"Perhaps someone loves you and your sons. Do you know who this might be?" Sivelia persisted.

A humming started in Nadine's lower abdomen and swelled between her legs. Sivelia tapped the card. A buzzing filled Nadine's ears as her face tensed. She kept her mouth pressed shut, even while the *manbo* scrutinized her. She shifted in her seat, trying to relieve the pressure in her crotch without shaking the *pànye*.

"Your brothers, your sons' uncles, when you think of them, what do you see? What are they telling you?" The pressure dissolved.

"Just like before. They're calling me."

Sivelia regarded Nadine with impatience. "Money is coming. It is a mistake to give money worries too much power." She swept up the cards. Nadine cut the deck. Sivelia laid them out once more.

"This is very interesting," she said. "Again, quite clear. This is a time of great change for you in work, in love, in your household. Comings and goings. Transitions, cross-roads. A death here—not a close relative.

"And a return. Perhaps one of your sons is coming home? Perhaps it is your own return home? Perhaps both? That part is not so clear to me."

Sivelia dealt the cards one more time. "Do you have any questions?"

"If, if, I am saying only if, there was a man. We can say, maybe a teacher. Who wanted to help my son." Nadine pressed her fingers into her hair and massaged her scalp. "What if he was old? And white? And might want to be more than a friend to me?"

Sivelia waited, surveyed the cards, and sat quietly.

Nadine folded her hands in her lap. "I would like to know what to do, if that happens."

"You must be honest with people, your sons, any man who might love you," she said. *"Verite se tankou lwil nan dlo, li toujou anlè."*

Nadine flinched. Truth is like oil in water, it always comes to the surface. Truth had been surfacing lately.

"Pray," *Manbo* Sivelia said. "Make offerings. Come back to see me."

Sivelia walked her to the screen door. Gary Watkins leaned against his car, sucking on a giant iced coffee. *Manbo* Sivelia raised her eyebrows. "Oh, oh?"

Nadine flushed.

"You must have faith, *cheri.*" Sivelia kissed her cheeks. "And be honest. Be honest most of all with yourself." The *manbo's* knowing little smile burned into Nadine's shoulder bones as she walked toward the car. Gary raised his coffee at her.

"How'd it go?" He opened the car door. She didn't answer.

Settled behind the wheel, he went on talking. "Had three glazed at Dunkin' Donuts. Forgot how addictive those things are. And this giant coffee. Couldn't even finish it." He shook the cup at her again, the ice sloshing. "Want some? No sugar in it though."

Nadine waved it away. She wanted quiet to reflect on the reading, but she'd been silent on the ride over and he'd devoted a whole evening to this trip. She owed him the politeness of a little conversation. "Coffee with no sugar is no kind of coffee," she said.

"Sorry. I should have grabbed some." He fit the cup into the holder and turned on the air conditioning. They drove through quiet suburban streets. On the ramp to the highway, while checking the side mirror, Gary asked again, "How'd it go? Any surprises? Useful advice?" They joined the rush of cars driving toward Boston.

"Anything about an older man?" Gary laughed, as if to show he wasn't serious, but his hands gripped the steering wheel as though he needed to steady himself, and he wouldn't look at her. "Short, white, and ugly?"

"I need to go home," Nadine said.

"Taking you there now." He changed lanes and sped up.

"No. Home to Haiti. I need to go to Haiti and bring Henry and Chance."

Gary Watkins's forehead wrinkled. He watched the road.

"Do you think Chance would be permitted to leave while he is on probation?"

They'd play soccer in the red dirt field near the big mango tree with their cousins, grind peanut butter with their aunties, and, with their uncles, ride motorcycles, build furniture, plant fields, and play dominoes. She'd pray with them at their grandparents' tomb overlooking the ravine and the dark mountains rolling to the sea.

"I think we could find a way to make it work," Gary said. "If you're sure that's what you want to do. Some people think there's too much unrest right now—with the elections coming up later this year."

"That trouble is in the cities," Nadine said. "Not on Lagonav." He'd said *we*. Why did she have to like this *we* so much? But when she imagined home, she did not see Gary Watkins. Did he think he would be traveling with them?

"I should have told Chance and Henry the truth about their fathers," she said. "Secrets are no good. Shame keeps people stuck with a secret. I was ashamed."

Light flickered across Gary's glasses.

"Shame is heavier than a sack of salt. *Wont pi lou pase sak sèl.* I am tired of carrying that. *Manbo* Sivelia reminded me of another proverb. *Verite se tankou lwil nan dlo, li toujou anlè.*"

Gary half-turned his face. "Translate please. Something about oil and water—not mixing? Like us—we don't mix?"

"No. Not that." Nadine, full of appreciation for the ride, for the attention he gave her sons, for future doors he could help her to open, wished she could care about him more. She wished he were younger and at least part Haitian. If he spoke *Kreyòl*, they would understand each other better. "It translates: Truth is like oil in water, it always comes to the surface. But it was not up to you to tell my boys about their fathers."

"I'm sorry about that, Nadine. But while waiting for the truth, a lot can happen—a whole life. A whole life of secrets and lies."

"People have too much power to make others feel ashamed. The church, the society ... I should tell you the truth right now," she said.

"Oh, please do. Go ahead." Gary sounded mean, angry. Hurt.

"My heart is tired," she said.

They drove in another long stretch of silence all the way to the toll booth. They crossed the river into Cambridge. He stopped in front of her house and parked the car, but kept the engine running.

"That's it?" Gary leaned toward her, palms outstretched. "Seriously?"

She denied the flicker of yearning in her belly, unbuckled her seatbelt, opened the car door, and put one foot on the sidewalk.

"Nadine, wait. I—" He laid a hand on her thigh. "Please."

She turned toward him. Truth surfacing. Her chest, her stomach, and the secret place between her legs bubbled with truths. She wanted someone to hold her. She wanted to ease his loneliness. She wanted him to help her. He had helped her. She didn't want to owe him anything. She didn't want to need anything. No. And she didn't love him like that. This was too much, too complicated. That was the truth. She pulled away, breathing hard.

"I am more comfortable if you are, my friend," she said. Without waiting for his response, she pushed herself out of the car and closed the door.

Their mother insisted on front row seats. The alternative school's graduation was in the youth center's gym. It looked pretty good—an official podium, rows of shiny folding chairs with cushioned seats, a flower arrangement. Henry put a program on a chair for Sage who insisted on joining them—she still hadn't met Chance—and looked around for Gary Watkins—strange he wasn't there. "We should save a spot for Coach, right?"

"There are many empty seats," his mother said.

When Chance heard he didn't have to wear a cap and gown at this ceremony, he'd gone out and gotten himself a fancy-ass suit—Henry didn't want to think about where the money had come from—blinding white jacket and pants with an apricot-colored shirt, open at the neck, gold cross on a thick chain. Since when had he gotten religious?

The graduates stood along the wall. Chance held some pages ripped from a spiral notebook—they still had the raggedy edges hanging off them.

A woman, long dark hair swinging over her smooth brown back and shoulders, her summery flowered dress swirling around her legs, walked back and forth along the line of students, adjusting a collar here, a strand of hair there. When she stopped in front of Chance, she straightened his gold cross and laughed.

"That's the guidance counselor," his mother said. "*Li bèl!*"

"Mind if I sit here?" Rosie stood over him, her bare knees

almost brushing his leg. She answered his what-are-you-doing-here look before he had to ask the question out loud. "My cousin's graduating."

"Go ahead," Henry said. Coach would have to find another spot. "Save that seat next to you for Sage."

"You've never met my cousin, Jewell." Rosie pointed to an animated dark girl in a bright blue dress standing near Chance.

Henry didn't have to turn around to feel his mother's interest. She leaned into and over him, her happy energy up another notch. "Rosie! *Dat mwen pa wè w.*"

"Did Henry tell you we're working together?" Rosie opened the door for his mother's excited questions in *Kreyòl*. Is he doing a good job? Is he a hard worker? Did he make good decisions? Was he on time? Did she enjoy working with him?

Rosie answered his mother's questions, while tracking Chance in her peripheral vision. *Manman* nodded so repeatedly and smiled so big, her neck and face were going to hurt later from the strain. She patted Rosie's knee and invited her over for dinner.

Sage slid, out of breath, into the seat beside Rosie. "Sorry, I'm late. Hello, Ms. Antoine. Hi, Henry." His mother nodded, lips tight.

"This is Rosie," Henry said.

"Let me switch seats with you," Rosie offered. Nadine sucked her teeth.

"It's okay," Henry said. "It's starting."

Chance and his classmates filed over to their chairs, as applause filled the gym up to the ceiling. You wouldn't think the number of people in the room could have made such noise. His mother was the first to stand, and the rest of the crowd followed in clumps. Stamping, clapping, hollering—a room full of people who hadn't thought they'd see the day when these kids would be done with high school made a lot of noise! The tears sliding down his mother's cheeks messed with Henry's resolve to stay cool with Rosie and Sage right there beside him. Fuck it, they were yelling as loud as anyone. He spotted Coach Watkins over by the gym doors. Henry put an arm around his mom. She rewarded him with a quavery smile. Sage winked in approval.

The principal stood at the podium and motioned for people to sit. After another long minute of applause, the noise subsided and people settled. The principal began his generic graduation talk about pride and Cambridge and hard work. "Faculty and students of this extension school have chosen today's speakers—Wilma Taylor and Chance Antoine. Ms. Taylor?"

A skinny girl with huge glasses, big teeth, and bony elbows, hunched over the podium. She flattened her paper, glanced at the crowd, and back down again.

"I moved here to Cambridge from Alabama to live with my father. I'd never been up north before." Her voice rang out, big and sure. In a strong southern accent, she went on to talk about her mother's death, the grief she suffered, the help she'd received at the alternative school, how it was like the family she'd left behind. She didn't look up again until she'd finished. The microphone amplified her relieved sigh, and the audience laughed, an appreciative laugh full of support, before the applause rang out.

"It is my great pleasure," said the beautiful counselor, "to introduce this next speaker. This young man has spent his short time at our school working hard to complete his graduation requirements and apply to college. He embodies that rare ability to work when it is time to work and play when it is time to play, and brings his passion to everything he does. I know you'll all join me in giving Chance Antoine a round of applause."

"What's that in his hand?" Henry asked his mother. It looked like a tiny brush and Chance was rubbing the bristles between his thumb and forefinger.

"Shh." Nadine stared at Chance.

"It's a makeup brush," Rosie said, blinking. "It calms him."

How do you know? he almost asked. "He doesn't seem nervous."

Chance loved the spotlight. He adjusted the mic and threw back his shoulders.

"When I was chosen to be one of the graduation speakers, I thought it was a joke. My brother, Henry, right there, is the smart one in our house. He's also the older one, so teachers knew him first and they expected me to be just like him, serious, studious—a great guy, but completely different from my kind of greatness. You feel me? I think I disappointed everyone including my Mom right there—hi *Manman*—right from the start with my inability to take things serious."

Henry heard his mother suck her teeth. She shook her head. He turned to look at Coach Watkins, who was nodding, arms folded across his chest, leaning back against the wall, as if settling in for a long story. Chance paused and lifted his chin at Rosie.

"Life is full of haters, right. Life is a drawer full of knives, especially for the Black man, right? So why not laugh? Laughing, joking, enjoying the moments as they come doesn't mean you don't got—have—don't have something important to offer to the world. We have a proverb, *Se kouto sèl ki konnen sa ki nan kè yanm.* Only the knife knows what is in the heart of the yam. Can't judge by appearances. People must be put to the test. Difficult times reveal a person's true character."

"Mmhmm," Rosie said and rolled her eyes. Chance took an audible breath.

"No doubt we have it easy compared to our enslaved ancestors. No doubt we have it easier than our parents, who came from other places, had to learn a new language, a new culture, but everyone's got knives stabbing their hearts. Everyone's got a knife with their name on it. Your knife might not be my knife, but it hurts anyway. You gonna walk around radiating negativity or try to smile through the pain? That's a choice.

"People around you be having difficult times and you want to be there for them, you want to help them, and sometimes you don't know how. When you look at a person, you don't know what they been through. You don't know how they getting by. You have to watch and see. The same man can be a terrorist or a freedom fighter, a hero or a war criminal, depending on who's judging.

"Brother Malcolm, Malcolm X, said, 'There is no better teacher than adversity. Every defeat, every heartbreak, every loss, contains its own seed, its own lesson on how to improve your performance next time.' Us at this school, we know trouble, and today we are graduating. May our performances keep on improving. I thank the staff of this school, especially Ms. Garcia, Coach Gary Watkins over there for keeping an eye on me, my brother for handing me books, especially Malcolm's autobiography, and standing by me even when I act the fool. Most of all, I thank my Mom for working so hard to raise us right, no real help from anyone.

"Malcolm said, 'If you don't stand for something, you'll fall for everything.' It's time we figure out what we stand for and live it with a whole heart. Don't fear the knife. Congratulations, class of 2005."

Chance raised his arms as if he'd just scored a really big touchdown. Their mother was crying, clapping wildly, Coach too. Chance found Henry and raised his eyebrows in a question. Henry nodded, and Chance gave a small pleased smile, unlike the oversized grins Henry was used to seeing on his brother's face. Chance wove through the crowd toward him, accepting compliments on the way.

"Congratulations," Henry said.

"Now you know. You ain't the only scholar in the family." Chance rubbed his knuckles across Henry's scalp. "Damn, that line for the food is long. Let's go outside so's I can breathe."

Sage, Rosie, her cousin Henry, and Chance clustered together, squeezed in by the surrounding crowd. Their mother stood talking with Wilma Taylor's father over near their seats.

"Congratulations, Chance," Rosie said.

"Thanks." Chance bit his lip. "Didn't expect to see you here."

"Wouldn't miss my cousin's graduation," she said.

"I'm Sage," Sage said. "Congratulations."

Chance gave his smirky, flirty smile. "Where you been hiding?"

Their little group squeezed through the crowd in the direction of the door. "Wish I had a blunt right now," said Chance, the minute they escaped the building.

"I got one," Jewell said. "Where we gonna light up?"

"Back there—behind those bushes." Chance pointed across the field and began walking in big bouncy strides before Henry could object, one arm around Sage, the other around Jewell. "Henry, Rosie, you coming?" he called over his shoulder.

"Nah," Henry said. "Not me."

"Rosie?" Chance asked.

Rosie shook her head. Henry put a hand on her back.

Sage tilted her head and raised her eyebrows at Henry.

"Go," he said. "You don't need my permission."

"That's okay," Sage stopped and slipped from under Chance's arm. "I'll wait here. I've been meaning to check out this mural." She gestured to the wall of the youth center.

Chance and Jewell ducked into the bushes.

"You didn't have to hold back on my account," Henry said.

"I don't need to get high right now," Sage said. "This is the mural you told me about, right? I was late cause I was trying to find that panther you said you painted." She wove her fingers between his and pulled him away from Rosie, close to the painted wall, pressing her body against him. He didn't want to want her right now, but he'd slept at home the last few nights and his body missed her.

"See you later, Henry." Rosie edged away. "Tell my cousin I went home."

Sage kissed him, and he tried to relax. No Cambridge cop would be looking to arrest a kid for a little weed at graduation.

Chance and Jewell staggered toward them, laughing and bleary-eyed.

Sage studied the mural. "I give up," she said. "Show me your panther."

"Show me your panther?" said Chance. "Is that what you said? Panther, that's what girls be calling it now?"

How could his brother be so fucking smart one minute and such an idiot the next? Some people might blame it on the weed, but it was more than that.

He knew exactly where on the wall the panther crouched. The little black face that he'd meant to look mysterious and menacing, but turned out cute. It looked like a cuddly kitten. He didn't really want to show it off.

"That right there," Chance tapped it with the toe of his brand-new, bone-white kicks. "That sweet little pussy is Henry's."

"Awww," said Jewell. "It's cute."

"Rosie said to tell you she went home," Henry said.

"He was eleven," said Chance. "He painted it over and over, trying to get it right. Finally, Coach had to make him stop. 'But that's not what I see in my head,' he kept saying. 'I need to fix it.'"

They all laughed. Why was that funny? Why couldn't they have let him keep trying until it met his expectations? He remembered thinking it would be around in a public place for a long time, and he wanted it to be right. Look, here they were, eight years later, laughing at it, proving his point.

"I knew right away that the panther was Henry's animal totem," Sage said.

Chance and Jewell laughed again, not realizing she was serious. Henry faked a laugh too, and put his arm around Sage's bare shoulders.

"Bet the food line's gone down," he said before Sage could start dropping knowledge about all the panther symbolized and all it revealed about him. Chance would laugh his ass off. Henry would be hearing about it for the rest of his life.

The reception swirled around Nadine, everybody talking, sweating, drinking warm punch from cheap little paper cups, hers soggy and threatening to collapse in her hand. She swallowed the last mouthful as Gary Watkins headed her way. Chance and Henry with Rosie's pretty Haitian cousin and Sage stood near the food table, laughing together, eating cookies. Chance shoved a handful into his mouth.

Gary squeezed between groups of chattering, hugging people.

"*Zanmi m,*" he said and stood still in front of her, hands at his sides.

"My friend," she said. "*Wi.*" She kissed one cheek, then the other, careful not to bump his glasses, careful not to brush his lips.

"Good speech!"

"Yes."

She crumpled the paper cup, and drops of sticky punch spilled onto her fingers. She and Gary faced each other, the only silent, unsmiling people in the room.

"Na—"

"Gar—" They interrupted each other, spoke again, interrupted each other again, then dropped into silence.

Gary blinked, scratched his ear, then his head. He looked at the floor and rubbed the back of his neck. She remembered his hands on her back and how good they'd felt.

"Brand new floor," Gary said. "And they have to serve food in here." He stooped to pick up some crumbs and wipe at a spill with a shred of napkin.

"This is a nice place," Nadine said. "Very cheerful."

"You didn't see it before they fixed it up, did you?" he asked. "Pretty dingy then." He held the crumbs and napkin in his hand as if he didn't know what to do with them, then along with her paper cup put them in his pocket. He took her hands.

"I still can't believe it—all those years of knowing your boys, all those basketball games and homework hangouts and you right around the corner—"

"I was working!" she said. She would not feel bad for not being one of those American—what did they call them? Soccer moms. Startled, he dropped her hands. She hadn't meant to be so harsh. "I'm glad they had the youth center to come to."

"Those boys are good people," he said. Together Gary and Nadine watched as Chance slapped Henry on the shoulder and Henry bumped back into him. "They always took care of each other—even when they were little guys. I used to think Henry, being older and all, took care of Chance, but when Henry hesitated at the edge of the playground or sat alone on the bleachers, it was always Chance who noticed and called him over to join the game."

Her sons didn't look as though they'd suffered any, without fathers. She'd done it—alone, raised two fine young men. She was only thirty-six. Time to think about her own future.

"Nadine." Gary's voice was husky. Her stomach clenched as she prepared herself for some unwanted declaration of love.

"I want to give you this." He pulled an envelope from his pocket. "A graduation present for Chance, for your family. From my mother. I sold the trailer. It should cover tickets and whatever else you need for that trip to Haiti—gifts for family, whatever."

Tears gathered in her throat. "I ... I ..."

He shoved the envelope at her. "Take it. We're friends, right?"

Nadine's hand shook. She wanted that trip. She'd even considered going to the deacon since he'd escaped child support all these years, but she hadn't been able to do it. Gary folded her fingers around the envelope and patted her arm. "We're friends, Nadine. Okay. No strings attached. I care about you and the boys. I love you and the boys."

"I'm sorry," she said. "Thank you."

Three short phrases that almost covered the human condition. I love you. I'm sorry. Thank you. Useful in any order.

Henry sat on the steps of Sage's porch in the thickening summer twilight. She was late coming from class. Maybe he should have accepted the key she'd offered him a month ago, but her eagerness to give it to him had only triggered a strong reluctance to take it. He almost pressed her number on his phone—two on speed dial after Chance at number one—then decided to wait. He considered calling Chance. Since graduation they saw each other at the center, where they kept busy—Henry helping kids spell their stories and Chance helping them perfect their team work, shots and picks. Chance and Rosie talked again, more with each other than Henry did with either one of them. No, he'd see his brother tomorrow; calling while he sat locked out of Sage's apartment seemed pathetic. What would he even say? He'd only be calling to pass the time.

He had the syllabus for the linguistics class Professor Edmund asked him to TA in fall. If he'd brought that article by Yves Dejean, he could make good use of what was left of the daylight. He had to let Sage know he was staying in Boston. He'd hinted, but people heard what they wanted to hear and didn't hear what they didn't want to. His whole life, the whole father lie, was a good example of that.

He heard Sage's glittery laugh even before he saw her round the corner. She approached, surrounded by three other chattering people—friends from class. Henry recognized Ally, a very tall blonde girl; Kenny, an Asian guy with a spiky hair cut, and Paul, a raggedy looking white guy who reminded him of Bear back at school. Maybe they were just walking her home, but they carried Market Basket bags, and the good time they were having didn't seem to be winding down.

"Henry! Sorry, I'm late. I told them you'd understand 'cause you know how long those Market Basket lines can be. We're going to make dinner."

"Hi, Henry," Ally said.

Sage went on. "Kenny brought the vegetable slicer his

mother brought back from Japan. It makes noodles out of zucchini! We're going to make veggie pad thai."

Did she really expect him to be excited about that?

"Hey, man," said Kenny.

"I wish you'd told me people were coming over," Henry whispered.

She rolled her eyes and pushed past him to unlock the door, Kenny right behind her. Ally stepped back to let Henry go ahead, and Paul took up the rear.

Henry hadn't been in the apartment with anyone but Sage, and his mother that one time. These new friends settled in quickly—Ally unpacked the groceries at the counter, Kenny clamped the fancy veggie slicer to the table, and Paul filled a pipe with weed.

"Don't be boring," Sage murmured, handing Henry an onion. "Can you chop this?"

He reached around Ally for a knife and cutting board and resisted making a comment about putting the onion in Kenny's machine.

"Henry, slice the cabbage and peppers too, okay?" Sage thunked them down beside his cutting board. "Henry learned all about cutting vegetables at school, working in the dining hall. He could probably even make zucchini noodles without that machine."

He was sweating and steaming his glasses. If he took them off, he'd start tearing up from the onions. Caught between pride in his knife skills and fury at being treated like a kitchen boy, he told himself he was overreacting and chopped as fast as he could without slicing off a tip of a finger.

The sweet smell of weed filled the air. Kenny shoved zucchini into the slicer while the others, except Henry, gathered close. At first the "noodles" came out in short, broken pieces, but Sage figured out that success depended on the size and shape of the squash and cranked out a giant bowl of zucchini strips that had no end, while her friends applauded and praised her.

"Want a hit?" Paul held the pipe toward Henry. "Weed's going to make this food taste real good."

Henry accepted. He'd be more able to get through dinner with his edges blurred.

Ally shook up a jar of peanut sauce. "This food will be good, weed or no," she said.

Sage collected Henry's evenly chopped vegetables, added them to the bowl of zucchini, threw in cubes of tofu. "Grab plates, people. I almost whacked my elbow on that machine," Sage said. "Henry? Move it?"

He looked at her across the table. She looked back. Along the tense thread between them was a silent scary place around which spun the serving, eating, talking.

"I'm not your boy, Sage."

Her face scrunched up. He felt a pang of sympathy before Kenny's laugh squelched it.

"So sensitive," Kenny said. "Our own government put my ancestors in concentration camps—my grandfather lost his whole agribusiness—worth millions. But Japanese people know how to get by, move on. My grandfather's a millionaire again two times over."

Henry put down his fork.

"Never mind," Sage said quickly. "I can do it."

Kenny scraped back his chair and stood. "I'll take care of it."

"I can't believe you just said that," Henry said.

"Oppression isn't a contest," said Paul. "Everybody relax."

"What do you know?" Ally said. "As a white man, you have no idea."

"And you do?" Kenny asked.

"Yes, sexism is alive and well. I could give a million examples. Even today in class, that girl who said 'I'm not a feminist,' like being one would be so terrible."

Relief smoothed Sage's face as she chimed in with Ally. "The women's movement was the biggest peaceful revolution in this country," she said.

Kenny returned to the table having packed up the slicer, a smug look on his face.

"Besides," Sage continued, "anyone who really cares about social justice would be vegan, for so many reasons. I even convinced Henry that a plant-based diet is necessary in order to feed the world and slow global warming."

Henry hadn't ever been this heated except at his brother. He didn't want to flip out in front of these strangers. He focused on his plate, but couldn't imagine taking a bite. What would Chance say? He'd tell a joke, a good joke. Professor Edmond? He'd give a lecture on the historical roots of racism with an emphasis on Haiti, slavery, and Creole. Gary Watkins? Gary Watkins would combine those approaches, but talk about the racism right here in Cambridge. Henry avoided Sage's attempts to catch his eye as he tried to figure out what to say or do next. She and the rest laughed at Kenny's imitation of the "I'm not a feminist" girl.

Echoes of Malcolm X pounded in his head. He wanted a good quote to throw at these people. But he kept fixating on something he'd read just a few days ago—a 1963 interview in which Malcolm criticized Black people for marrying outside their race. When he read it, he'd strongly disagreed. In this moment he understood the reasoning. In the Africana Studies department of UMass Boston, he would not be the one trying to educate everyone around him, even as a TA, and that was going to be a big relief.

"Are there feminists in Haiti?" Ally asked.

Everybody stopped talking and looked at him.

"Never been to Haiti, but I know the country is full of strong women." Henry's agreeable tone surprised himself. He could get through this dinner, then talk rationally to Sage, tell her it had been great—especially the sex—but he wouldn't be in Minneapolis in the fall and in a few weeks he was going to Haiti, so they might as well end it now.

"Guess they'd have to be," said Paul. "Poorest country in the western hemisphere."

"And Haitian men aren't very reliable, right?" Ally said. "I don't mean you, Henry. I know you're American."

Henry slammed his fist on the table, knocking over his water glass. "Really?" he said. "Am I really hearing this?"

"Never mind." Sage leaped for a dish towel and leaned over him mopping the water, one hand on his back. "You know, Henry told me that whenever his mother spills something it's like a libation to the ancestors—when she spills coffee, it's like sharing coffee with her dead mother." She talked quickly and brushed her lips against Henry's cheek.

He was finished. "I need to go. It's been fun."

"Wait," Sage grabbed his arm.

"I'm leaving." He pulled away without giving her friends another look. She followed him down the stairs.

"Henry, please wait," she said.

"Your friends are up there," he said.

"I don't care." She clutched his arm. "They don't know any better. Drop some knowledge on them. They're not bad people."

"Look, you're a good person, but this isn't good. What we have isn't good."

"The sex is good." She touched his neck just behind his ear in the way she knew made him crazy.

He shook her off. "The sex was really good. Really really

good. I'll remember it my whole life. But I can't do this. And I'm staying here in the fall. So there's no point."

"Staying here? Not going back to Minneapolis?" She wasn't crying. He was thankful for that. She'd go upstairs, and her friends would be waiting with dessert and more weed. Sage would be fine.

He turned from her sad face. "Hope the rest of your class goes well. And your summer."

Anything she'd say would only make him feel worse, so he took off down the steps and around the corner before she could reply.

A block away he pressed the one on his cell phone and Chance answered.

"Yo, Bro," Henry said.

"What up? You okay?"

"Yeah, why?"

"I don't know—you sound funny."

Henry walked fast through the warm evening, big strides, noticing nothing around him, no destination in mind.

"I think I just broke up with Sage."

"No shit?"

"No shit."

"Wanna ball up? I'm at the center, 'bout to lock up, but I can wait. Coach'll let me drop the keys at his house."

"Yes!" Henry began to jog. One-on-one with his brother was just what he needed right now. Chance always ended up winning at first, that height advantage, but if they played long enough, three out of five, to twenty-one, he might end up ahead.

F ull Gospel looked more like an old school than any image Henry had of a church.

"Because it *is* an old elementary school," Chance said, pointing out the words Lincoln Elementary carved in the stone over the metal doors. Chance rested the basketball on his hip, reached deep in his pocket for a scrap of paper, and checked the address. "But now it's a church. Look." On the scrap of browning lawn stood a small white sign that said in black block letters "Full Gospel Church" and just below that an inspirational quote: "Forbidden fruit creates many jams." Henry wanted to comment on the irony factor, but had a feeling Chance wouldn't take it well.

Nothing moved on the quiet street, a block off busy Blue Hill Ave. In an ad for the church in the phonebook, they'd read that the deacon led a Wednesday night Bible study at 7:00. Henry hoped they could catch him before it started. Though he'd do it for his brother, he didn't feel like going to the class itself on such a warm summer night when the evening shadows had taken the edge off the heat of the day. They could be shooting hoops on the court by the river.

Their first instinct was to crouch behind the cars parked along the street, but Henry pointed out that they wouldn't want to look suspicious. To the deacon, they'd be two anonymous guys.

"Let's do this thing," Chance said and led the way up the worn steps, onto a dangerous looking mat made of sharp metal rectangles, designed to scrape dirt from parishioners' shoes. It bit into the soles of their sneakers and crunched against the stone beneath it in a way that hurt Henry's teeth and prickled his neck.

Chance pulled one door and then the other, but they were locked tight.

"Let's check the back," Henry said.

A driveway on the side of the building opened into a big empty parking lot. A chain link fence separated the lot from the backside of a row of businesses. The barbecue wafting from a restaurant competed with the rotten smell of the dumpsters.

A silver-gray convertible, Al Green's "Let Stay Together" blasting from the radio, ripped into the lot and pulled up into the space closest to the building. Chance dribbled the ball a few times.

"That's an Audi A4," he mumbled. "Guy's got gwop."

"Is it him?" Henry asked.

"Who else would it be?"

The man sat in the car while the roof replaced itself in a choreographed series of moves. The music stopped. They leaned against the building, next to the back door, stone hot against their backs. Chance palmed the ball, looking at his own fingers instead of the man stepping from the car. Henry knew how hard he'd worked exercising his hands to be able to do it.

The man wore a gray suit in spite of the heat with a lime green vest and bow tie. He saw the boys and nodded. He didn't look much like Chance—thick dark eyebrows over startling gray eyes, a neat moustache, no dimples, a small mouth, hair in deep waves. Like Chance, he walked as if for an audience, but his walk was tight, not easy, and he paid a lot more attention to his costume.

"Here for Bible study?" the man said. "You're early."

So it was the deacon. But wouldn't he be glad to see people showing up for Bible study? Wasn't that his job? Shouldn't he sound more welcoming? Chance still hadn't looked at the guy directly.

"You're Deacon Joseph?" Henry asked.

"Yes, I am." The deacon's eyes darted around, taking in the deserted parking lot, as if he was afraid they were about to jump him. "And you are?" Henry nudged Chance. Had he ever seen his brother so quiet for so long?

Chance slammed the ball against the pavement. Deacon Joseph and Henry jumped. "Let's go." He began dribbling the ball across the lot without looking back.

The rhythmic smack of the ball on the asphalt reverberated in the heated silence between Henry and this stranger. The deacon raised a caterpillar eyebrow. Henry kept his face still. There was something he should be saying right now, but he couldn't figure out what it was. A muscle jerked in the deacon's cheek.

How easily a father could ignore a child. A mother couldn't do that. Well, maybe. But their mother hadn't. Rosie would remember the abortion for the rest of her life. How often did Chance think about it—even now just months after it happened? And Nadine better never find out. She'd never get over it. Henry felt guilty relief that he had escaped being born a woman. He pinned the deacon with a deadly glare.

"Well, who are you?" the deacon asked again. "What do you want?"

Henry knew he couldn't, shouldn't answer this question. Chance had chosen to walk away.

"Nothing," Henry said. He gave the deacon what he hoped was a withering look and loped after his brother.

On the walk to the T, Henry had to half run to keep up with Chance. They sat side by side in silence on the train back to Cambridge.

"Not too late to shoot some hoops," Chance said finally.

The court, surrounded by the summer dark, gleamed under bright lights like a movie set. Chance dropped the basketball and sat on it, leaning back against the fence. Henry stood beside him, and they waited to play winners. Rosie, the only girl on the court, raced back and forth. "She's a great defensive player," Henry said. "Seems like she has more than just two arms."

Chance gave a grudging nod.

"Thanks," Chance said, eyes on the ball. "When you decide to find your father, I got you."

Henry watched Rosie grab rebounds, her little unpregnant body running, jumping, and wanted to tell Chance that he knew about the abortion, but why? And now was not the time.

Samba beats popped and sizzled through Yara's screens into the steamy afternoon. An unfamiliar black SUV with New York license plates filled the parking space in front of the house. Nadine, prepared for another evening alone on her back porch watching her tomato plants grow, brightened and danced up the steps.

She knocked hard on her friend's door and when no one answered, turned the knob. "Yara!" she hollered through the crack. So much had happened that needed telling. And she was ready to talk, about the boys' fathers, Gary Watkins and the money for their trip, her determination to go to school and become a speech therapist, but first she would brag about Chance's graduation speech and college opportunities.

Luiza, Yara's older daughter, appeared, a white towel around her slim body and another tucked around her hair. Of course, the SUV was the son-in-law doctor's car. Nadine's stomach tightened. She wanted to be happy to see this girl who, along with her sister, babysat for Henry and Chance and Rosie, taught them to ride bicycles, build snow forts, and make lemonade stands.

Luiza kissed her on both cheeks. "Nadine! Come in. Come in. My baby needs to meet his auntie. Mom!"

The baby! Nadine's disappointment evaporated at the prospect of holding Yara's grandson. Auntie! Yes. She liked that.

"Mom's dancing with him so I could take a shower. You could have come to visit me, you know? But thanks for the cute outfits."

Why hadn't she visited? A nice trip to New York with her friend. Because she had to work and was afraid to leave Chance, so tangled up in her own life she hadn't even thought about getting away for a weekend.

She followed Luiza into the living room, where Yara cradled the baby in her arms and rocked her hips and shoulders to the music.

"You look like the happiest person in the world," Nadine said from the doorway.

"I think I must be," Yara said. "He has just now stopped crying. He screamed his way across Massachusetts, even when Luiza took him out of his car seat. I'm afraid to stop moving. What is more precious than the quiet when a baby finally stops wailing?"

Nadine stepped closer and wrapped her arms lightly around her friend, breathing in Yara's familiar perfume. She swayed with her and regarded the child.

He crinkled his forehead. Nadine clucked at him. Helpless under the spell of his toothless smile, she stared and grinned back. Yara handed him over. Only a few months ago he'd been that grainy black-and-white smudge in the sonogram picture, and now here he was charming her.

"Nico. Nico." Yara touched his cheek with the tip of turquoise fingernail. "He looks like his father."

The doctor, Nadine thought. "Where is he?" she asked.

"In New York. Too busy. I need to get back to work myself so Luiza came to stay here for a couple of weeks. That way

274

I can help her and do what I need to. She wanted to see friends. I missed home. I missed you. You'll have to tell me everything."

Fathers. Too busy, far away, or absent all together. What difference did it make? The busy ones were more likely to help with money. Luiza didn't have to work right now.

Nadine pressed her nose against the baby's head of fuzzy dark hair, the familiar weight of a tightly wrapped little body in the crook of her arm, his ear against her heart. The muscle under her left shoulder blade twinged sharply just the way it had when she carried and nursed Chance and Henry. The muscles don't forget. She sat down. Nico began to fuss, and she stood again.

"I can take him," Yara said. "But if you hold him, I can heat up something to eat. I had to cook meals to freeze for my son-in-law. He can't always be eating at the hospital. So I made enough for us too."

In the kitchen she dumped a plastic container of chicken stew into a pot. Nadine positioned the baby against her shoulder and patted his back.

"So how are the boys?" Yara asked. The caring in her voice encouraged Nadine to tell all.

"Chance gave a speech at graduation!" Nadine said. "Henry has a girlfriend."

"A speech? The last thing I knew, you worried he wouldn't graduate at all. I told you, right? Chance is a good boy." She stirred the stew and beamed at Nadine as if she, Yara herself, were responsible for Chance's success. Nadine's hand moved fast and hard against Nico's little back, and she breathed deep to slow it down.

"And the girlfriend?" Yara asked.

"She's not right for him," Nadine said.

Yara set a bowl of stew on the table and reached for the baby. "Sit. Eat. Why not right?"

Nadine put a spoonful of stew into her mouth. Delicious, of course. No matter what she said about Sage, Yara would respond with a cheerful remark. If she said Sage was too chatty, Yara would say that a serious boy like Henry needs a girl like that. If she mentioned her nose piercing and her toe ring, Yara would say lots of girls have them and a sense of style is always good. If she talked about tofu, Yara would pat her belly and say they could all do with some healthier eating.

Nadine swallowed. "It's Henry's decision, not mine."

"Yes, but you can have an opinion! You can tell me. Mothers have a right to opinions. And the best way not to make trouble with him is to give your opinion to someone else. I'm your friend, Nadine. Talk to me."

A friend who is never home anymore. Too busy, too far away, or absent all together—what difference did it make with fathers or friends? Yara with her accomplished daughters, her cleaning business, her house, and now a grandson, family here in the States. She had everything but a boyfriend, and for all Nadine knew, she might have one there in New York.

She could tell Yara about Sage's locs and the unmade bed, but what did she really know about the girl? Not much. She would have to try harder the next time they met—ask her some questions. Henry had seemed so nervous, Nadine hadn't wanted to do anything to make the situation more uncomfortable than it already was.

"She's nice enough," Nadine said. "He likes her."

"Not right. Why not? Tell me!"

Who knew what went on between two people? The story of Sage was Henry's to tell. "You said you'd be here for awhile. We'll talk."

Nadine picked a piece of chicken from the stew, sucked it

off the bone, and considered telling Yara about Gary Watkins and how she could have a boyfriend right now if she wanted one, but decided against it. For Yara to really understand, she'd have to include background, maybe even Uncle and his lap. She cracked the bone, sucked the marrow, and decided she would tell Yara but not now, not with Luiza in the next room. The baby provided ample distraction. They talked to him, about him, and took turns walking him around the kitchen.

She bent over little Nico to kiss him goodbye. Chance banged on the window.

"Hey, baby!" Yara called. "Come in, beautiful! Your mom's here and my little grandson. Believe it or not, he's as handsome as you are." She gave Nico to Nadine and threw open the door to the apartment. Chance wrapped her in a nice hug. No nasty drug smells followed him. He looked at Nadine over Yara's shoulder with clear eyes and a relaxed smile.

"Whoa, let me see the competition!"

Yara pulled him over to Nadine and Nico.

A look she'd never seen passed over his face, naked sadness. He touched the baby's ear, the complicated curves of his own ear bent close to Nadine's face. She had a sudden desire to whisper something into it.

"Okay, Mom," he said. "You the judge. This baby cuter than me?"

"No," Nadine stage whispered. "But don't tell him."

Chance laughed.

"So you were the valedictorian?" Yara handed him stew in Nadine's just-washed bowl.

"Hah!" Chance laughed again and around his mouthful of food said, "Kids and teachers chose me. It's kind of like the girl who loses the beauty contest but wins the award for personality."

"Well, beauty doesn't last and personality does," Yara said. "But the last I heard you were getting into some trouble and making your mama sick."

Nadine's face clenched. Her heart squeezed. Chance and Henry couldn't stand her talking about them to anyone.

She stared at Nico's little drooping eyelids to avoid Chance's angry face.

"I'm done with that," Chance said. "My friends is all in jail with stories I don't want to be part of. Stories so bad I don't want to be saying them in front of innocent baby ears. And now teachers be saying I can go to college, get money. Got to grab that while I can. That's all. When a man sees it's time to wise up, he wises up. Got to be ready."

Yara grabbed his shoulders and stood on her toes to kiss him hard on the cheeks. "I sure am glad to hear that, baby. Your mother and I both knew you had it inside you."

Nadine dared to look at Chance's face; she wouldn't lie even if it made him angry. "For awhile I wasn't sure," she said. "I wondered."

"Me too," he said.

"Where's Henry?" Yara asked.

"Who knows?" Nadine said. "He has his own life—working, girlfriend. Sometimes he doesn't come home at night."

"Do you worry?"

"Why should I?" Nadine teased. "Henry is a good boy. Both of my sons are good boys."

"Men!" Chance corrected her. "Good men. When you going to see that we grown?"

"I see it." Nadine pressed her lips together to keep from saying anything to provoke him.

"So what else is new, baby?" Yara asked Chance. She refilled his bowl, and he sat to eat his second helping.

Henry's familiar footsteps clattered in the stairwell along

with someone else's. Nadine opened the apartment door and called up. Henry and the girl, Sage. She'd never been to the house before.

"Tell him to come meet Nico," Yara ordered. "Henry, quick, get yourself down here. I want to see this girlfriend I've been hearing about."

Nadine flinched again, worried Henry would know she'd been talking to Yara about his love life. She was so tired of her sons being angry with her. She dipped her head to smell the baby's sweet head. Her breasts ached remembering the fullness of milk.

"Thought they broke up," Chance mumbled as Henry and Sage sidled into the kitchen.

"Smells delicious in here," Sage said.

It's chicken stew, Nadine thought. *You don't eat that. Why would it smell good to you?* Sage had a funny hat on with a cloth sunflower pinned to the brim. The girl headed straight toward her and the baby. *How did people learn to walk, dance, just be at home in the world like that?* Henry followed her, a shy grin on his face.

"What a cute baby!" Sage put her cheek against Nadine's. She smelled like licorice. Her locs were gone.

"Your hair!" Nadine said without thinking.

"I gave her a haircut," Henry said. Sage lifted her hat to show short hair, almost like Nadine's own.

"I asked him to," she said. "I feel so much freer now."

Chance made a clownish face and shook his head. "Henry better stay in school. He ain't gonna be no barber."

"Henry has lots of skills," Sage said. "He can be whatever he wants."

Henry smiled at the floor.

Yara introduced herself to Sage and began to ask her how she liked Cambridge, what she was doing here, how she and

Henry met. They sat around the table. Nadine stood to rock the baby, listening, like watching a movie on TV, everyone talking, just a few feet away, but separate.

Then Chance said, "Right when you came in, Yara was asking me what's new. I was about to say fathers. Yara, did you know about all that?"

Nadine clutched the baby hard, and he startled awake. Before Chance could continue, she herself blurted the truth. "Yes. Chance and Henry have different fathers. I never told anyone." Except Gary Watkins.

"And mine's a jerk," Chance said.

Nadine willed Yara to look her way and when she did, Nadine told her in the silent eye language of friends not to get into it now, not to ask questions. Sage's lack of surprise said that Henry had already told her everything.

"Jerks can have great children," Yara said. "And you've been raised by a strong and smart mother who couldn't have loved you more. Look at you—a graduation speaker."

Chance bit his lip and studied his sneakers. When he'd gotten his face under control, he asked to hold the baby.

Henry put his arm around Sage.

Nadine handed Nico to her son and stretched her arms high, her back, for now, free of pain. She looked around the table, at Yara, Henry, Sage, Chance, Nico, memorizing the moment. They'd all been babies. Yara in Brazil, Sage in California, herself in Haiti. Luiza. Rosie. Gary Watkins had been Hazel's baby. Hazel had been a baby. All the Riverview residents had been babies somewhere in the world with their troubled and astonishing lives ahead of them, never knowing they would someday meet and depend on Nadine Antoine. Even as she marveled at this thought, another struck her— people were being born right now who would impact her life, in ways she might know and ways she wouldn't.

Thank you. I love you. I'm sorry. I love you. I'm sorry. Thank you. I'm sorry. Thank you. I love you.

Yara and she exchanged a smile over Chance's bowed head as he passed the baby to Henry, a small smile, that for one long moment, held all that mattered in the universe.

ACKNOWLEDGEMENTS

This book has been years in the making with many voices contributing to the volume you hold in your hand.

Thank you to all who gave me advice and support. You know who you are. I appreciate your help with this book and your presence in my life.

VINE LEAVES PRESS

Enjoyed this book?
Go to *vineleavespress.com* to find more.